PEAK
PERFORMANCE

David R. Kauss, Ph.D. (adjunct assistant pro-
fessor, Department of Medicine, UCLA), has
made a lifelong study of the psychology of
athletes, the psychology of competition, and
the psychology of performance. He has written
numerous articles on emotions and athletic
performance and is an active clinical and sport
psychologist with college and professional
athletes.

DAVID R. KAUSS

PEAK
PERFORMANCE

mental game plans
for maximizing your athletic potential

A SPECTRUM BOOK

PRENTICE-HALL, INC., Englewood Cliffs, New Jersey 07632

Library of Congress Cataloging in Publication Data

Kauss, David R
   Peak performance.

  (A Spectrum Book)
  Includes index.
    1. Athletics—Psychological aspects.   2. Coaching—
(Athletics).   3. Sports—Psychological aspects.
I. Title.
GV706.4.K38   796'.01   80-15169
ISBN 0-13-655332-X
ISBN 0-13-655324-9 (pbk.)

10 9 8 7 6 5 4 3 2 1

Editorial/production supervision by Eric Newman
Interior design by Christine Gehring Wolf
Manufacturing buyer: Barbara A. Frick

Prentice-Hall International, Inc., *London*
Prentice-Hall of Australia Pty. Limited, *Sydney*
Prentice-Hall of Canada, Ltd., *Toronto*
Prentice-Hall of India Private Limited, *New Delhi*
Prentice-Hall of Japan, Inc., *Tokyo*
Prentice-Hall of Southeast Asia Pte. Ltd., *Singapore*
Whitehall Books Limited, *Wellington, New Zealand*

To my Dad—my first and best coach.

CONTENTS

Contents

PREFACE

Peak Performance is a book about the mental side of competitive athletics. It deals with the attitudes, emotions, thoughts, and behaviors that create positive athletic performance. Addressed to athletes and coaches, the book discusses the many psychological factors that are recognized in sports today but about which there has been little useful, specific information: concentration, motivation, team spirit, confidence, poise, aggressiveness, and pressure. A glossary is included to help provide meaningful descriptions of these oftentimes confusing and hard-to-handle mental factors.

   Peak Performance is about getting ready to perform. It is for both athletes and coaches, at all levels of competition. For the athlete, there are proven individual techniques for harnessing thoughts and emotions to perform better. For the coach, there are tools and strategies to use in handling player preparation, both in practice and in pregame settings. This book is written for coach and athlete, together, for an important reason: Complete psychological preparation is best done when coach and athlete work as a team, when each person is aware of what the other is trying to accomplish when using the various techniques described.

   The techniques and coaching suggestions are applicable to any sport (or to any other performance activity) at any level. This book is for novice athletes and coaches involved in Little League Baseball, AYSO Soccer, and Pop Warner Football, right on up to professional athletes and coaches looking for one more useful edge on the competition.

People at all levels will find new things to think about and to try that will improve their competitive skills. This book tells you exactly what to try—in the game, in the locker room before the game, and on the practice field.

Peak Performance is about how to prepare, compete, and win. It is about how coaches and athletes can get the most out of themselves. As Chapter 1 points out, if you're going to put time, energy, and commitment into your sport, you might as well get the best possible results. This book shows you how, through The Readying Approach to improved athletic performance.

I would like to thank the following people for their help in making this book a reality: John Arvanites and Dr. Raymond Bakaitis, for many discussions about competitive sports and help in finalizing the manuscript; Shirley Van Alstyne, for her patience and skill in so many facets of manuscript preparation; and Dr. Beth Meyerowitz, for her insightful criticism and her invaluable encouragement.

All illustrations are by John Arvanites.

A NOTE TO COACHES

This book is written for athletes and coaches. Since each performer is different, the book aims to teach each athlete how to use the thoughts and feelings that he or she experiences, in order to perform better.

It is precisely because each athlete is an individual that this approach works, but this very fact prevents me from offering a general "how to" for coaches to use with *all* athletes. The coach's job is to help the athlete to learn what needs to be done to perform better. Although the coach usually knows very well the physical requirements of preparation, psychological preparation all too often becomes a matter of "demanding" concentration, relaxation, and so on. Unfortunately, the athlete can't give you what he or she doesn't know how to produce.

Peak Performance is a tool you can give to your athletes. It will give meaning to words like *concentration, effort,* and *poise.* Instead of hoping that your athletes are emotionally ready, you can give them a method for making sure that they are.

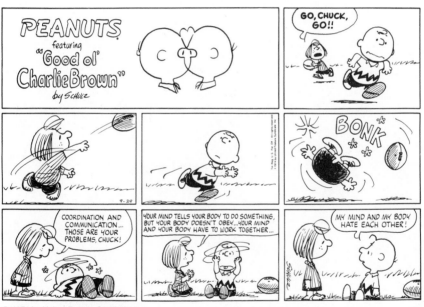

THE READYING APPROACH TO SPORTS

This book describes a comprehensive approach to improving your athletic performance. With the international explosion of sports activity during the past fifty years, many physical training procedures have been refined, making today's athlete the best trained, most highly skilled competitive performer ever. Along with these advances in training procedures has come the awareness that psychological and emotional factors can also influence athletic performance. Coaches, reporters, athletes, and others involved in the athletic scene comment almost daily on a player's or team's attitude, emotionality, fear, confidence, and knowledge, often attributing to such factors the responsibility for success or failure.

Although everyone agrees that the athlete's state of mind has a lot to do with his or her physical performance, very little has been done to specify those factors that tend to bring about positive performance, and even less to apply what meager knowledge of performance and emotions we do have. This book does just that: It describes a two-step, readying approach for helping you (1) to *observe* your own thoughts and behaviors prior to and during competition to learn what leads to good performance and what doesn't, and (2) to *control* these factors, once they are identified, to learn how you can bring about those psychological and environmental circumstances which usually lead to good performance.

The Readying Approach

Our focus, then, will be on the *readying procedures* that athletes can use to prepare themselves to perform well. We can think of these readying procedures as extensions of some physical readying activities with which we are all familiar. For example, sprinters take a certain position in the blocks, baseball infielders crouch as the pitch is delivered, and tennis players receiving service usually hop or move before the ball is actually hit toward them. All of these activities occur before the competitive activity itself, *because they help the athlete to be in the best position, or to be moving in the best way, when he or she is called on to act.* The athlete is bringing about circumstances that will lead to good performance one or two seconds later.

If we speed up our athletic clock, we can see that psychological and environmental readying procedures can be thought of in the same way: they, too, are activities that are done not because they have value in and of themselves, but because they make the next act (the important one as far as competition is concerned) easier. Psychological readying procedures are the thoughts and feelings the athlete tries to have prior to performing—thoughts and feelings that usually leave him or her in the best position, or moving in the best way emotionally, when competition itself begins.

But what are these thoughts and feelings? The ones usually mentioned are concentration, relaxation, motivation, confidence, and other psychological states that mean different things to different people. A coach may talk to a team about being poised or feeling relaxed, but these terms are bound to mean different things to various team members.

When social scientists have tried to study athletes and their emotions to discover the particular feelings that lead to good performances, they have met with little success, because *no one emotion or set of emotions helps bring about good performance for all athletes.* Every athlete is different, and each athlete needs to develop individualized readying procedures. As you go through this book, try to learn what you feel like prior to and during a good performance. Then figure out how to bring about those feelings and thoughts.

What you do to get ready to perform should depend on the thoughts and feelings that define who you are. If thinking about your opponent or feeling angry helps you, then learn to do so more effectively. If, on the other hand, feeling good and relaxed helps you to play better, then learn to do that more effectively. You should also learn to get rid of thoughts and feelings that you usually have but that inhibit other, more positive, feelings. This approach will help you learn to employ your thoughts and feelings to your own advantage.

But even though you will be dealing with feelings—and possibly quite strong ones—it is important to realize that I am not talking necessarily about deeply rooted psychological issues. An athlete does not have to undergo ten years of intense psychoanalysis, or engage in mystical practices like hypnosis or Zen, just to improve athletic performance. This book will deal with feelings that are at or just below the surface, that you yourself can identify with only a little time, energy, and thoughtfulness.

One of the problems that has prevented athletics in this country from making use of the behavioral sciences is the common conception that using such an approach requires dealing with long-standing personality structures that may have little to do with athletic performance, and that coaches and athletes feel nervous about handling. There seems to be the feeling that calling on a psychologist will lead either to teams discussing how to love one another, or to athletes lying around on couches talking about their mothers. The approach of this book, while concerning itself with the thoughts and feelings of individuals, does not involve anything like that.

States of mind—not your lifelong "personality"

Instead of talking about the athlete's "personality," we will consider a few of the feelings, thoughts, and behaviors to which the athlete already has access—things you probably already know but are not doing. The distinction here is an important one: A person's long-standing personality traits are less relevant to producing good athletic performance than are the *individual states of mind*, like anxiety or excitement, that the athlete can bring about at particular times for the purpose of readying.

If we think about the many things that we are all capable of thinking or feeling in the course of our lives, we can see that we usually use only a small percentage of these emotions most of the time. One person may be usually cheerful, another usually nervous. But every person knows what certain other feelings are like, and, with practice, can even feel them, at least for short periods of time. The gentle giant can turn into a raging hulk for the length of a game, and the nervous worrier can create an oasis of calm thoughts for the few ticks of the clock it takes to go into competition. I am talking about selecting what you need from the range of attitudes and behaviors you already possess.

You may find strange the idea that a person can "choose" to feel a certain way simply because it leads to good performance. This, however, is exactly the skill every coach expects his or her athletes to have. The coach sees an athlete behaving in a certain way and instructs him or her to behave differently: to stop, for example, lifting one's head and instead to keep one's eyes on the ball. At first, this is quite difficult. You've never done it that way before and you're used to doing it the old way. This is part of your physical *personality*. But you know what the coach is talking about, and after a few awkward attempts, and perhaps a little coaching help, you can learn consciously to do a new thing.

In much the same way, you can approach thoughts and feelings as *internal behaviors*. (Actors do this all the time.) Just as with the change in physical behavior, at first it will seem impossible, then awkward and unproductive, and then, finally, possible and useful. The process is one of bringing into play a behavior (a movement, a thought, or a feeling) that you may already know but have not yet learned to use in that situation. Thought of in this way, using one's emotions for one's own purposes seems much less imposing.

Because we don't yet have rules for changes in emotional behavior, as we do for physical ones (e.g., "keep your eye on the ball"), we must take a more individual approach in helping the athlete to develop appropriate readying activities. This approach aims at improving athletic performance *within the performance limits of the individual*. Each athlete has a range of capabilities; a bowler, for example, may bowl anywhere between 110 and 200, depending on how *ready* he or she is. With proper readying, you can perform at the top of your particular range more and more often. Usually, as this occurs, the range as a whole will move up, and you will be able occasionally to perform beyond what seemed to be your upper limits. You can play better, and more consistently! Thus your performance can improve, even though you maintain an attitude of playing under control, as opposed to overreaching.

A self-improvement approach

Winning is not necessarily the object of this approach. Winning in athletics has been both maligned and praised during the last two decades, with opinions ranging from "winning is the only thing" (the credo of one of America's most famous and idealized coaches), to those who point out the destructive aspects of our competitive athletic system. Without addressing the merits of either argument, this readying approach stresses the improvement of the individual's performance, given his or her abilities. The goal is to work hard to better yourself, to locate the factors that help you to perform as well as you are capable of, and then to bring these factors to bear when you are readying to perform. As such, the approach has applicability far beyond the realm of athletics or even of competition; it is an approach designed to foster positive change in any endeavor, whether competition is relevant or not. The athlete's goal becomes doing the best job he or she can do, and not simply beating an opponent.

I hope it is already clear that this approach places most of the responsibility on you, the athlete. Rather than waiting for your coach's edict about how to prepare, you must put forth some time and effort yourself. Having committed yourself to improving your performance, you are expected to go beyond the merely mechanical preparations that are common today; you are expected to figure out what circumstances lead to good play *for you,* and then to practice creating those circumstances, using the techniques described in this book. If athletic improvement is worth committing yourself to, then it is worth doing well, even if that means thinking about it in ways that are new and awkward at first, and that require taking the time to think about seriously. This book will help you learn what the appropriate athletic factors are, but you must discover how each factor affects your own performance.

Factors—internal and external

Just as the readying approach is divided into two segments, observing and controlling, so is this book. I will first discuss the factors for you to consider while observing your own readying, and give some tips how to observe as objectively as possible; then, in the last part of the book, I will discuss specific techniques and applications. Throughout the book there will be things for you to think about, things for you to observe in yourself, and things for you to try. Use the many tips and techniques according to the results of your own observations. Find what leads to effective readying and positive performance for you as an individual.

As you will soon see, this approach does not deal only with emotions. One of the important aspects of the observation phase is to see what factors, both internal and external, affect your performance. The *internal factors* go on inside your head; in other words, the thoughts and feelings during readying. The *external factors* can be thought of as everything else; the weather, practicing, talking, watching television, and so on. It is important to identify the internal and external factors affecting your performance, and then to try to extend your control over as many of these as possible. There will of course always be factors that you cannot do anything about, but the more factors that you can gain control over, the better your performance is likely to be. We will look at these many factors to see how they affect performance.

Until very recently, the internal factors were considered out of our control, or even beyond our understanding. While recent trends in sport have pointed out the vital importance of these factors, they have done little to explain exactly how what is in the head affects what the body will do. Thus, coaches and athletes often believe that a very important (if not the most important) performance factor—namely, the athlete's state of mind—is precisely the one they know and can do least about. No wonder, then, that they experience so much pressure and frustration, especially during readying.

A major goal of this approach, therefore, is to provide a framework, an outline of performance factors that athletes and coaches can start observing and controlling, so that we can leave behind the "athletic dark ages" of merely hoping and praying that gameday will find the athlete in the proper mood to do well. An overview of these factors is presented in Chapter 9. Chapters 2–6 go into more detail about the four major types of relevant factors: characteristics of tasks, characteristics of persons, recent task-person history, and immediate task-person performance conditions. This will all become clear as we go along.

Assumptions behind the Readying Approach

I hope that this description has raised as many questions as it has answered: Just what are these factors? How can I better observe my readying? How can I change my precontest thoughts, feelings, and behaviors? Before answering these questions, let us consider some of the assumptions implicit in this approach, so that you will have a better idea of what you are getting into.

This approach to readying is meant primarily for the athlete who takes his or her performance seriously and wants to play better. The basis of athletics has always been simple recreation done for the fun of it. If this recreational aspect is all you want from your play, fine; it doesn't make sense for you to invest serious time and effort to improve your performance. The casual athlete may require only participation to derive the benefits of physical play.

For most athletes, however, more is required. There are many reasons why even weekend tennis players and doctor-prescribed joggers may want to improve their performance. Use this approach in whatever way you see fit. Even if you usually play just for the fun of it and only occasionally care about performing well, this book can help you.

If you do have even a slight urge to play better—to stop always losing the first set, or always buying the drinks—or even want to improve to championship level in your sport, read on. Having made this decision, remember this: No one fully understands all the factors relating to athletic performance today, so you will have to adopt the attitude of a scientist whose laboratory is yourself. Rather than relying on experts in the field or experienced coaches to tell you exactly how to improve your performance, you need to look carefully at your own readying and performance, with the attitude that maybe tomorrow or maybe next year you will be able to discover the precise formula for determining your own level of performance. It's a process of finding out and trying, and thereby learning.

This approach should be particularly helpful to young athletes, accelerating what is usually called the *experience factor*, but is nothing more than knowing about how to prepare and conduct oneself so as to perform consistently well. With this approach, you will learn more about how you can play your best in a shorter period of time. What takes the ordinary athlete ten games to learn, you can learn in two or three. And you'll be learning the most important lesson of all: how to be ready to do your best when you really need to.

A full commitment to observing yourself and then doing what is necessary to perform better is crucial. As I said earlier, if it's worth doing, it's worth working at. While coaches can be very helpful, it is you, the athlete, who must take up this individualized approach, for you are the only expert at what is going on inside your head. The guidelines in this book will help you to become even more expert, and a better observer and controller of your own activities. This can not only improve your athletic performance but can also help you to feel more successful, to move toward the top of what John Wooden calls the

Pyramid of Success: "Success is peace of mind which is a direct result of self-satisfaction in knowing you did your best to become the best that you are capable of becoming."*

That's what *Peak Performance* is all about.

---

*John Wooden, *They Call Me Coach* (Waco, TX: Word Books, Publisher, 1972). Used by permission of Word Books, Publisher, Waco, TX 76703.

The Readying Approach to Sports

2

EMOTION IN SPORTS:
How you feel is how you'll play

Any coach can tell you that how you feel will affect how you perform; there's really very little argument about that. The question then becomes "How does what I feel inside of me affect what my body does?" There must be some specific mechanisms through which these feelings work. Feeling "psyched-up" is not a magical thing that transforms a poor player into a star; on the contrary, feeling "psyched-up" (and other emotions) determines performance level in ways that have their basis in the body's overall construction. In this chapter we will look at some of the ways in which emotions affect performance, and I will discuss specific emotions and their uses.

Coaches often deal with these complicated matters by oversimplifying. They want their players to feel some vague kind of sensation that they call "emotional." I've heard coaches say, "You can't play this game well unless you get *emotional* about it." Well, in a sense that's correct. How can you perform well if you are totally uncaring and have absolutely no energy to bring to your competitive event? But the problem with this oversimplification is that it equates being emotional with being ready to play well, or with being motivated enough to win.

To make sense of the emotion-performance link, we need to try to specify exactly which emotions do which things for an athlete's performance readiness, and how much of each emotion is good or bad for a particular athlete. Every coach has seen a variety of emotions work, depending on the people and the situations involved. Worrying about playing an opponent who is physically superior has caused athletes (a) to be too preoccupied with this fact to be ready to play well, or (b) to become so motivated that they give an excellent performance. No one can say that worrying about this kind of situation is necessarily helpful or harmful, or that these two types of athletes, both of whom can be said to have been "emotional" before competing, performed equally well. The key to understanding this and the other emotion-performance links we will be looking at is to consider the specific person and situation involved.

Emotions—Emotions are feelings and are to be distinguished from thoughts (words that we process inside our heads) and physical sensations (like hot and cold, and sweet and sour). We may at times be able to give words to our feelings, but they are not necessary for a feeling to exist. Why we have emotions is a subject that social scientists and philosophers have debated for thousands of years, and I will not try to improve on their work here. It is sufficient to say that emotions are a critical part of our ability to respond to our environment. They are our strong reactions to things that happen around us, and they help our bodies to react physically when the need arises. When we are physically threatened, for example, by a car coming toward us while we are crossing a street, we usually respond physiologically and emotionally, and both reactions help us to get out of the way quickly.

Most of the time, however, we are not being threatened by immediate death and we still go on having feelings. This is also true in precompetition readying periods. These feelings still represent our reactions to our world, but we usually have more time to reflect and plan. Emotions like sadness and joy, for example, are some of our long-standing responses to events: We are sad because of losing a friend, or happy over getting a high score on an exam. In this context, emotions can be thought of as one of our internal feedback systems, telling us when something *feels* good or bad, whether we want to seek it or avoid it in the future, and other self-management and survival decisions.

Social scientists, when trying to determine the basic emotions we are capable of feeling, usually limit the list to seven: joy, sadness, anger, love, fear (worry), shame (guilt), and surprise. We can recognize these emotions in ourselves, and other people identify them in us by noticing our reactions to events. Obviously, we are capable of feeling many other emotions—anxiety, confidence, trust, horror, and disgust—all of which can probably be traced back to the basic seven. Then there are the finer distinctions within these emotional categories.

Joy, for example, can be broken down into levels and types of joy: gladness, pleasure, quiet satisfaction, unrestrained glee, and so on.

In actuality, however, none of these emotions exists as "pure" feelings. The words are simply labels that we use to describe what is going on inside of us. Seeing emotions in this way is important because it allows us to realize that *each of us feels things individually and uniquely.* You need to keep an open mind about what feelings can be, in order to use the techniques described in this book.

Essentially, there are four qualities of your emotions that are important in emotional readying: your *emotional personality* (or usual way of feeling), your *reactivity level* (how strongly you feel things), your *ability to control* your emotions, and your *emotional flexibility* (the ability to feel different things at different times). People differ in these qualities, just as they do in strength, speed, and so on. The better you know your own emotional qualities, the better you can ready yourself to play. Let's look at each one briefly (see Figure 2-1).

Figure 2-1. Emotional Qualities.

Emotional Personality—Each of us has a personality: a common and consistent way of thinking, feeling, and behaving. Your personality is nothing more than the set of feelings, thoughts, and activities that you characteristically experience in many different situations. Some people, for example, are typically very bubbly and outgoing with other people, whether they are friends or strangers. Others may usually feel depressed, or happy, or worried.

These steady, normal moods form the context into which everything that you do, think, or momentarily feel is placed. It is ridiculous even to think about which emotions will help you to perform better without first taking stock of your usual mood. Only in comparison to this overall mood will your momentary or deliberately evoked readying emotions have any meaning. To say that Muhammad Ali is very quiet before a fight is very different from saying that Bill Walton is not talking to anyone before a basketball game, and the difference is that the activity—being quiet—is much more characteristic of Walton's personality than of Ali's. The two athletes may seem to be doing the same thing, but they are probably experiencing very different emotions and thoughts.

Reactivity Level—You also have a reactivity level, which is the strength with which you usually feel things. Some of us respond to everything in a calm, unemotional manner, so that our range of reactivity is relatively low. Other people are very excitable and respond strongly to events; their range of reactivity is high. It is important to recognize what your range of reactivity usually is (and it is equally important for coaches to know this about individual athletes), and not to compare yourself with others. What is a very high level of feeling for you may be quite a moderate display of feelings for someone else, and that person's level should not be used as a guideline for your own readying. Instead, set whatever emotion you may be trying to achieve during readying to your own standards of reactivity. Don't be concerned if a coach or teammate says you are not "high" enough, because only you can tell where in *your range* of emotional levels you really are.

Control—People differ, too, in their ability to control their emotions. While a person can often change this with practice, his or her ability to control emotions can be seen as part of the overall personality, and will often be consistent from situation to situation. In general, the more you can control your emotions, the easier it will be for you to make use of the Readying Approach; but this kind of control also includes the ability to allow yourself to go *out of control* for short periods of time. There is much more discussion of control later in this book.

Flexibility—The aspect of your personality most important in producing appropriate readying is *emotional flexibility*. This refers to how easily you can feel different emotions at certain times. We all have one or two ways that we normally feel, but we don't have to feel that way all the time. Your flexibility in being able to feel other things, especially at those points in your readying where you want to control specific emotions, is a skill to be worked on, just as you practice your physical movements.

These four emotional qualities are factors that each athlete should know about him- or herself, and that every coach should know about his or her athletes. They form the raw material of the athlete's emotional makeup, just as the individual's speed, strength, and so on make up the physical portrait. Just as you have learned to capitalize on your physical advantages and to minimize your physical disadvantages through practice, so you should begin to approach your emotional personality. See where your strengths are, and try to shore up your weaknesses. Any readying that involves using specific emotions has to take into account the person's overall emotional capabilities. (I might also suggest to coaches that these four emotional qualities deserve as much attention as do physical attributes in the selection and assignment of individuals to certain sports tasks.)

In making use of these four qualities in your own readying or in coaching someone else, the main rule of thumb is this: Do not try to force the individual outside his or her normal pattern of feeling and functioning. For example, don't try to make a generally unemotional person into one who feels things very strongly or into an emotional leader. Similarly, don't try to force an athlete into feeling certain ways that are not a comfortable part of that person's flexible feeling pattern; this will result only in confusion and the dissipation of whatever energy that individual athlete may already be bringing to competition. Instead, try to work within the individual's (or your own) existing patterns and levels of feeling, helping the athlete to sharpen his or her thinking and preparation with that emotion *in small steps*, always staying within his or her overall level of responding.

Perhaps a case will illustrate this point. A college football player came to me with the complaint that his coach felt he wasn't aggressive enough to play well. The athlete wanted me to help him work himself into a rage of hatred before games, so that his anger would inspire him to savagely attack his opponent, thereby displaying all the aggressiveness any coach could want. What this rather easygoing, quiet young man wanted was to experience feelings that were almost completely outside his realm of functioning, and were at levels far above his calm approach to life. I pointed this out to him and suggested alternate sources of energy, like eagerness and excitement, which he could use to "psych" himself up. With a little practice he learned to use successfully the positive imagery technique described in Chapter 7. Luckily for him, I had earlier tried to do with another athlete exactly what he had requested. What ensued were terribly frustrating attempts on the part of the athlete to hate his opponent, followed by feelings of guilt over having to stoke himself up in this manner. The consultation was not effective, and both the athlete and I realized that it was useless to try to turn an unemotional competitor into a raging storm of emotional energy, especially by trying to use a "negative" emotion like anger, which the athlete did not naturally feel inside. It's not so much that this is dangerous or harmful—it's simply not very effective. Coach and athlete are much better off trying to build on some emotion that the athlete does feel, using this as the source of energy. What we could call the "Billy Martin Approach"—I'm going to beat you to show you that I'm better than you are, not afraid of you, and that I generally hate your guts—works fine if those feelings are already inside the individual athlete and need only to be increased a little, but it is much less likely to succeed in athletes who characteristically take a completely different approach to their sport.

Emotions, energy, and performance

The major positive role that emotions can play in the preparation of the athlete is supplying the necessary energy to perform well. Generally, the more emotional a person is feeling, the more raw energy that person is capable of bringing to competition. Unfortunately, the relationship between energy and performance is not direct; that is, it is not true that the more overall energy an athlete has, the better he or she will perform. (Overall energy here refers to physical, mental, and emotional energy, or any source of arousal.)

Arousal is a key concept, and it is used roughly as the equivalent of energy. In studies of athletic performance dating back to 1908, what has generally been found is that as arousal increases, performance improves, up to a certain point. Then after this peak performance level has been reached, additional arousal actually makes performance more difficult, and the quality and speed of performance deteriorates. This relationship between arousal and performance is presented in the following diagram, called the "Inverted-U" (see Figure 2-2). This relationship is essentially the same as the one described in Chapter 7, which relates tension and relaxation to performance. It indicates that at very low levels of arousal, the athlete does not have enough energy to perform well. Performance is slow, lethargic, and not coordinated with everything else taking place during competition. As the person's arousal level increases, the pace and accuracy pick up, until the individual reaches a level of arousal that is perfect for him or her and the task involved. Beyond this point, the more aroused the individual gets, the more performance suffers. At very high arousal levels, performance

Figure 2-2.

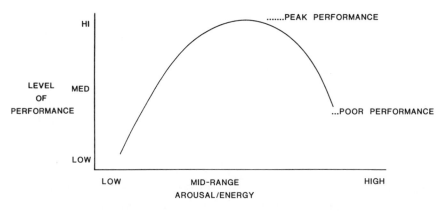

is erratic, inaccurate, and very poor. This is particularly true when the task calls for performing complex or precise movements, using what is called *fine motor coordination*.

Obviously, then, the goal is to get yourself into the mid-to-high range of arousal, taking into account what your usual range is. More will be said about this in Chapter 7. For now, it is important to realize that *arousal* and *energy* are general terms that do not necessarily denote specific emotions. Arousal and energy are the results of your readying; they are not useful mechanisms by which to get ready.

The useful mechanisms are the *sources* of arousal and energy, and this is where the specific emotions enter into your readying. *Any single emotion can be a source of arousal and energy for you.* You can think of every emotion you might feel during readying as a separate contributor to your overall arousal level. The amount of anxiety you feel contributes to your arousal level, as do the amounts of anger, excitement, and other emotions.* Because these emotions contribute cumulatively to your arousal level, and because arousal level is one of the major determinants of performance, you need to pay attention to each separate feeling. This is where you can control your emotional readying, not by waiting until competition time and then trying to adjust your overall arousal level. Athletes who attempt the latter are attempting something as complicated as juggling a dozen eggs, with the expected messy result.

Since these individual emotions are the keys to your overall emo-

---

*You can think of this relationship in the following way: Arousal = anxiety + confidence + excitement + fear + anger + team spirit + any other feelings of energy.

Figure 2-3.

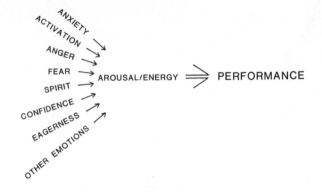

tional readying and level of arousal, let's take a look at them one by one. I'm going to focus on seven emotions most commonly encountered in athletes trying to prepare themselves. (But this does not exhaust the list of emotions that you can use.) I am going to discuss these emotions and give examples of their use; this will help you to choose which of them you may want to concentrate on in your readying. Specific techniques for controlling the level of each emotion are discussed in Chapter 7.

Anxiety

Of all the emotions that relate to performance, by far the most common and least understood is anxiety. There are many different words that we use to denote anxiety: tension, worry, being upset, being preoccupied, ruminating, and distress; the list could go on and on. What all these terms have in common is that they refer to a state of mind in which the individual is responding with discomfort to some event that has occurred or is going to occur. This discomfort is over something unsettled, something that prompts the person to worry about the consequences of his or her actions, either in the past or in the future.

This ambiguous, unsettled, confused nature of the discomfort is the hallmark of anxiety, and it is this aspect that distinguishes it from other "negative" emotions like fear and anger. The person who is anxious is caught in some incomplete phase of an action. In athletics, this usually takes the form of worrying about impending events. The more imminent this event becomes, the more intense the anxiety is likely to get.

But this is just a general definition of anxiety, and relies heavily on the notions of discomfort and potentiality—what one might do or might have done. As was pointed out, even negative, uncomfortable emotions can be excellent sources of arousal. Coaches and athletes have

Emotion in Sports

long recognized this dual nature of anxiety, seeing that the real task involves not avoiding or creating anxiety before competition, but using it in controlled doses. In sport, anxiety has the reputation of being both a crippler of sensitive performers and a motivator of athletes.

Should you try to raise your anxiety or to lower it? It depends on you. In our society, the answer is usually to lower it, for one simple reason: The external pressures the athlete is under force his or her anxiety level up too high to begin with. *The issue really is not whether anxiety is good or bad; the issue is determining which direction your anxiety level needs to go before competition to put you in the best range to perform well.* Even at low levels of competitive sport in this country (like Little League baseball, Pop Warner football, and AYSO soccer), there is a great deal of pressure to win, from peers, coaches, observers, and the athletes themselves. Obviously, the higher you go as a competitive athlete, the greater the pressure to win becomes. It is only natural that most athletes need to lower their anxiety levels to perform well, and need to learn ways of controlling their worries so that they will not interfere with performance. For this reason, most of our discussion of anxiety will focus on lowering and controlling anxiety; there is, however, a section in Chapter 7 on raising anxiety for those who might find it helpful.

The Two Kinds of Anxiety—For now, however, let's think about what forms anxiety takes and what you can do to deal with it effectively. While everyone experiences anxiety differently, there are two general kinds. One is called *somatic* anxiety, which refers to symptoms of anxiety that are experienced in the body. Some common signs of this type of anxiety are muscle spasms, cold hands, and hyperventilation. More serious developments can include headaches, ulcers, and hypertension. Perhaps the most common manifestation of somatic anxiety occurs in the stomach, as "butterflies" or even as nausea. Because athletes are usually very aware of their bodies, this type of anxiety is probably the more common of the two.

The other, *cognitive* anxiety, refers to worries inside the person's head, which may or may not have external symptoms. Cognitive anxiety can consist of unwanted negative thoughts, worries, inability to concentrate, and inability to prevent the mind from racing or from considering the negative side of past or future situations. It is often typified by the vague, lingering feeling that something bad is going to happen or that you have done something wrong.

Either type of anxiety can conflict with athletic performance.

Somatic anxiety is more likely to affect the physical side of performance, while cognitive anxiety will disrupt attention and other mental activities. The two types of anxiety often appear together. However, one is usually dominant, with the secondary type posing little problem for the athlete and probably even being a healthy sign.

These two types of anxiety require different approaches to control them. For somatic anxiety, interventions that work directly on the body, like massage, yoga, and biofeedback procedures, are most useful. Less formalized activities, like soaking in hot water, sleeping, and sex, can also be helpful. Obviously, most of the activities that are helpful in reducing somatic anxiety are things that will feel good to the body. In choosing your approach, try to focus on the specific part of the body that gives evidence of your tension. And be regular in your efforts. (See Chapter 7 on Relaxation.)

If your anxiety is primarily cognitive, the best way to deal with it is through mental activities, to engage your thoughts in something other than your anxieties. Engrossing games, reading, watching television, and writing letters can be helpful. While this prescription sounds easy, you may find it difficult. Distracting yourself from worries works for some people, but for others this can only be done as part of an overall program for reducing anxiety. The attention-clearing technique discussed in Chapter 7 can be used as well. A great deal of attention will also be given to cognitive anxiety in the section on negative imagery and creative worrying in that same chapter.

Athletes who experience a combination of the two anxieties, without one dominating the other, will surprisingly have less difficulty in lowering the anxiety level. This is because the best method of dealing with such a combination is to engage in physical activity: active sports, dancing, or just plain hard work. If you are training hard in your sport and still experience a combination of anxieties, try to find some other physical activity that you can *play at* without stress or performance requirements. For example, if baseball is your main sport and you are experiencing anxiety about your performance on the diamond, you might find that tennis or golf can actively engage both your body and your mind as *pure play*. Younger athletes are doing this already as a natural part of their activities. The older we get, the more we have to be aware of reserving energy for specific competitions. Also, avoid activities that involve either exactly the same or conflicting body movements as your main, competitive sport; failure to do so can result in fatigue and excessive strain, as well as physical mistakes (for exam-

Emotion in Sports

ple, the different types of hand and wrist motions required by tennis and squash).

All of these activities are remedies to be used in response to anxiety problems before competition begins. But they will be more effective if you can structure them naturally into your life, instead of applying them sporadically, like medicines. Even though you may initially try one of them specifically to reduce your anxiety, you should try to fit the activity into your daily or weekly routine, so that the new activity becomes something that you do in and of itself. These approaches to somatic and cognitive anxiety are not meant to be used immediately prior to competition, but rather as habits that will in the long run make your anxieties less prominent in your mind and body. There will be much more to say about tension and anxiety in later sections.

I have said absolutely nothing about what your anxieties might be, or where they come from, or even how much they really bother you. In terms of athletic performance, these things are not that important. Obviously, the content of the worry will be different for each athlete. Overall, I have found that it is the type of anxiety (somatic or cognitive) and the level you wish to reach that are the important determinants in the successful management of anxiety. You do, of course, have to recognize what your source of worry is. But once you have done so, the suggestions given here and the techniques described later can be applied regardless of what it is you are anxious about. It doesn't even matter if the anxiety comes from within your sport (like pressure from your coach or teammates) or from other sources (like pressures and problems with your family, girlfriend, job, or school). In the long run, what's important is that you recognize it for what it is and try to do something about it. The worst way to handle anxieties is to try to ignore them. Athletes who do so are usually the ones whose performance suffers the most in high-pressure competition.

Do's and don't's

Anxiety is a volatile emotion. How you respond to it can greatly affect the level of anxiety that you feel. Trying to ignore it usually only encourages it to grow. But equally destructive is the tendency to "worry about worrying." Many athletes are so aware of the possibly negative effects of anxiety on their performance that they overrespond at the first sign of it. This causes them to worry about the fact that they are worrying, instead of concentrating on the upcoming event.

Worrying about worrying is almost always harmful, and it is not the same thing as honestly addressing yourself to your concerns. The appropriate mental activity of recognizing your anxieties and thinking about them seriously, well before competition, as an aid to clearing your mind of them when competition actually begins (again, see Chapter 7) is very different from getting spooked by the fact that you are worrying. For the athlete who tends to worry about competition, the watchword is this: The fact that you are worrying is perfectly natural for you, so don't try to fight it or worry about it. Just recognize it and let it be. An internal message like "I'm nervous but that's okay, that's just me and it's perfectly natural" is a good approach. (Obviously, a coach who can communicate this to a nervous athlete will be doing him or her a tremendous favor.) It's not the initial level of anxiety that is usually the culprit in causing poor performance, but the athlete's reaction to that initial level and to what it might mean.

My own research suggests that, for the athlete who usually does worry, precompetition anxiety is the best source of overall arousal. In a two-year study with a nationally ranked college football team, I found that the typically anxious athlete was much better off when he *was* nervous before competition, and that such athletes did not do as well when they were not nervous on the day of a game. If anxiety is part of your life and you accept it for what it is, then you should use it on game day, instead of (1) trying to ignore it, (2) worrying about it and thereby increasing it, and (3) trying to use other emotions, like excitement, eagerness, and confidence, to be the source of your overall arousal.

This last point is an important one. If anxiety is something that you usually feel before competing, then trying to psych yourself up through rousing, confidence-building thoughts or pep talks is a mistake. It usually serves to combine the arousal from one emotional source (excitement) with that from another emotional source (anxiety), leaving your overall arousal level too high for top performance. If you get anxious before competition (assuming that you are not so anxious that your functioning is impaired), accept it and use it as a source of energy to do well. Don't be afraid of a little pregame anxiety; it can really help, if you don't fight it.

One athlete among those I studied typified these relationships. A high-strung wide receiver, he was usually quite anxious before a game, often to the point where he could hardly talk to anyone or hear what they were saying. Sometimes he even experienced nausea and vomiting. But this was a natural part of the readying process for this athlete, and the absence of such anxiety left him unable to reach top performance levels. In addition, he responded negatively to further encouragement and prodding from teammates, coaches, and even friends who were kindly exhorting him to have a great game. Because this athlete had come to accept the fact that he would be nervous before a game, and that he shouldn't fight it or worry about the effect of his anxiety on his performance, he was able to use his own anxiety as a stimulus and energy provider.

Unfortunately, I have too often seen responses to anxiety work against athletes. I once coached a young baseball player who had a great deal of talent but who constantly fought any feelings of anxiety before a big game. His parents contributed to this problem, with his father's well-meaning comments about the necessity of "playing relaxed" only serving to escalate the athlete's own concern. Needless to say, on such occasions he did not perform up to his usual high standards. Equally shackled by his own reactions was the football player who so feared being nervous at game time that he would spend the whole day trying to distract himself from his anxiety, trying not to worry even though it was a simple fact that he was worried. By the time the game rolled around, this athlete was often emotionally and physically drained by the constant effort it had taken to "not think," and his performance suffered. He would have been much better off if he had simply worried about what was on his mind, seen it for what it was—a natural part of his readying that might have actually contributed to his performance readiness—and gone on about his business. Obviously, then, the first step in using your anxieties for your own advantage— even before you turn to Chapter 7 for specific readying techniques—is not to fight your own anxiety. Just let yourself worry a little.

A final word on anxiety is appropriate here, especially for coaches and well-meaning friends or parents. Anxiety should be seen as a personal reaction of the individual athlete to his or her situation, and trying to control it externally usually doesn't work. A nervous athlete can sometimes be calmed down, but this often calls more attention to the anxiety than is warranted. During competition, ignoring it is usually the best approach for the coach, while encouraging the athlete to get into the physical part of the sport. And it is usually very dangerous to try to stimulate an athlete to be more nervous before competition. Some coaches will try to do this if they feel that the athlete or team is too cocky to play well, but this is a tricky business, and the coach needs to be exactly right in his or her estimation in order to achieve a positive result. The best strategy for the coach is to become aware of the individual readying needs of each athlete, to help the athlete to become aware of these needs, and to take cues from the athlete prior to competition. Let the worriers worry, and help them to see it as a natural part of the game. And when in doubt, use some other pathway, like pure excitement or confidence building, to get the athlete's attention, and let anxiety alone.

Anxiety, is an individual emotion, and is best handled on an individual basis by the athlete him- or herself. The tools for doing so are discussed in Chapter 7.

Confidence

Another emotion commonly considered in the production of positive athletic performance is confidence. Technically speaking, confidence is more of a state of mind than an actual emotion, but its use as a device that explains the successes and failures of so many athletes warrants its inclusion here. Moreover, most athletes think of confidence as a gut feeling that they either have or don't have—not so much the thoughts they might be having about an opponent, as the inner sense of how things will go in competition. It can best be handled as the other emotions are, rather than as a series of thoughts or ideas.

What is meant by confidence? It can usually be defined as a sense of well-being, a generally positive outlook on whatever competition is upcoming. It is almost always a good sign for an athlete or a team to be expressing real confidence before a contest. (I mean real confidence here as opposed to blustery, overstated claims of confidence and "what we're going to do to those other guys" before competition. Such boasts are often signs of an inner lack of confidence, and should be avoided.)

When working on confidence, consider the difference between confidence and your *anticipated outcome*. Anticipated outcome refers to whether you expect to win or lose in competition. Confidence, on the other hand, refers to the feeling that you will *perform* well. Even if your opponent is physically superior, so that even a good performance will probably not result in victory, you can still feel confident that you will play well. The extent to which you can separate these two factors may help to determine how well you play.

Many of the great coaches in American sports emphasize this distinction. Before games, they concentrate on what their athletes are doing to prepare *themselves*, on building confidence in their own ability, without stressing the toughness of the opponent. Even after games, these coaches comment almost exclusively on the performance of their own athletes: whether they played to their own capabilities, and not whether they were able to win. This approach keeps the athlete's attention where it should be: on his or her own performance, and not on comparisons with other athletes, which are often a source of anxiety and can undermine the individual athlete's confidence. I will have more to say about anticipated outcome in Chapter 3.

Confidence can refer to a number of different elements, including confidence in yourself, in others who will be competing alongside of you, in your emotional readiness, in your physical ability, in your knowledge of your opponent or of your own assignments, goals, and strategies, in your physical condition, and in your coach. None of these should be overlooked in your preparation; confidence is more notable when it is lacking than when it is abundant, and uncertainty in any of these areas can contaminate an athlete's otherwise high level of confidence. Confidence must be based on good feelings about all of these areas, and it is usually of little value to try to build confidence in one area without attending to the others.

Some athletes are able to focus on the positive rather than on the negative in assessing their own potential for performance; this is obviously a good approach. You may find yourself focusing more on some of the confidence areas than on others. Since life is not perfect, a complete survey of these areas would leave you with some things to feel good about and others that would concern you. With practice, you can learn to choose which of these you will attend to: As a basketball player, for example, will you spend your readying time thinking about how well you and your teammates work together on defense, thereby building your overall confidence level, or will you dwell on the fact that you are not one-hundred percent sure of the new plays your coach has put into the offense? If your coach is sharp, he or she will work to minimize your concern over the offense and will talk up your team's defensive skill.

You can work on this selection process yourself in techniques like the Readying Spot and Imagery techniques described in Chapter 7. The first step is becoming aware of all the forces influencing your confidence level, before you can begin to choose what to focus on. Of course, I am assuming that when you do spot a source of lowered confidence, you will try to do something about it, either by approaching the people involved or by giving yourself extra practice on the activities that are undermining your overall confidence level.

Raising and lowering confidence levels—when and how to do it

Confidence is usually seen as a good thing, as it is usually easier to bring down an overconfident athlete than to build up an underconfident one.

But probably a more accurate representation of the effects of confidence on performance is the inverted U. As with anxiety, performance will improve with confidence up to a point (different for each athlete), after which more confidence will result in a poorer performance (e.g., the play of the overconfident athlete). Each coach and athlete needs to be able to raise or lower confidence, depending on the individual's needs and the immediate situation. Here are some guidelines.

Let's start with situations and athletes that require raising the confidence level. The overriding rule in building confidence is that success builds confidence. This may sound simple, but it is certainly true. It is very difficult to build confidence with a last minute blitz of pep talks; what works much better is the steady use of positive reinforcement (see Chapter 4) in practice situations that are designed to help the athlete feel successful. This means structuring your workouts so that they can be liberally sprinkled with rehearsals of behaviors and decision-making situations with which you are familiar and can do relatively well.

This does not mean practicing what you are already good at to the exclusion of other activities; it simply means including some successes in your practices, especially toward the end of each practice, and in workouts immediately prior to a given competition. The athlete will do well to focus almost exclusively on such successes before a big competition, so that he or she can remember what has been done successfully in the past, and (perhaps most importantly) have the sense that the upcoming competition is going to be essentially a matter of doing those things which he or she does best. Lack of confidence often comes from the fear that competition will demand things from the athlete that go beyond his or her knowledge and capabilities. This can be especially dangerous if the athlete is concerned about the coach or teammates demanding something extra in a big game. On the contrary, confidence is usually the result of feeling that you know what will be expected and have practiced, so that you and your coach are happy with your current readiness. Remember, the goal is not to make the athlete ready for the opponent, but to help him or her to perform in the upper portions of his or her range.

A second rule, especially applicable to coaches but also to athletes who can take a leadership role with their peers, is that confidence is spread not through fiery speeches but through example. When athletes sense that a coach is fully ready for whatever competition may bring, they themselves are readier and more confident. Although nervous apprehension will probably never be eliminated, the coach would do well to epitomize an attitude of eager anticipation and confidence.

Third: Events outside of sports can affect the athlete's performance. Oftentimes the individual's *learning history*—the prior events in life that have affected his or her self-image—will overlap into sports. Thus athletes who do not feel generally confident have a difficult time feeling confident in their athletic abilities.

This kind of outside effect is often situational. In certain situations or in the presence of certain people, the athlete's level of confidence may go up or down. I have seen Little Leaguers and high school athletes, for example, play at a certain level most of the season and then have their whole approach to the game changed by the presence of a parent. For some athletes, the effect is positive: he or she feels more confident with a loved one there to watch. For others, however, the effect can be devastating, completely undermining the athlete's self-confidence. The presence of other people, like buddies, can do the same thing. I had a PONY League baseball player, for example, who played at a fairly high level throughout the season but who tailed off toward the end of the year. It turned out that once school let out for the summer, some of his friends could come to practices and games in the afternoons. This boy, who had been quite confident, was nervous when his buddies were there. Apparently the "teasing" relationship these boys had, along with the athlete's sense that they were better athletes than he, conspired to undermine his confidence. The solution was to invite the boys to hit a few balls during practice. They had not been playing organized baseball all spring, and were unable to do much with the pitches I gave them (especially since I held nothing back). When my ballplayer saw how ineffective they were, and how well he was doing in comparison, he felt much more confident, and their teasing stopped almost immediately.

This is only one example. Often all that needs to be done when a confidence-undermining factor is identified is to eliminate it (e.g., ask the boys not to come, or ask the parents to sit out of the athlete's line of vision). Other situations can be handled similarly. If, for example, it makes you nervous to watch the opposing pitcher warm up before you go to bat, then don't do it.

More complex and tougher to deal with are problems outside of the sport, such as problems at school, or with a girl or boyfriend, that interfere with confidence building. If you are worrying about flunking a test or about doing something that may have put you in a bad light with a friend, anxiety can diminish your confidence in your athletic ability. The only solution is to settle the issue outside of your sport as well as you can. Don't underestimate the power of confidence-shattering events in one part of your life to affect your feelings and performance in another, namely, your sport.

Providing steady success with appropriate positive reinforcement, giving and using examples of confidence, and arranging your performance conditions to avoid confidence-cutting people and things—these are the keys to keeping your confidence level up. But remember, too, that you do have some choice in how you feel. The world is full of many happy, sad, discouraging, and encouraging things, and the ones you focus on in your sport will make the difference in how you feel. In short, develop self-confidence, the knowledge that you are doing your best, that you have worked hard at your sport, and that you are answerable to no one but yourself for how well you perform.

Overconfidence

At the other end of the scale is the athlete who is overconfident and therefore does not play well. Every coach has at one time approached an event with that sinking feeling in his or her stomach that the team is too cocky, and not taking preparations for the upcoming contest seriously enough. Unfortunately, the athletes themselves are usually blind to this phenomenon, which makes it doubly tough to do anything about it. What's the best approach to take in such a situation?

The rule of thumb with confidence problems is to try to affect the athlete through example, not by talking about the dangers of overconfidence. All too often coaches find themselves giving the team a tongue lashing to try to bring them down to earth; this usually has only a temporary effect in practice, perhaps forcing the athletes to be serious only for the rest of that day. Then, in competition, the overconfident athletes find themselves in more of a contest than they anticipated, remember the coach's heated warnings, and panic, trying too hard to overcompensate. Occasionally, athletes in this situation find themselves close enough at the end of a contest to pull it out, once they have regained some emotional stability, but all too often there is not enough time.

Emotion in Sports

Much more effective is demonstrating to that athlete that he or she is not infallible. With lower level athletes this is not difficult. The coach of a high school athlete can usually perform the sport better than the athlete. Or older athletes (ex-team members, for example) can be brought in to work opposite the current squad. The point is to remind the athlete that he or she has not reached the top rung of the ladder. I've even seen coaches use this approach to embarrass a particularly cocky athlete, but this can be a tricky business, leading to broken rapport. When an approach like this is used gently and surely, merely as a reminder of relative strengths and weaknesses to the athlete, it can be very effective.

The coach who has the luxury of films or tapes of the athletes can use these devices as tools to fight overconfidence. It is very humbling to see yourself playing poorly, making mistakes, and performing at a low level, even if some of those activities have since become part of your positive performance repertoire. Showing always works better than telling.

When using a method like this, the coach must follow the lesson with some conciliatory, fence-mending contact. At some point after you have gotten the athlete's attention and moved the confidence level back toward the normal, positive performance range, let the athlete see what you have done and point out the reasons. This does not always have to be done immediately; with thick-skinned athletes, it is often a good idea to let them sleep on the lesson for a night or two (more sensitive athletes, and especially younger ones, need quicker reassurance). The main idea is to (1) make your point through demonstration and not through words, and (2) go back to the positive, building approach that is the hallmark of consistent, good coaching. If the coach has already established good rapport with the athletes before these confidence-lowering methods are used, this second step is usually no problem at all. The athletes know what you are doing and will accept it.

In fact, it is precisely *because* the athletes can see what you are doing in trying to cut down their cockiness that words alone won't work. Some kind of demonstration, on the other hand, gives the coach time to get past the initial inattention and "yeh, sure Coach" attitude; the athlete is actually being *shown* that there is still room for improvement.

But in using this approach, keep some words of warning in mind. Don't try to bring your athletes back down to earth very soon after a big success. Let them enjoy it; it is probably the best positive reinforcement they can ever have for working hard and achieving.

But beyond this, be careful in trying to lower an athlete's level of confidence at any time. After all, we know that high confidence is usually a positive sign in the athlete and will encourage good performance. The wise coach should be absolutely certain that his or her hunch is correct—that the athletes are really overconfident—before trying to bring them down.

What is the bottom line? When it comes to confidence, there is a lot that coaches and athletes can do. Athletes can give it some individual attention, as described in the section on specific individual techniques. For the coach, the watchword is success. Confidence building and regulating speeches may occasionally get through to the attentive athlete, but it is demonstration and example that will really do the job.

Feeling "psyched"—activation

Let's concern ourselves with that mysterious expression that has been used to describe every feeling from fear to joy to the shaking fits: feeling "psyched." We have all heard athletes talk about feeling psyched, and we usually get the sense that they mean they have been well-prepared, emotionally or psychologically, to perform well. What the word really means no one can explain: Having one's head in the right place comes close. But despite its imprecision, the term has proven to be a useful one, denoting for many athletes a certain excited way of feeling prior to performing.

We are all familiar with that general feeling of anticipation and excitement that can precede any big event. It is often a sense of eagerness, of feeling strong, active, and full of energy. You just can't wait for the fun to begin; you are eager, as though a thousand pep talks have gone through your mind and left you "wired."

To avoid confusion with whatever your concept of being psyched may be, I'm going to call this feeling *activation*. Activation can be thought of as the pure mental energy of eagerness and anticipation; it is an arousal-producing state that is completely positive (unlike nervousness, fear, and anger). It is excitement for positive reasons, and the root of all play.

We have all experienced such a feeling, and we have all known or heard of athletes who developed this sense of activation to such an extent that it became their primary energy source for performing: for example, Pete Rose, now with the Philadelphia Phillies. Pete was often heard to say things like "I love to play this game. I feel lucky just to be able to get up everyday and play baseball. I can't think of anything in the world I'd rather do. Even if they didn't pay me I'd still do this just because I love it." His source of energy was pure activation, the simple excitement of the activity itself.

This approach to sport is not meant for everybody, and many great athletes have excelled without such wide-eyed enthusiasm. But if you do have at least a streak of this kind of feeling running through you (and I'd say that most competitors do), you would do well to develop it. You can learn how to produce and control it.

Compared with many other feelings and energy sources, activation has a number of advantages. It is a natural, positive emotion with which everyone is familiar. It doesn't have the disadvantages of emotions like anxiety and fear. It's fun, and therefore usually provides the athlete with a steadier source of *controllable* energy than do other feelings. It goes hand in hand with confidence, as each feeling enhances the other.

Activation is especially useful for athletes whose sports involve demanding muscular activity for short durations. The short but power-laden sport of weightlifting, as well as football, wrestling, and shot put, are ideal activities in which to use activation as a source of arousal and energy. Where speed and strength are required, activation is a definite plus; where fluidity of motion and muscular relaxation are required, it may be less crucial. Overall, however, it is often both the foundation and the result of a positive attitude toward your sport.

How and where can you get the feeling of activation? It can be produced individually by using imagery techniques and pregame mental readying procedures. (See Chapter 7). There are also natural sources of it. Activation is often the product of the rhythm, or cycle, of the athlete's preparation. Especially in sports that require a lot of steady practice and in which competitions occur regularly, the supply of spontaneous activation can be pretty low at some times, and abundant at others. When the athlete who is used to practicing long and hard is given some time off or asked to engage in less rigorous physical exertions in practice, his or her feelings of activation will rise. Thus coaches can sometimes arrange practice routines to slack off just before a big event.

Similarly, in patterns of competition in which a number of lower priority, "routine" games are played prior to an important game, the athletes usually have no trouble feeling excitement and strength. Scheduling competitions is sometimes not entirely under the coach's control, especially in organized sports, but it can be done, or at least adapted to intelligently. As any coach will tell you, it is impossible to be up for every contest, or for a long string of tough competitions. Coaches and athletes need to be aware of these fluctuations in activation level, and should guard against demanding it when it is not naturally there. Activation cannot be forced; it needs to be allowed to grow. In eager, competitive individuals, it always will. The athlete must play through periods of low activation at an acceptable level, and then use the activation that naturally cycles through him or her to produce top level performances on those occasions *when they are needed most* in competition.

Another good source of activation is the athlete's performance itself. Most athletes get pleasure from playing well, and so a good performance is positively reinforcing for the athlete. If you think about those times when you hit a particularly good shot or ran a very fast race, you will feel a surge of activation. The wise coach capitalizes on this phenomenon, so that the athlete's own performances serve as activating forces. For example, by letting the athlete do the things he or she does well and likes to do in a practice before a big event, the coach raises the athlete's activation. Immediately before competition, the coach can remind the athlete of those times when he or she has done particularly well and was pleased by the performance; the coach can also screen big plays and great performances before a major contest. Focusing the athlete's attention on positive efforts raises his or her arousal level. You should realize, however, that this depends on doing so fairly regularly. Unless the athlete feels this performance-related activation energy to be part of an overall style, last minute pep talks about great performances and big opportunities will not have much punch.

Activation can even be successfully raised during performances. I have seen a coach take advantage of his team's first half performance in a basketball game to spur the athletes on to bigger and better things in the second half. The situation was this: The team had an up-and-down season and was facing the conference leader, a very strong and highly regarded team. Half time found our team trailing by only two points. Some players were amazed at this. The coach, contradicting the players who thought that the other team wasn't really all that good or hadn't played well in the first half, instead emphasized the skilled performance of his own team. He pointed out the many things that each player had done well. When the realization began to sink in that they were a good team and were beating what they had thought to be a superior team, the athletes couldn't wait for the second half. What made the critical difference between seeing things this way and the usually disastrous phenomenon of having a team "wake up" at half time to the realization that they had been playing over their heads or had been lucky was the coach's repeated emphasis on how much fun they had been having, and on how positive it was to meet a challenge like this. The team won by nine.

The issue of letting activation grow instead of trying to force it is critical. Activation is best utilized if it is not expected all the time (e.g., "this is a big game and you *should* be up for it"). If athletes cannot look forward to a contest with anticipation simply because the game itself is fun for them, then no pep talk is going to get them up. As is the case with respect, admiration, love, and other positive human feelings and attitudes, activation cannot be demanded; it must be allowed to build at its own rate and in its own rhythm, in an atmosphere of disciplined effort.

In trying to make use of activation as an arousal source, keep two more factors in mind. First, even though activation is almost always a positive feeling, your sense of excitement may not be completely separate from other, negative feelings. One of the great dangers of trying to artificially build up your own eagerness (and of other people, like coaches, trying to do so through verbal encouragement and cheerleading) is that the arousal you get from this source can combine with the arousal from other sources, like anxiety or fear. So if you are already nervous or scared, the addition of a lot of activation energy may increase your overall level of arousal too much for you to perform well. Remember that you must consider the arousal you get from all sources of energy, since they usually do combine. The rousing pep talk from your coach, or even the more gentle encouragement from friends and teammates, when added to anxiety or some other uncontrolled, negative emotion, may put you past your optimum performance range. (Recall the inverted U.) The best bet is to use activation only when you are not feeling other emotions—when you (or the athletes you are coaching) are in danger of being flat and listless. But in the presence of any other motivating emotion, you would usually do well to avoid further arousal through activation, since the arousal from the other emotions (and the natural excitement that occurs during competition) should be enough to carry you through the contest.

Secondly, individual responses to activation will vary. Depending on how much arousal the athlete is experiencing from other emotions further excitement can either hurt or help his or her performance. Some athletes seem to thrive on the excitement of a big event, while others need to minimize the excitement in order to play well.

Preparing an entire team by pumping them up with verbal exhortation will be good for some but bad for others. The coach who makes an entire squad get very excited, jump up and down, and yell and scream before a contest is actually ensuring that some of his or her players will play poorly. If the athletes who can benefit from such stimulation can be identified and separated from the others, then vigorous exhortation is fine; but, when it is done in a large group, some players will benefit while others will suffer. I consider it a sign of questionable readying when, for example, an entire football team comes onto the field yelling and pounding on each other, jumping up and down like excited ten-year-olds. For some of them to do so is fine, as long as the others can prepare themselves on the sidelines as they see fit and are not required to join in the mayhem.

With these qualifications, activation in moderation is almost always helpful to the athlete. For most athletes it is a great source of arousal. Activation in moderation means the application of a brief, focusing technique (like a short pep talk or imagery session), and not a scathing harangue that builds to a crescendo of uncontrolled emotion. Keep in mind the cycles of excitement we all go through, and try to save the activation push for when it's needed most. But most importantly, the more you can make competing in your sport fun, the better your use of activation will be.

Fear

A couple of years ago a basketball player came to me for help with his readying. "Doc," he said, "before our last game I was so scared I could hardly think straight. I was going to be guarding this really big guy on the other team, and I was actually worried about getting beaten to death under the boards. Before the game, I was practically sick to my stomach about it. But, you know, I played great that day, maybe the best I've ever played. So that made me think that maybe if I could get that scared all the time, I'd be a really great player. Can you help me do that?"

I complimented this athlete on his willingness to try new things, and on his awareness that whatever had helped him to play well—even though it may have been a negative feeling—could be used again to aid his performance. We worked on finding out exactly what that feeling was for him, and eventually he was able to use a modified version of it

Emotion in Sports

in his readying. But before I set out on such a course with him, I had to make absolutely certain that it was a good idea, and that no other pregame feeling would do just as well.

Although fear can work in the manner described here, more often than not using fear as a readying technique is replete with problems. In this section, we'll examine both the uses and the drawbacks of fear as an arousal source. Keep this one thought in mind: You probably should try everything else before using fear as a motivator.

Fear can spring from many sources. One common source in athletics is physical fear: being apprehensive about physical injury occurring in competition, either to you or to others around you. Especially in sports where there is a lot of physical contact and muscular activity (like football and wrestling), or where a lot of speed must be controlled to avoid injury (like pitching a baseball), it is not unusual for athletes to worry about the physical danger. In younger athletes, and particularly in those who are very strong or big for their age, the fear of harming an opponent is quite common, and can be a deterrent force in getting the athlete to compete fully. Fear of physical injury to oneself is natural, an essential part of our biological makeup. Other sources of fear can be spectators (fear of embarrassment), coaches (fear of negative consequences), and simple fear of failure.

Whatever the source of the fear, there are always both a physical and an emotional component to it. Fear of, say, physical injury involves a physiological response as well as the recognition of the fear itself. Your body is built to respond almost immediately in emergencies, and this "fight or flight" reaction is provoked by a rush of adrenalin that activates your entire body. Obviously, this can be an excellent source of arousal, but the problems of dealing with the negative aspects of the fear arise equally quickly and dramatically.

The main problem in using fear as a source of energy is that it tends to completely dominate the mind, making other, necessary thought processes next to impossible. The basketball player said it

Figure 2-4.

FIGHT   FLIGHT

himself: "I was so scared I could hardly think straight." If you're just going to be running like crazy from a bear, then this kind of response makes perfect sense: Run as fast as you can, using all your physiological tools. But if your activity involves thinking, responding to varied moves of your opponent, or carrying out complex and delicate physical behavior, then fear can interfere with these activities and harm your performance. Obviously, almost every sport involves some of these complex procedures.

Still, fear can be of value to some athletes, in certain sports more than in others. The key is control. If you are able to create a fear that you can also control, so that it raises your arousal level to your optimum performance range and no higher, then it can be a plus.

The most common fear that can be managed in this way is *fear of failure*. This does not involve fear of physical harm, which usually elevates one's arousal level much too high for successful use. It has to do instead with the athlete's sense of self. Social scientists who have studied what motivates us to strive for achievement have identified two major motives for success. Some people simply want to be successful very badly, so the rewards of success are the "carrots in front of the mule." These people keep their minds on where they are headed, and contemplate how great it would be to get there.

The other motive is fear of failure. These people work hard to do well because the thought of failing is repulsive to them. They are working to avoid the embarrassment, anxiety, depression, and loss of self-esteem that would come with failure. While the other motive, desire for success, is probably better suited to high achievement, fear of failure can be a very powerful force as well. Unfortunately when this fear gets very strong, it often paralyzes the person. This is the kind of athlete who freezes during big games.

Athletes cannot be molded into one or the other type, but seem to fall into either category and pretty much stay that way. The task of the

Figure 2-5.

DESIRE FOR SUCCESS   FEAR OF FAILURE

fear-of-failure athlete is to learn to control his or her fear, keeping it out of the paralyzing, upper range. He or she should also realize that a certain amount of this fear is necessary in order to do well, and that the absence of such fear (for example, in an attitude of overconfidence) indicates that performance will be less than optimal. (See Chapter 7 for specific techniques of fear production and management.) Fear of failure can be harnessed in individuals who naturally experience it, but it should not be prescribed for others. Make sure you know which category you, or the athletes you coach, fall into, and prepare yourself accordingly. Whatever you do, don't try to inject fear of failure into the athlete who doesn't naturally feel it; you will only dampen his or her natural enthusiasm to try hard for success.

There is another, more damaging type of fear, which is a definite impediment to top performance: *fear of success*, fear of commitment, fear of finding out just how good an athlete you really are. While some athletes love the challenge that a superior opponent offers, others have a fear of actually finding out what their level of performance can be. These people are sometimes discouraged from going into competitive athletics at all, even though they may be prime physical specimens. This kind of fear is of being revealed, and it can be deadly to performance.

When we are young or trying something new, everything is in the future. Every ten-year-old can dream about running like O.J. Simpson or growing up to be president, without facing the sometimes harsh dictates of reality. In our lives we have no choice: We must age, thereby finding out very clearly that we will not become rich or be a star. But sport is voluntary. No one has to compete at any sport, and even after choosing to compete, no one is forced to work hard at it. For some potentially good athletes, the prospect of finding out that they are not the best is enough of a deterrent to keep them from trying. This can take the form of simply not competing, or, for the person who has some of this feeling but who does not let it totally dominate his or her life, it can involve never truly testing the limits of his or her capabilities. If I don't try my hardest, don't do all the work I need, put in all the time required, play my hardest so that there are absolutely no excuses for winning or losing, then I can keep alive the self-image that I am on top, or at least that I really could have been if things had only worked out that way.

This kind of fear can have many sources, like one's role in the family or methods of dealing with other important people in one's life. Unlike most of the other emotions I have described, it usually requires deeper, longer-term attention to really overcome it. This does not mean, however, that it is beyond reach for the coach and athlete. On the contrary, sometimes the simple, straightforward explanation of such a pattern to an athlete by a coach can make a great deal of difference. The key is to do it in a nonjudgmental way. The focus must be on the implications of this pattern for the athlete, and not for the success of the team or of the coach. By exhibiting this pattern, the athlete is already saying "Don't challenge me" to his or her sport, and is implying, "I'm afraid of what I might find out if I go all out for athletic performance, for my coach and for my team." Unless this fear is respected, no outside help will be of much use. Focusing the conversation on the positive rewards and fun of competition is the best strategy. After all, it is fun to try to do something as well as you can. Comparisons with some external standard like your opponents or heroes or coaches are much less important than the value of competing with yourself, to make yourself as good as you can be in your own eyes.

We can see that fear is a delicate emotion in relation to performance. It can be used effectively in moderation, and is best utilized when it comes from within the athlete. The inducement of fear by coaches is a dangerous practice, especially on a teamwide basis; it insures less than top play from at least some of the team (namely, those motivated by desire for success). And, all things considered, perhaps it is too personal an emotion (remember things like personal pride, machismo, and saving face) to be brought in simply to try to prod a person into performing better at an activity that was supposed to be fun in the first place.

Anger and hate

What place does hating one's opponent have in the repertoire of readying emotions one can use in sports? Answering that question is difficult, and it makes little sense to try to settle the moral issues here. It is a fact, however, that many athletes, especially professionals and those involved in physically punishing sports that are derived from fighting (wrestling, boxing, and to some extent football), use hate and anger as a source of arousal, often with much success.

I think of anger as a motivating force in terms of the "Billy Martin Approach" to competition. This fiery and successful manager of championship baseball clubs is fond of saying that he sees the game as a war, a battle between two opposing forces who are out to defeat, humiliate, intimidate, and generally punish each other into submission. He seems to see his side as the one that can never be intimidated or overcome as long as the team's fighting spirit is strong enough. The other guys are weak-willed and inferior, and have to resort to underhanded, dangerous tactics just to have a chance. The psychology is simple: "Are we gonna let them do that to us, or are we gonna get out there and do it to them first?" Only one answer is possible within this framework, and if you can't work up some good, old-fashioned dislike for your opponent, then you're not much of a competitor.

This approach certainly motivated Billy Martin to heights he might never have otherwise achieved; and perhaps it has more merit than meets my eye. But frankly, this type of psyching has always struck me as being basically out of one's control, disrespectful, and ultimately self-defeating. If you think that you may find it helpful (and I know that many athletes have), then keep it in mind when you read Chapter 7.

If this emotion is to be used successfully, it seems most likely to be so when used individually, *without* external prodding. If working yourself into a rage makes you a better tackler or runner, fine—work on it and refine it to its utmost. There will be specific techniques to deal with that later on. But I am not going to offer any interpersonal techniques (e.g., for coaches to use with athletes) for raising anger. There are better, more controllable sources of arousal.

The feeling of anger is usually the result of frustration. Social scientists describe anger as the emotional response we make when no overt, behavioral response to some source of frustration is possible. We get angry when we get stuck in traffic, or when a referee makes a bad call against us; the impediments to our progress are there, but we can't really do anything about them, so we get angry. In using anger as a source of arousal, we can provide a real or imagined object of frustration, allow anger to build, and then release the arousal along with the anger in competition, against an object (the opponent) we can do something about. The result, if such a technique is used properly and within reasonable limits, is that we experience energy-filled performance along with the feeling of satisfaction that comes with venting any pent-up emotion.

But there are problems with trying to use anger in this way. All the warnings about the drawbacks to using negative emotions for arousal also apply here. In fact, the danger of having the feeling spread to noncompetitive areas is even more pronounced with anger than with other feelings, simply because the tension, struggle, and often physical contact of competition can all contribute to feelings of dislike between opponents, even without employing prearranged feelings of anger. In addition, anger can easily wind up being the source of arousal that pushes the athlete to too high a level on his or her performance curve. This is as dangerous as being lackadaisical, especially because the overaroused athlete who is angry will probably not be able to calm down during competition, even when that is clearly called for by performance difficulties early on.

Often the imagery the athlete uses to build up his or her anger before a contest is overshadowed by the realities of the competitive situation: that is, there's really nothing to be all that angry about. While excitement, eagerness to compete, tension, and anxiety can usually be maintained with relatively little effort over time and during competition, anger is more volatile. It comes and goes in a shorter period of time, leaving the athlete who was raging with energy at the start of a contest limp as a noodle in the final, more critical stages of the game. This suggests that the longer the competition, the less useful anger will usually be. For weightlifting, hammer throw, and jumping events, it can be more helpful.

The main determinant in assessing the positive and negative effects of anger on competitive athletes is control. If you are comfortable with anger and feel in control of it even when you become very excited, then it may be useful for you. All too often, however, the pregame rage of the athlete leaves him or her out of control. In such cases, mental errors multiply, and concentration can be very poor. Moreover, hating the opponents as if they were enemy soldiers who deserved loathing and punishment can lead to other excesses of arousal, sometimes with very damaging effects (e.g., Woody Hayes's striking an opposing player in the Gator Bowl). The athlete who chooses to use anger as his or her source of arousal is doomed to be always riding the fine line between positive aggressiveness and destructive rage. If you feel you can do so (and some great athletes have), try it out a few times. My own consulting experience tells me that you'll probably be disappointed in the results.

Overall, the individual responses to anger will determine its usefulness. Some athletes can handle being angry and even benefit from it, while others go to pieces. A few examples from the NBA will suffice to illustrate this point. We have all seen players who have been angered by their own misplay or by a bad call try to overreach themselves, and simply compound their problems by committing mistakes (usually a foolish foul). On the other hand, we have Kareem Abdul-Jabbar, the perennial all-pro and Most Valuable Player, who often responds to his own anger with a visible burst of exceptional performance. Either response is possible and normal; the careful observer will notice, however, that it is much easier to recall examples of anger destroying an athlete's performance than of it helping.

If you find that you have problems with your anger, that competitive events which anger you detract from your play, then you need to be able to plan for these occurrences. There are three main points to consider in dealing with this problem. First, time is often the best medicine for cooling down. When anger starts to get in the way of the physical and mental relaxation and attention necessary for top performance, it is best to sit down, take yourself out of the game, gather your thoughts, and then go back in. Coaches sometimes do this when they see an athlete getting too angry to play well; this is a great idea, provided that it is not done punitively. It is easy for the athlete to feel that he or she is being removed from play as punishment for poor performance. This kind of misunderstanding can be avoided by (1) taking the athlete out calmly, and (2) having the understood expectation (through discussion between coach and athlete during practice times) that the time out is just for calming purposes, and is not a punishment.

What to do during such a time out brings us to the second point: Try to give yourself some alternate response to occupy yourself with, instead of dwelling on the anger. For example, one baseball pitcher I consulted with found that questionable calls by the umpire got him very angry, and this affected his ability to concentrate. I encouraged him to chat with one of his infielders at those times, or to do some ground work on the mound. These time outs did not endear him to the impatient batters and umpires, but they did serve to calm him down. Obviously, timely visits to the mound by his manager were also helpful. Similar kinds of rest periods can be arranged in other sports. I often suggest that athletes go back and do some of their initial warmup routines, both physical and mental readying. A few moments of such activities on the bench can work wonders in a tough spot during competition.

The third point is probably the most central: Your mind belongs on your own performance on the next play, and not on the opponents, officials, or the last play. It is especially critical to get this point across to younger athletes, who tend to let events stay with them from situation to situation. If this awareness is already part of the athlete's readying, and if he or she knows that the coach actually sets a good example for this by not overreacting to negative events, then the athlete will be much better prepared to deal effectively with the anger-provoking events that naturally arise. I'll have a lot more to say about the coach as an example during games in Chapter 8. Briefly, time outs and good coaching models are the best medicine for anger-prone athletes.

Team spirit

This is the intangible, that certain something some teams have and others don't. We refer to teams that have it as being "cohesive," a "family," working together as a unit, or complementing each other. But nobody can pinpoint what it really is and where it comes from.

In one sense, discussion of team spirit doesn't belong in a chapter on emotions. Team spirit is not a true emotion; it is more of an attitude, a sense of togetherness. I've found that most coaches and athletes respond to team spirit, or the lack of it, as they do to confidence: Whether or not the members of a team have a feeling of unity determines how their team spirit will affect their performance.

Since most of the terms used to describe team spirit are positive ones, it is easy to assume that this feeling aids performance. This is not always the case. Social psychologists have not been able to show that teams with high team spirit do any better than teams without it. Even teams with a noticeable lack of friendliness and unity can perform just as well as their back slapping opponents. It seems to depend on the team.

Team spirit is most easily defined as friendly, positive interactions between team members. From a social scientist's point of view, the more times one team member says or does something positive for another team member (like shout encouragement, or shake hands), the higher the team spirit will be. Unfortunately, it has become quite clear that friendly, happy teams are not necessarily successful ones. In baseball, for example, the New York Yankees of 1977–78 seemed to be fighting all the time, but it didn't adversely affect their play. The same was true of the Oakland A's of the mid-seventies. In fact, players on both these squads commented on the positive effects of the fighting: the more clubhouse hassles there were, the better the team played.

No one can really know if that is true. There are also teams that openly show affection among team members and enjoy much success, even attributing their success to good team feeling (e.g., the 1979 Pittsburgh Pirates, whose motto was "We Are Family").

Maybe all we can say about team spirit is that some teams do well with it while others don't. For most teams, some minimal level of good feeling is probably essential for good play, and higher levels can inspire top performance. This would seem especially true for younger, lower-level teams. It may be fine for professional athletes to fight with one another and then fall back on personal goals, contract incentives, and an air of "professionalism" on the field; but for younger, amateur teams, fun and good feelings usually make a better environment in which to perform well.

These are some of the things that make team spirit more likely:

Common Bonds—Common goals, common enemies, and common hardships usually lead to team unity. When team members are able to see a mutual target, unity grows. The same is true of opponents who raise strong feelings in many team members. The common hardships, like long practices, physical punishment, and strict coaching demands on all team members, make for at least a small degree of unity on almost every team. It has been said that athletes who have been dead tired together after a long, hard workout (or who have "sucked wind" together after wind sprints) form a bond that cements them into a unit, whether they are friendly or not.

Peer Leadership—It is difficult for a team to rally together emotionally without someone to rally around, and the coach can only go so far. When one of your peers steps forward, you are then able to respond from a sense of shared struggle and achievement. Peer leadership can take many forms: There's the silent team member who leads by example; the "holler guy" who keeps everybody alert; the peptalker or cheerleader; and even the practical joker who keeps people laughing. The most commonly recognized leader is the self-sacrificing person who puts team success ahead of personal glory. It is important for coaches to realize that any or all of these approaches to leadership can work. Instead of trying to mold one or two athletes into specific leadership types, the coach would do much better to let each athlete do it his or her own way. It's okay to encourage individuals to take a leadership role, especially if your team has no natural leaders, but trying to give specific instructions on how to do it can backfire. Give your prospective leader a choice of roles, and never push it. Leadership cannot be drafted.

Coaching Emphasis—Team spirit can be aided by coaching directive and verbal emphasis, though it is not usually enough simply to demand it. Team members must be taught, by instruction and example, to recognize team play, and must be rewarded for exhibiting it. Coaches should encourage conversation unrelated to sports, for example, unless it directly interferes with a lecture or meeting where one person needs everyone's attention. Examples of team cooperation and unity should be pointed out and encouraged: for example, thanking a teammate for an assist in basketball.

Continuity—The longer-lasting and more stable the workings of the team, the higher the team spirit will be. This includes the stability of the people on the team, the routines the players go through together, and the ups and downs of competition they share. Players who have experienced together "the thrill of victory and the agony of defeat" will naturally feel commonality and spirit as a group.

Physical Signs of Unity—Uniforms, insignia, and the like can give individuals a sense of cohesiveness, and are therefore to be encouraged at every opportunity. Any athlete who has worn blue clothing or a blue uniform into an arena dominated by the red colors of the opponent knows the unifying force of this kind of "branding." Displaying your insignia (school or team letters, for example) becomes a statement of your team affiliation. Even physical appearance (length of hair or facial hair) can help, but it's hard to give such directives these days, and there are drawbacks to extreme regimentation of any sort. It's usually best to let the peer pressure of the team itself dictate these standards, but minimum levels of dress when a team is traveling are reasonable.

Success—Aside from sharing the ups and downs of competition, athletes who share team success come to have a sense of team identification, whether they began by liking one another or not. Emphasizing the team nature of a victory is always a good idea.

On the other hand, there are factors that can lower the likelihood of your team feeling like a unit:

Favoritism—If all team members are not rewarded or punished equally for their efforts, team spirit will suffer. The word *efforts* is a key one, since that is what should determine coaching response, and not simply success. This applies just as much to ignoring some things, not merely to praising and punishing. It is common, for example, to see some team members yelled at for a mistake while others who do similar things are ignored. This doesn't help team spirit. Incidentally, this is one of the few places where an individual approach to coaching—

Emotion in Sports

gearing responses to each athlete based on what he or she needs to hear—conflicts with another aspect of readying, namely, team development. When individual differences in response are necessary, make team members aware that this will be going on and tell them the reasons for it.*

Uneven Practice Demands—Not everyone on a team will need to do the same things in practice, but there should be equality of time and effort required. This kind of daily comparison goes on all the time, and for that reason it can be an even more damaging problem than favoritism.

Spotlighting and Scapegoating—This is often the most obvious form of inequality within a team, and one that can lead to unspoken, backbiting disharmony. The coach who singles out particular players for praise or blame, especially after competitions, is asking for trouble. Scapegoating (singling out one or two individuals as the source of the team's failures) is particularly damaging to young athletes. Postgame explanations of success and failure must take on a team aspect. The players know inside who has done well and who has done poorly, and they will respond accordingly. Even when the coach does not single out a player, the other players may. This is especially prevalent with younger athletes, where peer pressures and status seeking are rampant. Poor players are often singled out and ridiculed for their ineptitude, even though they may have been trying hard and are certainly working for the good of the team. This kind of behavior is very different from the good-natured teasing that can go on among friends, and which may be effective in prodding a very good player to try harder. The coach should not tolerate the teasing of a less talented teammate.

These are some of the factors that contribute to or detract from team spirit, but they don't tell the whole story. Specific quirks of your team may dictate how you can best approach the issue of team spirit, or even whether it is necessary. Do whatever works for your team, but give team spirit some thought, instead of just demanding it. As with confidence, eagerness, and other feelings, it is best to try to create an atmosphere in which team spirit is allowed to grow, and in which it is actively encouraged. Mutual respect for each team member's efforts

---

*One of the reasons for writing this book for both coaches and athletes—and not one book for each group—is that things work best when the athlete knows what the coach is trying to do, and vice versa.

and abilities can be just as strong a unifying factor as liking each other. A certain amount of cooperation is necessary for all teams to be successful, and any source of such cooperation can suffice. The bottom line in team spirit is a sense of common goals, a sense that you and your teammates are all working together to perform well and win. And, luckily for the coach, nine times out of ten the very fact that all team members are competitive and want to win will make this commonality of goals an established fact, and some team spirit will naturally grow up around this bond. Moreover, the entire atmosphere of team competition works in favor of team spirit, and, in the absence of damaging factors like those described above, it will be there.

The *feeling*

There is one final emotion that is different from all the others. I call that emotion the *feeling*. The *feeling* is described in detail in Chapter 7, with explicit instructions on how to get and use it. It is the single best emotion you can use to improve your performance.

What is the *feeling*? It is that one feeling, unique to you, that defines when you are ready for your best possible performance. It does not always feel good to you, but it is the feeling that prepares you best. The *feeling* can be anything at all, but it differs from the emotions already discussed in two ways. First, it is usually not a pure feeling at all, but is more likely to be a combination of thoughts and feelings that mingle in such a way as to make things just right for you to do well. Second, it is completely individual, so that the words we usually use to describe our feelings to others, and which others can understand because they have felt similar things, are inadequate. The *feeling* is different for each of us and is very powerful. Later on we will look at how to build it and why it works.

Overview

These are some of the emotions that you can try to incorporate into your own readying. Let me briefly summarize a few key points:

1. Mid-range arousal usually produces the best overall performance, depending on the sport and the athlete.

2. The arousal you get from different emotional sources is cumulative. Use specific individual emotions as your tools for putting your overall level of arousal and energy where it helps you to perform best.

3. No emotion is simply good or bad; nor, for that matter, is any factor I will discuss in this book. The need for more or less of any particular emotion depends on how much more or less arousal you need to compete well on a particular day.

4. The use of any emotion should depend on how it naturally fits into or grows out of your overall personality. Different levels and types of emotion are applicable to different athletes. In addition, you need to fit your own use of any emotion to the specific situation you find yourself in. Trying to come up with only one readying routine won't work, because different tasks call for different levels of arousal.

5. You have probably noticed that all emotions are linked; they interact and are not pure. Your level of confidence can affect your level of activation, your level of anxiety can affect your ability to use anger, and so on. Part of readying will be to determine just where you are and how you are feeling *naturally* before going ahead to apply an increase or decrease of some specific emotion.

6. You can't force emotions to exist or to disappear. You *can* create an atmosphere in which they are fostered or diminished, and you can practice specific readying techniques that will allow you to feel them for short periods of time. Luckily, these short periods of time are all you need to perform well in competition.

Proper readying is an exercise in *recognizing* and *controlling* your emotions for a few minutes or a few hours, putting you in the right frame of mind to do well. This is best accomplished by steady practice, as are all of the skills you need in order to perform at a high level. Chapter 7 will lay out all the specific ground rules for handling your emotions, as well as for handling your attitudes and thoughts—which will now be discussed in Chapter 3.

3

ATTITUDES AND THOUGHTS:
Controlling your game

"She has a good attitude about competing."
"He's got a bad attitude about practicing."
"If she only had a better attitude. . . ."

Attitudes are closely related to emotions, but they differ in one important respect: They have a strong *cognitive* component. They consist mainly of thoughts, and this enables us to distinguish them from the often indefinable feelings we also experience. In athletics, emotions usually supply the arousal and energy necessary for top performance, while thoughts provide the direction and control; or, to put it another way, emotions put the fuel in the tank and thoughts provide the steering, the braking, and the other skills of driving.

Attitudes can be thought of as networks of thoughts that cluster around a central theme. I may have one thought about Guy Lafleur, another about Phil Esposito, and still another about Marcel Dionne, but together these begin to define my attitude about hockey players. We can think of attitudes as the tracks along which our minds run. Every thought I have about a sport can be seen as a separate entity, but it makes more sense to see them in the same context they came out of— namely, my overall attitude about that sport. The individual thoughts make up the attitude, and at the same time the attitude affects each of the thoughts (especially new ones). Somewhere in the midst of this complicated relationship I can usually pinpoint the focus of my attitude about a particular thing.

Attitudes help to determine which emotions we will feel at any given time. If I were to meet you, how I feel about you and the terms in which I might describe you would stem from my attitudes about people like you. This suggests that attitudes are more stable and last longer than emotions. Feelings are, in healthy people, states of mind that come and go with relative ease, while attitudes tend to be more deeply entrenched. They are more like personality traits. (See Chapter 1.) If I like baseball, that attitude will affect my perceptions and feelings about baseball players I encounter. I may be nervous about one game, scared of another, and confident about a third, but my underlying attitude about baseball remains intact.

This is not to say that attitudes are permanent, but their cycle of existence is longer than that of most emotions. Whereas a feeling of anger or anxiety may last for up to a few days, an attitude can last for years, surviving all the shorter, more superficial feelings I may have about specific things during that time. Attitudes have a life span; they are born, grow to a peak, decline, and often disappear from our minds entirely. They encompass emotions and other readying cycles, like physical readiness cycles, mental readiness cycles, and so on.

One of the most important qualities of attitudes is that they color our emotions. *Attitudes* help to determine our *perceptions* of the world, which in turn affect our immediate *feelings*, which have a lot to do with our *performance*. This chain—attitude–perception–feelings–performance—is operating all the time, whether we are aware of it or not.

Figure 3-1.

ATTITUDES → PERCEPTIONS → FEELINGS → PERFORMANCE

Let's take a specific chain and see what it looks like. I am an athlete whose attitude is that it is good to hustle. Because I have such an attitude, I tend to see the world of athletes in terms of how much or how little they hustle. I probably also assess my own performances in terms of how much I hustled. This, in turn, affects my feelings about myself and my performance: If I have hustled, I am likely to feel good about my performance; and if I can easily see myself hustling in my next competition, I will probably feel confident about that contest. My level of confidence will then affect my performance. So we see that this simple attitude can have many effects, changing my perceptions, emotions, and other performance factors.

This chain is also important in another way. Scientists studying the relationship between attitudes and emotions have found that we often call the same physiological feelings by different names, depending on our attitudes and our perceptions of the situations. For example, let's say that my heart is pounding, I have a strong feeling in the pit of my stomach, and I'm sweating. What emotion am I feeling? How can I figure out what emotion is causing this reaction? Well, if I'm walking in the woods and have just seen our old friend the bear, fear is probably what I'm feeling. If I'm watching a teammate score the winning run in a critical baseball game, excitement and joy are probably better descriptions. If I'm waiting in the on-deck circle in the bottom of the ninth, however, anxiety could well be the best label. Similarly, if I feel a rush of emotion at a critical time in a tennis match, my attitude about how things are going will determine whether I call the emotion anxiety or excitement. It depends on the individual situation.

Figure 3-2. One physiological reaction can be interpreted as different emotions, depending on the situation.

My thoughts and perceptions about the situation will go a long way toward determining whether I will call my state of mind *fear* or *excitement* or *nervousness*. And the clearer the picture I have of my own thoughts and perceptions (i.e., attitudes), the better I will be able to control my feelings, as I must to perform well. Emotions are the immediate readying factors that supply us with the arousal we need to perform well; attitudes are the background mental patterns that help us to control these emotions when performance time rolls around.

Attitudes provide the context in which specific emotions exist.

Attitudes and Thoughts

For example, the Montreal Canadiens have a long tradition of hockey excellence; this fosters an attitude of superiority in their players. This *attitude* of superiority leads the players to *perceive* weaknesses in their opponents and strengths in themselves, which in turn leads to *feelings* of confidence, which in turn lead to *good play* on the ice. Even if temporary anxieties do come along, such as the pressure of a big game or the threat of another top team that is playing well, they will have much less of a negative effect on the Canadiens than they might have on some other team. In fact, such anxiety can be easily turned around and used as a source of arousal. The attitude itself thus underlies the specific emotions that the Canadiens may feel from one game to another.

This attitude can also have a more direct effect on play, without operating through emotions. It may lead the players to spot specific weaknesses in their opponents that can then be exploited, but which may not have even been noticed without the attitude of superiority to begin with. This attitude might also inspire the players to try more difficult maneuvers on the ice, thereby expanding their repertoire. The examples could go on; the point is that the attitude becomes the foundation of many other performance factors.

It is more difficult to list common attitudes than it is to list the seven basic emotions. Because our minds differ from one another, our thought patterns are unique. Still, a person's attitudes toward his or her sport can usually be broken down into two categories: an overriding attitude toward the sport, and a number of smaller and less influential ones, often derived from the first. I have found that the overriding attitude is usually the strongest and the toughest to change, and that the smaller ones are more accessible to intervention. This chapter will address itself to both types of attitudes.

Early developmental set

The most important attitude in the production of good athletic performance is what I call *Early Developmental Set*. This attitude can be roughly defined as one in which the athlete has had, from some time early in his or her life, thoughts, images, and motivations concerning the playing of a particular sport. A positive Early Developmental Set (or EDS for short) means that the individual has always leaned toward sports as an activity central to his or her life. In general, the more specific the EDS thoughts and images, the better. It's a good sign for an athlete to love sports in general, an even better one for him or her always to have daydreamed about playing basketball, and an even better one if the daydreams focused on a certain position—namely, the position that is now to be played. When all these factors combine, and when the athlete even winds up on a particular team or at a particular school that was part of the EDS, the positive effect can be very powerful.

A strong, positive EDS is not essential for good performance, but when it is present, it can be capitalized on. We can say that some Montreal Canadiens are born and some are made. The born Canadiens—those athletes who have, from a young age, focused much attention, effort, and thought on being a superior athlete in one sport or another—have a built-in performance edge. This EDS becomes the edge that coaches look for in selecting and recruiting athletes, and athletes who have such an early history of devotion to sport often make good leaders. Performing well is almost always on their minds, and it shows.

Where does a positive EDS get its start? Parental encouragement and exposure to athletic heroes and leaders are among the more common sources, but more important is the youngster's own choice of a sport. Through interactions with peers and the simple joys of competition and play, the young athlete learns to channel more and more energy into sport. He or she plays a great deal and follows the exploits of others through the media. Early coaches can also exert a great influence. And, as will be discussed shortly, you yourself can practice having this kind of attitude. As with other attitudes, a positive EDS is born in our experiences and in the examples that others set for us. When the young athlete has a strong, positive, older athlete on whom to model his or her own efforts and images, it is almost impossible to prevent a good EDS from developing. And when this early attitude is combined with some success and pleasure in sport, the combination is superb.

"Good" and "bad" attitudes

How often have you heard coaches say things like "That kid has a great attitude," or "He'd be a fine player if only he had a better attitude," or "She's not motivated to work hard enough," or "If only my athletes had her kind of attitude"?

Coaches love to talk about athlete's attitudes and what could be accomplished if only a bad attitude could be replaced by a good one. Unfortunately, simply talking about attitudes and motivation doesn't

Attitudes and Thoughts

get the job done. What coaches need are new ways to understand attitudes and new approaches for changing them.

What does a coach really mean when he or she refers to good or bad attitudes? Well, it is usually not the attitude itself, but the observable behaviors that the athlete is exhibiting. The athlete who is described as having a "good" attitude is usually attentive and active, brings a great deal of energy to practices and competitions, and tries to attack his or her problems and weaknesses. The athlete with the "bad" attitude, on the other hand, often appears inattentive and preoccupied, and lets the coach know that other things are on his or her mind besides the sporting task at hand. This athlete comes across as lazy, with a limited amount of energy, and generally avoids problem areas and competitive weaknesses. There is little sense of challenge and accomplishment when this type of athlete practices, and too often this becomes apparent even in competitive events themselves.

The factor that makes the difference between these two extreme kinds of competitors is universally called *Motivation*, with a capital *M*. Motivation, or the lack of it, is the one major force that most coaches pay attention to when they try to deal with an athlete's inner thoughts and feelings. It is the bottom line for many coaches when sorting out the winners from the losers.

What is motivation? What motivates us to do what we do, or to not do some things we might be better off doing? The complete answers are more complex than the scope of this book allows for, but there are some basic, simplified ways of looking at motivation that can be useful to coaches and athletes.

Sources of motivation

Motivation to work hard and do well in athletics is essentially no different from motivation to do other things. In this context, we can identify three major sources of motivation: our innate drives, or needs; our social requirements and goals; and the rewards and punishments involved in sport.

The most basic sources of motivation are our *drives*. They are the most basic because they require nothing outside of our own bodies and minds to set them in motion—that is, to *motivate* us. Drives are simple things like hunger, thirst, or the sex drive. They keep us alive, and they are always part of our motivational makeup, no matter how complex and sophisticated our lives might become.

The drive most relevant to athletic performance is the drive for *mastery* or *competency*. We share with our primate cousins some inner need to act on our world, to manipulate our environment, and thereby to learn more and more to help us survive. Our incredibly complex and adaptable brains are probably the result of such a mastery drive in our evolutionary ancestors. Every athlete is engaged in satisfying this need by learning to attack, defend, and otherwise control the "world" of the sporting event; you are learning to manipulate, and hopefully to master, your opponent and your game.

Somewhat more sophisticated are our *social* needs and goals. Among these, there are two that are directly relevant to sport: the *need for achievement* and the *need for affiliation*. The first of these was briefly described as the opposite of *fear of failure* in the section on fear in Chapter 2. It is the need to succeed, to achieve, and to be recognized as doing well at whatever we choose to do; obviously, this is present in many athletes. The need for affiliation is most clearly involved in team sports. It is the need to feel and to be accepted as a part of some group of people. Even athletes engaged in individual sports are anxious to be recognized as athletes, or as representatives of their school or state or country. The national pride displayed by Olympic athletes is usually motivated in this way.

Thirdly, there are the tangible *rewards* for sport participation, and the complementary punishments. We all operate on the pleasure–pain principle and are motivated to do things that are rewarded and not to do things that are punished. Athletics can be physically rewarding (and, at high levels, financially rewarding, too), and this physical pleasure is what gets many kids into sports in the first place. Other rewards include the kinds of social recognition described above, as well as direct approval from parents, coaches, and other role models. The well-motivated athlete is usually the one who is more aware of the rewards he or she is getting or hopes to get from sports, while the unmotivated athlete is often unclear about the personal pros and cons of sports participation.

How to handle motivation and attitude

Each of these sources of motivation has implications for how the knowledgeable coach can deal with athletes. The guidelines for building and maintaining positive attitudes are clearer than those for remedying negative attitudes, since it is easier to build toward something

Attitudes and Thoughts

than to try to move away from an existing bad habit. This is just as true with mental and emotional activities as it is with physical behavior.

To oversimplify a little, all the coach needs to do to build positive attitudes is to provide positive experiences for his or her athletes in relation to the three motivation sources: drives, social needs, and rewards. Make sure that your athletes do get a sense of mastering, and of learning new skills. Giving the athlete this sense of mastery by structuring victories and obvious signs of progress into workouts makes the athlete much readier to accept criticism and work assignments in his or her areas of weakness. It satisfies the most basic of the motivational needs by enabling him or her to feel that, through effort in sport, he or she has become a more competent individual.

The need for achievement is also satisfied by providing periodic successes for the athlete, and the positively motivating result can be further enhanced by the coach publicly recognizing this success. A pat on the back in front of the team can work wonders for an athlete's social motivation. The need for affiliation is most easily met through the comradeship born of both positive and negative experiences, as long as the experiences are shared by all.

Rewards that motivate are most effective when they are kept simple. Best is the good feeling of doing something well, and this is often the prime source of motivation of the less verbal, very physical athlete. Giving him or her a channel along which to feel good during a long practice session can work wonders for motivation. A basketball player who needs work on free throws, for example, will probably maintain a much better attitude about it if he or she mixes the fun of running and jumping with the work itself. When frustration and the start of negative attitudes set in, a quick dose of physically pleasurable activities can be very helpful. Mix the good stuff in with the work. Remember fun? It is a direct motivating factor, a long-range producer of good attitudes, because it is among the best rewards we can experience.

The building of positive attitudes has as its watchwords the following: Do all you can to keep both goals and progress visible to your athletes. It is when such goals and progress become forgotten that attitudes begin to sink, and the repetitive work of practice becomes the most obvious, dullest, aspect of sport. Keeping goals and progress in the mind of the athlete lays the foundation on which all positive attitudes are built: feeling good about oneself. The well-motivated athlete is the one who is getting what he or she needs from sport, and who can therefore feel good about participating.

Handling the "bad attitude" athlete

Here's where the coach's task gets stickier. You have an athlete who is not well-motivated, who gives you a hard time, and who displays one of the various bad attitudes that coaches typically see. How can such an athlete best be approached?

It would be impossible to list all the possible sources of a problem attitude or all the complaints an athlete might have. But there are some general guidelines for dealing with such athletes, and they follow from the sources of motivation described above.

1. Discourage halfway efforts. One of the real dangers of having a negative attitude about a sport is that this often leads to less than maximum effort. Once such a pattern is established, it is very difficult to dislodge. Consequently, when a coach sees an athlete who is down and is not fully competing, it is usually a good idea to bring this to the athlete's attention. Insist on the athlete giving full effort even if his or her attitude is not strictly positive. The attitude and the behavior can be separated, allowing for full effort without inspired, eager play.

The purpose in taking this step is to force the issue with the athlete, and to prevent the negative attitude from lingering and affecting his or her performance. Force the issue by demanding top effort or dismissing the athlete entirely, but avoid giving the athlete an ultimatum. This distinction is a tricky one, but it can be made with a little care.

If you say to an athlete, "You better shape up or you're off the team," you are taking a gamble that is probably unnecessary. Some athletes can respond to this and will try to change their approach to the game, but others will be unable to do so. The very fact that an athlete is exhibiting a bad attitude is a sign that he or she is *confused*. If the athlete clearly wanted to play, there would be no attitude problem; if not, he or she would simply quit the sport or the team. The athlete who does not totally dissociate him- or herself from the sport, but who is obviously not wholly committed to it either, is in a limbo that can be very uncomfortable. An ultimatum can force such an athlete to make a premature choice that can have negative effects: It can force some athletes to quit altogether, while forcing others to stay and make an outward show of eagerness without the inner attitude to back it up. The way I like to handle this dilemma is to make the athlete aware of what is going on and to insist that, for whatever period of time he or she is practicing with me, only a one-hundred percent effort will do. What he or she does at other times is up to the individual; I don't expect this

Attitudes and Thoughts

athlete to be a cheerleader or peptalker. When practice time approaches, the athlete must decide *each day* whether he or she is going to go all out; if not, then I tell the athlete to stay home. If this results in more absences than I am willing to tolerate, I tell the athlete that since he or she appears to have made a decision, not to bother coming anymore. In effect, I have given the athlete a day-by-day ultimatum, a grace period during which some change must occur. This middle stage between the appearance of the bad attitude and the final dismissal gives the athlete some time to get things straightened out within his or her own mind, without the pressure of having to fake it in practice each day.

This approach is offered with the assumption that the coach will also use some of the other guidelines presented here, especially talking with the athlete. Simply to deliver the ultimatum, even in the mid-range severity described here, doesn't really help to settle the issue; it merely buys the coach and the athlete some time, and takes the problem out of the realm of the exasperating, everyday struggle that can destroy whatever is left of a positive attitude in the athlete. Discouraging half-hearted effort is essential once the athlete begins to have a negative effect on other athletes through his or her negativism. Frankly, I think the coach is doing the athlete a favor by telling him or her to stay away whenever he or she isn't ready to go all out, and no more than one or two halfhearted practice efforts should be tolerated. I am suggesting, however, that the coach doesn't have to be angry and punitive in demanding that the athlete get it together; it can be done best in a spirit of concern and with a clear, firm desire to help the athlete settle whatever issues are distressing and undermining him or her. Remember, it is a terrible feeling to be trying to do something and not to be able to give yourself freely to it; that is the battle the athlete with a negative attitude is facing, no matter how harsh and uncaring his or her portrayal of the negativism may be.

2. **Talk to the athlete.** Ignoring the problem usually doesn't work with bad attitudes, but expressing your concern over the problem you have in common does. Make the focus of your conversation *what the athlete wants:* what the sport, the upcoming event, or the practice sessions mean to him or her. Bringing up the athlete's Early Developmental Set can be very helpful here. When a bad attitude shows up in an athlete, chances are it can be traced to disappointment: Some predetermined expectation of the athlete is not being met by your sport. Talking about such a discrepancy between the expected and the actual can really help, even if the conversation turns up nothing that you, the

coach, can actually do about it. It is usually a matter of helping the athlete to readjust his or her expectations or perceptions of your sport.

In talking with the negative athlete, keep in mind the three sources of motivation: drives, social needs, and rewards. The better you can locate the areas in which the athlete's needs are not being met, and in which you may be able to help the athlete start getting some positive reactions, the quicker the negative attitude will begin to fade. Asking specifically about a list of motivation sources is often a good, direct approach to use.

I consulted with an athlete who had good skills in tennis but who was sluggish and resistant during practice sessions. I asked her, as directly as I could, what motivated her to play in the first place. When she couldn't answer the question, I gave her a list of things that usually motivate athletes—desire for success, fun, physical enjoyment, social status, rewards from parents or friends, the desire to win, and so on. Choosing from this list helped her to start telling me what she felt she wasn't getting. Then I had something to work with.

In talking with the negative athlete, do two basic things: Start with one or two general questions about how the athlete feels and what expectations are not being met, and let the athlete tell you about it (not the other way around); and, if this doesn't get things started, give the player a list of positive things to be gotten from sport, so that he or she can choose where to go to get some more of the pluses instead of the minuses.

3. Don't push. Yes, it is exasperating to have an athlete who does not perform to his or her potential and who constantly displays a lack of eagerness, attention, and effort. But all the yelling in the world will not turn this athlete's head around. Save your ultimatums and threats for your last effort, and start out more gently. *Clearly* and *privately*, discuss it with the athlete as a problem you *both* have. An athlete with a negative attitude is certainly hurting him- or herself more than anyone else, but as long as he or she is under your direction, it is your problem, too. Since sullenness is often the hallmark of the bad attitude, yelling and threatening the athlete will only serve to deepen the athlete's resistance to you and your sport. Bad attitudes can seldom be pushed away; more frequently, they respond to guidance. Try to guide your athlete's thoughts in a new, more rewardable direction.

4. Look for the hazard. This is related to talking with the athlete. The *hazard* is the event that has put the athlete in a bad mood or has spawned the negative attitude. It may have been a bad game, being benched, or something entirely outside of your sport. But what-

ever it is, it probably holds the key to changing the attitude. A hazard is almost always present at the start of a negative attitude.

Why is this so? Well, since the individual is playing your sport, presumably at some point in the past he or she did so *positively*, for at least one of the positive sources of motivation. Now, on the other hand, he or she has a negative attitude about the sport. We have all heard athletes say, "(such-and-such) used to be fun, but it's no fun now." Obviously, a change took place, and often a specific event marks that point. In talking with an athlete, the better you can get the athlete thinking about the *exact point* at which things started to go downhill, the quicker he or she will start to change the present attitude. In fact, you, as an athlete, should ask yourself these questions: "If it used to be fun and isn't now, what happened? When? What can I do about it?" After all, this negative attitude is cheating you out of a source of plea- sure you once had, and it may be worth some effort to get it back. This approach reminds the athlete not of the potential rewards but of the actual rewards that he or she really did enjoy. Negative attitudes have a way of weakening in the face of such solid evidence of other ways of thinking. Once the hazard has been located, the conversation will eas- ily carry itself.

5. **Some Positive "Faking."** Occasionally, in athletes who are not heavily saddled with a bad attitude but who are going through a mild slump, the following technique can be very useful. It also applies to the athlete who has never been all that excited about his or her sport, but who seems to approach it positively on a slightly lower level. The technique involves instructing the athlete to behave *as if* he or she were a great athlete who had always known that he or she would grow up to be great, and who had always wanted to be a great athlete more than anything else. In essence, this is practicing having a high Early De- velopmental Set. The purpose of doing this is to remind the athlete that he or she is still in control, and that the mild slump does not necessar- ily have to take over his or her mood completely. The athlete is demon- strating that he or she can behave in many different ways and is not locked into being down. You are saying to the athlete, "There are other ways of seeing yourself. Just imagine what it would be like to actually be ———————————" (fill in the name of a star in your sport).

This works best with mildly negative attitudes, and serves as a good mood breaker. It shows the athlete who has never really seen him- or herself as a great, fully committed athlete that he or she can do more and feel better by seeing things in a different way. It can be especially effective with young athletes who may not have been good performers at a young age, but whose recent physical developments give them a good shot at competing at a high level. It can also be used to build the confidence of the athlete who may be down from losing, but who still has the potential to do well in a new situation (like a new team or a new school). If the athlete can't easily behave or feel as if he or she were great, the coach should describe what such a feeling would be like. Talk the athlete through it; describe what it would feel like to be Earl Campbell or Jimmy Connors. Then let the athlete's fantasies take over. The coach's job is first to describe the right kind of feeling and then to encourage the athlete to practice it.

6. **Be a Model.** With attitudes, just as with emotions and physical behaviors, the best teacher is the one who can *show* what he or she wants to get across, not just tell the athlete about it. By being a model for your athletes, you give them an example of a positive way to approach sport. This is what people mean when they say that a team takes on the personality of its coach. Learning through identification and example is one of the strongest of all human learning capabilities, much superior to learning through lectures or demands. Unquestionably, when a positive coach-athlete relationship is established, the athlete does take on many of the attitudes and characteristics of the coach.

The key here is the positive relationship. Research has shown that people tend to learn best by example when the model, in this case the coach, is seen by the learner as being similar to him- or herself. The more the athlete sees the coach as sharing goals, pleasures, and worries, the more likely that the athlete will adopt the modeled attitude, emotion, or behavior. With the troubled athlete, the coach must, through honest conversation and attention, give the athlete the sense that he or she does care, is at least trying to understand the situation, and does have a feel for the athlete's own dilemma. This is a necessary partner to being a model. The main reason why athletes don't learn modeled behavior and attitudes is that they see the coach as distant and different. If the coach can change this perception, then he or she can reasonably expect that being an example of a person with a positive attitude will rub off on the team.

Judge the athlete's attitudes not by what is said but by what is done. An athlete doesn't have to be a peptalking, leadership-oriented eager beaver to have a good attitude, and it is unfair to expect such zeal from any athlete. The few athletes who do present the coach with such an attitude are giving a gift that should be seen and used as such. In

Attitudes and Thoughts

addressing yourself to athletes with attitude problems, stick to what you have seen in the athlete's behavior that leads you to suspect a bad attitude. The more specifically you can point out to the athlete exactly what he or she is doing, the better the chance that he or she will respond well and do something about it.

If you want a deeper view of what motivates people, there are numerous psychological texts on the subject. This condensation of attitudes is intended to cover the topic, but not to exhaust it.

One final thought: If you have unsuccessfully approached an athlete about an attitude problem, you can always have him or her read this section. It may provide some ideas about what is going wrong, and can serve as a starting point from which you and the athlete can consider what you see going on, and what you can do about it.

What can the athlete do?

Addressing this issue from the perspective of the athlete is somewhat complicated by the fact that most athletes who have a bad attitude probably don't think they do. Since everyone sees the world through his or her own eyes, it's very difficult to have enough perspective on yourself to be able to know when your attitude is getting in the way of your efforts. Usually, athletes are told by their coaches that their attitude is presenting something of a problem. Less frequently this information will come from a parent, loved one, or fellow athlete. Such a pronouncement is often in the form of an edict: "You'd better change that attitude of yours if you expect to get anywhere." This is never a pleasant thing to hear, and it usually comes to the athlete like a bolt out of the blue. "What do you mean? Who? Me?"

What's the best way, then, for the athlete to respond? If you have found yourself in such a situation, keep the following points in mind.

1. First and foremost—don't shut out the criticism. Try to look beyond the actual person who brought up your attitude and think about what that person is saying. Getting mad will probably do neither of you any good, and merely prevents you from determining whether or not there is any truth to the person's complaint.

It's important to realize that there may be some value in your thinking about the criticism *whether or not the person is right*. Chances are that you are not the degenerate child you may think the other person is calling you; but you may not be perfect, either. Even if the person's criticism seems unfounded, take the opportunity to review your attitudes and overall approach to your sport. You may find that some of your earlier attitudes are no longer applicable and are only getting in your way. It is not a question of proving the other person right or wrong, but of looking at yourself as objectively as you can so that you can improve as much as you can. Even if the person's criticism is dead wrong, consider this: you are probably doing something that put the idea that you have a bad attitude into that person's head, and you would do well to figure out how. Then you can stop doing whatever it is, or can set the person straight about what you are doing and why it is not really indicative of a bad attitude, and get on to the more important business of working on your game.

I once consulted with a young swimmer who was constantly hearing from her coach that she had to have a more positive, committed attitude if she were ever to excel in her sport. She insisted that her attitude wasn't bad, and that she was committed to doing well in the pool. Rather than try to convince her that her coach was right or that she really did have an attitude problem, I asked her to consider what she was doing to give her coach the idea that she had a bad attitude. This indirect approach to the differences between coach and athlete enabled her, for the first time, to think clearly about what her coach was saying. It turned out that some of her relatively meaningless, joking comments about how much work there was in workouts were being interpreted by her coach as signs of a negative attitude, especially since such comments were always made to other team members. The swimmer herself certainly did see the value of the hard workouts, and her jokes meant nothing more to her than complaints about the weather or the difficulty of her schoolwork; but those around her did not see them that way. Even though she felt that the coach was wrong, the swimmer was able to get some good out of the criticism by considering it reasonably from a perspective that she felt was relevant. Had she merely angrily insisted that her coach was way off base, nothing good would have come out of the situation.

2. This example serves to illustrate another point as well: When you receive a criticism about your attitude, ask the person what he or she wants you to do, not what he or she wants you to think. No one can see inside your head, so obviously you have been doing something that signified to that other person that your attitude could be better. Find out, as exactly as you can, what it is, and why that person feels it to be a sign of a bad attitude. Then you both have some common ground on which to build a plan for making things better. It is not fair for any other person, even your coach, to demand that you think a certain way. But it is equally unfair for you to ignore that person's comments, especially if

Attitudes and Thoughts

he or she can point out the specific things you do that indicate a bad attitude.

3. During practices or competitions, if you find yourself thinking when you should be acting, *stop what you are doing immediately.* Having extraneous thoughts come into your mind when you should be doing things quickly, easily, and without hesitation is the best message to yourself that there is uncertainty either in your attitudes or in your actual knowledge of your assignments. When the uncertainty comes from the latter, refer yourself to Chapters 4 and 5 on the mental side of learning. When these extraneous thoughts spring from uncertainty about where sport fits into your life, or about anything else related to your commitment and pleasure in your sport, you are experiencing attitudinal difficulties.

You are always better off trying to settle things off the field. If you try to ignore them or practice through them when they are breaking your concentration, you are only making things harder on yourself than you should. Taking one or two days off to get your head together, either on your own or by talking things over with your coach or other confidant, is much more efficient in the long run than trying to grit your teeth and practice anyway. Sometimes doing things one-hundred percent means not just running or swimming or concentrating one-hundred percent; it also means taking the time to be one-hundred percent confused when you need to be. It means giving yourself some time to spend one-hundred percent of your attention on just how you feel about your sport and what you'd like to do about it.

4. Ask yourself honestly, "Am I giving *one-hundred percent* to my sport?" When someone points out to you that your attitude is less than perfect, they are saying that, in their view, you are not giving as much of yourself to your sport as you could. Consider whether you, in your own mind, are doing as much as you can to enjoy and excel in your sport. Doing anything less is only cheating yourself.

Maybe you've heard this a hundred times before from coaches, teachers, and parents. And maybe giving your all to your sport means that you wouldn't be cool, that you might look silly when you misplay or exhausted when you hustle. If so, then your attitude is clearly not compatible with sports competition, and you can expect to have coaches on your back as long as you have contact with athletics. In fact, this conflict—the cool athlete who doesn't hustle and the coach who values hustling above all else—is almost always at the heart of coach-athlete differences. It is almost always the problem whenever the coach says, "He or she has a bad attitude." If you hear these words from your coach, you'd better be absolutely certain that you are one-hundred percent committed to your sport before you start thinking the coach is off the wall. He or she is merely commenting on the external signs, while you are the one who will have to live with the less than top effort and performance when the athletic opportunity has passed you by.

5. When you do find an attitude within yourself that works against what you need to do to excel in your sport, *try to figure out who or what helps keep that attitude alive in you.* If the bad attitude got absolutely no support, it would die a natural death. All of our attitudes are maintained by at least some of the people we know or by some reward that we get from them. The more clearly you can identify the sources of these bad attitudes, the more able you will be to get rid of them.

I once coached a baseball player whose attitudes toward the game fluctuated daily. Sometimes this youngster really got into the game, but on other days he appeared lethargic and unconcerned before a game. In fact, he and I eventually realized that he usually felt that the game really didn't matter when he arrived to warm up, but that as the game progressed, he became more and more involved. On good days, by the sixth inning he would be sweating out a tough game right along with his coach. I asked him what was going on in his world—what people, places, or things did he have contact with when he was not at the ballfield—that helped feed his attitude of not caring about his performance on the diamond. After some thought, he realized that some of his friends who didn't play baseball tried to pull his attention in other directions, and even directly discouraged him from playing ball. Since he liked these friends, he was swayed by their opinions and their subtle undermining of his commitment to baseball.

I am not saying that there was anything wrong with these friends. Their interests lay outside of sport, and there is no reason to think that they should be interested in sport or should actively encourage the ballplayer to work at it all the time. The athlete was caught in a classic conflict between the values and attitudes of his friends and those of his coach. He liked baseball, but he liked doing other things as well. Realizing this was the athlete's first step in coming to grips with the problem, the first step toward working out a system through which he could commit himself full time to baseball while he was on the field and still give energy to his friends and other activities elsewhere. As you might guess, the two main elements in reaching this arrangement were (1) recognizing and purposely reinforcing a quick and definite off-field–on-field attitude shift as soon as he came to play, and (2)

62   *Attitudes and Thoughts*

explaining the conflict to his friends and asking them to respect his desire to play baseball. His coach was already aware of the whole problem, but in another case in which the athlete attacks the problem, talking with the coach would of course be an equally important part of the solution.

6. This leads us to the next guideline: Be sure to *tell the people around you, especially your coach, of your desire to change your attitude.* This may be the most important guideline for the athlete, for announcing to your coach a commitment to change in order to build good performance is one of the best things you can do for the athlete-coach relationship. No coach will turn away the athlete with an honest desire to improve, and the coach will usually bend over backwards to help such an athlete figure out what needs to be done to correct the situation. Remember, you can state such a desire to your coach even if you are not sure that you agree with his or her appraisal of your attitude, and even if you haven't the slightest idea how to go about rectifying the situation. You are simply saying, "I do want to be the best player I can be, in mind as well as body, and I will try to achieve that goal." This is a solid foundation from which you and your coach can approach the problem, and from which you can then try some of the guidelines described here.

These guidelines can only go so far; you have to take the actual steps. What these guidelines are really saying is that the hardest and most important thing for the athlete to do is to be open to criticism. You don't have to swallow everything your coach or another critic is telling you, but you should realize that you need such outside criticism to grow, as an athlete and as a person. That is the stated goal of this book—to help you to become the best that you can be. But if the path for so doing were clearly laid out in our minds, there would be no need for coaches or for books like this.

The imagery techniques in Chapter 7 are also applicable to working on your attitudes. They are designed primarily to produce specific feelings or states of mind, but, with practice, they can be used to help you inject certain thought patterns into your mind.

Specific positive attitudes

Up to this point I have been talking about good or bad *Attitudes*, with a capital *A*, pointing out the characteristics of each. But aside from each athlete's overall attitude, there are other, somewhat more limited attitudes that can also play a part in the athlete's readiness. Certain attitudes are almost always positive and lead to better performance. These attitudes are well recognized by coaches and athletes alike, but in the hubbub of physical and mental preparation they usually don't get as much attention as they should. Also, they often run together in the coach's (and the athlete's) mind, when separating them might work better.

These positive attitudes come from the personal attributes that athletes need to be able to produce top sports performance. These qualities, and the attitudes derived from them, fall into four groups: energy-producing attitudes, control-related attitudes, team-related attitudes, and competition-related attitudes. All of these attributes are needed for top athletic performance. Let's look at each category separately.

Energy-producing attitudes are those which contribute to the energy level the athlete needs to perform well. They work in ways similar to emotions, providing the psychological fuel the athlete must have in order to compete at a high level. The most prominent energy-related attitude is *full effort*: the attitude that, whatever I may be doing, I am going to do it at full speed, focusing all my effort and attention on the task at hand. This applies both to practice and to competition; it is a sense of wanting to put all of myself into my activity because there is pleasure in doing so. Commitment and intensity are the words coaches commonly use to define this attitude, and they are usually very good about rewarding it whenever it is present. Athletes like Pete Rose and John Havlicek come to mind when we think of this attitude.

A related attitude, that also leads to high energy levels, is *love of a challenge*. Athletes who have this attitude respond with great energy to situations in which they are being called on by an opponent or by a coach to show their best. The athlete who can mobilize this kind of energy when the time is right has a clear edge over his or her opponent. Teams like the Green Bay Packers under Vince Lombardi, the Oakland A's in the early 1970s, and the 1977–78 New York Yankees exemplify this attitude, rising to the occasion when challenged in postseason play. The athlete who licks his or her chops at the prospect of a good challenge, who gets genuinely excited about the big game just because it *is* a big game, will definitely benefit because of such an attitude.

Equally important as energy in producing top athletic performance is playing with *control*. First and foremost among this set of attitudes is that locker room poster favorite: *poise*. Your coach has probably given you a detailed explanation of the meaning of this term,

Attitudes and Thoughts

and I will merely point out that poise means being under control at all times, acting and responding to your opponent without panicking. Poise is a full partner of confidence; it is the knowledge that no matter what happens to you or your team during competition, you will continue to play the same way, with controlled intensity.

Our next positive attitude is *playing your own game*. This involves knowing and being comfortable with your own limits of performance during competition. It is just as important *not* to try to do things you are incapable of during competition, as it is to go all out. Coaches usually refer to this attitude as *playing within yourself*. It is easy to see when an athlete is trying so hard that he or she is out of control, trying to do things that aren't smart (like swinging for the fence, taking the low-percentage shot, or trying to run through blockers). Knowing and accepting your limits frees you to put all of your energy where it belongs: on the things you can do to win. We all have limits, and it is foolish to pretend otherwise. Playing with poise, control, and confidence does not mean blindly believing that you can do anything you want on the field of play; rather, it means knowing that you have a firm handle on what it is you want to do to perform well, and that you can do these things.

Closely related to this attitude, but different in one important way, is *playing as well as you can, and not playing "against" your opponent*. The truly great athletes and teams focus not on beating an opponent but on playing at a high level. Their attention is on reaching as much of their potential as they can, and not on being better than someone else. Even in the face of severe competition, you don't have to feel that you are "against" someone else; instead, you can focus on your own range of performance and try to come as close to the top as you can. The issue of whether you are a better athlete than your opponents is one you can do nothing about; you have your equipment and they have theirs. What you *can* do something about is how much of your physical and mental equipment you will be able to put into use.

In Chapter 1, I established the top of John Wooden's "Pyramid of Success" as the goal of appropriate psychological readying and the goal of this book. The reason is perhaps best seen here: Of the many things Wooden's teams did well, the most prominent was in the area of control-related attitudes. The three attitudes described here—poise, playing within yourself, and playing for yourself (and not against)—were regularly displayed by his teams. It was rare to see a UCLA player lose control of himself or try to do things he couldn't. One of the reasons Wooden's players always looked good was that they put their energy into doing what they were capable of, rather than trying to overreach themselves with bad shots or fancy passing. What some coaches saw as Wooden's rigidity in playing only man-to-man defense was merely a reflection of his attitude, embodied on the court by his players, that one should learn to do the basics well and then focus all of one's attention and energy on *that,* leaving alone the elaborate strategies of attacking a particular opponent. This insistence on players' having full control over their games, and not trying just to beat someone else, was at the core of the "UCLA attitude" and was the foundation of the players' confidence and energy.

Next we come to *team-related attitudes.* Team-related attitudes are applicable, obviously, only in team sports, and they parallel the discussion of team spirit in Chapter 2. There are two primary team-related attitudes to consider: *cooperation* and *self-sacrifice.* These words are thrown around a lot by coaches, and their meaning should be relatively clear. Cooperation and self-sacrifice together comprise the attitude that the outcome of the efforts of the team is more important than the outcome for any one individual. Individual success is always appreciated and rewarded, but especially so when it contributes to the success of the team. This means both stepping to the fore when the team needs you (for example, wanting the ball for a critical shot or trying to take the extra base when it's really needed), and being willing to do the little, inglorious things that help the team to win. The baseball player who sacrifices in order to move up a baserunner, the basketball player who passes, sets picks, and plays tough defense, and the football player who blocks well all display an attitude of team importance. This kind of attitude can come only through the encouragement and, when necessary, the insistence of the coach.

Competition-related attitudes, for most coaches and athletes, means only one attitude, but it's often the most important one: *being a winner.* What does being a winner really mean, and why is it so positive?

Being a winner is not the same as wanting to win. In fact, wanting to win very badly usually has a negative effect on athletic performance, since it introduces anxiety and tightness into the athlete's readying. Being a winner—having the attitude that you are a winner—means firmly believing that you will win in the end. The attitude does not depend on the outcome of any particular event. The athlete who sees him- or herself as a winner thinks in terms of the top of his or her performance range, and always in terms of the *next* performance. In an athlete with this attitude, "wait 'till next year" is not sour grapes or an idle threat made in anger; rather, it is a positive sense about his or her own abilities and potential for growth.

Two well-known concepts are integral parts of this winning attitude: *pride* and *positive self-image*. *Webster's* definition reflects the closeness of these two terms. Pride is defined as "the quality or state of being proud; self-esteem; a reasonable or justifiable self-respect." All of these words dance around the heart of the matter: Having the attitude of a winner means thinking well of yourself, yesterday, today, and tomorrow.

I suppose being a winner can be seen as an attitude that combines all the positive attitudes and emotions that contribute to one's athletic success. Examples can be found in the truly great teams and individual athletes who excelled for so long: the New York Yankees, the Boston Celtics, the Montreal Canadiens, Babe Ruth, Bill Russell, Jim Brown, Jack Nicklaus. These names mean winning—not only because these athletes won and built their reputations, but also because of the way they carried themselves, of the pride and confidence and positive attitude they maintained without downgrading their opponents. These are champions. And the attitude of being a winner, a champion, has got to take root in your head before it can find expression in your performance.

Many times younger athletes will have such a positive winning attitude about themselves in other areas, like school, social life, or an endeavor like music or art. The coach of such an athlete would do well to help the athlete to bring this attitude to sport as well, using the thoughts and feelings surrounding the player's other successes as a model for how he or she could feel in competition. For example, if a basketball player has a positive, winning attitude when he or she is in history class, this attitude can be brought to the court as well, with some instruction and practice. (See Chapter 7.) It is always easier to transfer some positive attribute from one area to another than it is to create it from scratch.

Using specific attitudes in
player selection and development

How do you use the list to your advantage? There are two ways: One is in the selection of players, in the assessment of their potential contributions to athletic success; the other is in building these attitudes within yourself or on your team.

When selecting players, coaches at all levels commonly overemphasize physical attributes and ignore psychological ones. At high levels of sport, a certain minimum level of physical ability and size is obviously required for the athlete to be able to compete. This eliminates all but a few eligible athletes. Once the minimum criteria are met, however, physical characteristics should begin to give way in the selector's mind to psychological characteristics. Selectors should be asking questions about the athlete's attitudes and emotions. It is a mistake to think that you can pick a physically superior athlete and work on his or her attitudes and emotions as an afterthought. It's like a man marrying a beautiful but cold-hearted woman, expecting to change her attitudes and emotions so that he can take advantage of her physical attributes. Sure, there are things that can be done to change what goes on inside a person's head, but there are psychological limits just as real as the physical ones. (See Appendix A for a full psychological evaluation format.)

Early Developmental Set is very important in player assessment and selection. Once minimum physical levels are met, the athlete with a positive EDS is almost always a good choice, since he or she will not have to spend much time reshaping attitudes and can concentrate instead on learning new skills.

The athlete must be interviewed by the person or persons with whom he or she would be having the most contact. It is very difficult to rely on reports from other people about how well a particular athlete will work under a given coach. Even so-called psychological experts have a tough time making accurate predictions about how well two individuals will get along.

Pulling all this together, we can say that the selection of athletes should involve three steps: screening of the entire pool of available athletes for selection of the percentage who are physically able to compete at the higher level; screening of this smaller group by someone knowledgeable in interviewing and in the attitudinal and emotional aspects of top athletic performance; and interviews by the coach, whenever possible.

I hope the implication of what I am saying about the importance of psychological factors is clear. If, for example, the physical characteristics (speed, size, weight, and strength) of all the running backs in the NFL were compared, I doubt very seriously if, on the basis of these factors alone, even the most knowledgeable observer could pick out the starters, let alone the stars, in the league. The differences in actual performance level are much more likely to be psychological. Especially in sports where building a team is a necessity (as opposed to selecting individual performers as in track and field, swimming, or tennis), attitudinal characteristics are vital, since they contribute so heavily to peer leadership. Athletes with positive attitudes can often provide the models and peer reinforcements for others to learn good attitudes.

Athletes can develop these specific positive attitudes—full effort, love of challenge, poise, playing within yourself, playing for yourself and not against, cooperation, and being a winner—by using methods similar to those described for the one overriding positive attitude. They can be encouraged, rewarded, and actively taught. Think of these three avenues for teaching and molding these attitudes:

1. Talk about them. Describe them to your athletes, point them out when they occur so that they can be easily recognized by the athlete, and verbally encourage your athletes to work on their attitudes as tools for producing top performance.

2. Model them. As much as you can, demonstrate to your athletes the attitudes you are talking about.

3. Reinforce them. Whenever any of your athletes gives evidence of the positive attitudes you are trying to teach, reinforce them through rewards, verbal praise, and simple attention.

This list of positive attitudes can be included in your pregame, preparation checklist. This technique for assuring your own readiness and that of the team as a whole is described in Chapter 8.

Other attitudes: significance, anticipation, and luck

Other attitudes deserve at least a mention here. These attitudes, depending on the athlete and the situation, can work for or against positive performance readying. You'll have to look at them very carefully to see how they affect you.

As with positive and negative attitudes, there are many individual ones that can affect performance. There are potentially as many different attitudes as there are athletes. Three of the most common attitudes that can help or hinder your readying are the significance of the competitive event, the anticipated outcome of the event, and your attitude toward luck or fate.

The *significance* of the athletic event often affects the performance of the participants. We have all seen athletes who respond positively to big games, who love the attention, and who play their best when the world is watching. Other athletes, however, find that significant events work against them, raising their anxiety beyond their optimum performance levels. Performance then declines.

We can think of the significance of any given event as the extent to which the world takes note: the extent to which people outside the sphere of ordinary activities of the athlete, team, and coach focus their attention on the event. For the professional athlete, who continually practices and performs with media attention and criticism, the requirements for playing in a significant event are very high. It must be a championship game, or a rivalry, or an important test. When a team is on a road trip, for example, and only one or two of their games will be televised back home, those games can take on added importance to the athlete. Many major league baseball players have commented on the difference in attitude, effort, and intensity when noncontending teams find themselves on the television game of the week. (In the case of such noncontenders, the added pressure of a significant contest often raises their overall level of arousal up into the top performance range, while the added exposure represents a source of potentially damaging anxiety for top teams that actually have something at stake.)

But significance of event can be very different for athletes at lower levels of competition. Championship games still fit the description, but the Little League ballplayer may be aware of added significance simply because his or her parents have come to watch, or because the team is playing against a team that includes a close friend or an enemy. Any of these factors can lead the athlete to play with an attitude that the game is a particularly important one, and this in turn can affect performance.

Whatever the source of the attitude, the athlete him- or herself can almost always tell if the event seems like a more important one, and the coach can easily pick up such an attitude by observing the players' attitudes during the days or hours leading up to the event. The relevant question becomes: Given the added significance, what makes the difference between athletes who respond positively and those who feel the pressure and respond negatively? The answer, unfortunately, is not a simple one.

Individual athletes do tend to respond consistently. The first step is to determine which effect added significance usually has on your performance. This will determine whether you will want to key in on the added significance as a source of arousal or will want to minimize the differences you see between this event and others you have played in. You or your coach don't need to figure out deep reasons why you respond one way or the other, and it will do no good to berate yourself if you happen to be one of the many athletes who perform best in low-significance situations. The point is to prepare yourself as well as you can, knowing your tendencies and limitations.

Generally speaking, the greater number of significant events you have played in, the better able you will be to prepare yourself in your normal way, even making use of the event's significance as a motivating factor. The extent to which you have been successful in past events of high significance will determine your current attitude: if you've won or played well in previous big games, you will be more likely to have a positive attitude about other big events. If previous big games have not gone well for you, then you probably have learned to be wary of such situations; you may prefer to minimize the importance of a big game.

Either approach can lead to good performance in your next big game, if you apply yourself to it wisely. If you respond positively to big games, then you probably don't need to give that much attention to your attitude. If you respond negatively, there are things you can do and that your coach can do to help you out.*

There are three things you can do when it comes to minimizing the problem of negative response to pressure. First, have a firm readying routine that you always do before any game, big or small. Stick to your routine as fiercely as you can before a big game, so that you take yourself through all the usual, ordinary psychological and physical steps. While some extraneous things will inject themselves into your routine because it is a big game, make sure that you know exactly what they will be and rehearse them, if possible, so that you can go through them relatively quickly and without thought when the time comes. This applies, for example, to player introductions (either on television or to fans in attendance) before big games. Anything else that will happen to you during the last few moments, hours, or days before competition should be treated in a similar way. Most important, however, is that you yourself do what's completely normal for your own

---

*The fact that you have learned, or have been trained, to respond negatively is important. You do not respond negatively because you are a weak person or an inferior athlete. Your own attitudinal and emotional reaction to a significant event comes from your previous experiences in that kind of event, from having learned that they usually go well or poorly for you or your team. Your gut feeling about such events does not come from your soul and has not been with you since birth, any more than your jump shot or your pitching motion came down from the heavens—you have learned all of these things, through practice, through the teachings of others, and through your experiences. They can be unlearned and relearned, and changed to allow you to respond the way you want to. You and your coach should both know this.

readying, especially immediately after something extraneous comes up.

Secondly, don't try to kid yourself about whether it is really a big game or not. Some of the worst readying disasters I have ever seen have occurred when athletes concerned about being too nervous in a big game tried to pretend that it wasn't a big game at all, tried not to think that anything was different. As an alternative to this approach, I recommend that you purposely think about the significance of the upcoming event as much as you can, but do it days before game time. Then you can be finished with those thoughts when it is time to get ready to play. You burn yourself out on thinking about the significance of the event at a time when it doesn't really matter, and when it really does matter, you don't have to do it. This technique is described fully in Chapter 7 as the Attention Clearing and Focusing technique, and it really does work.

Thirdly, the way your coach responds to the pressure of big events can have a great effect on your response. The coach who can demonstrate honest excitement and joy at the prospect of meeting a big challenge helps his or her athletes to adopt a similar attitude, thereby minimizing the negative effects of the anxiety. In general, helping players to see a big game as an honor that they have earned or as a reward for their high level of play up to this point is a good tactic, especially if the coach believes it. After all, bad, lackadaisical athletes and teams don't play in that many big games.

A second attitude that can be a plus or a minus for an athlete is that athlete's thoughts about how an event will turn out. It is a simple fact that some athletes perform better when they think they will win, and some athletes perform better when they think they will lose. And there are all kinds of attitudes in between. This is not the same thing as confidence, because the athlete's anticipated outcome of the event doesn't necessarily have anything to do with his or her feeling about being ready to perform well. Anticipated outcome usually becomes relevant when there is a discrepancy between the physical abilities of two teams, or when there is a long history of success or failure in a given situation. If I were to play Bjorn Borg in tennis, I would definitely anticipate that I would lose, and this could affect my performance. I might give up early and look very bad, or I might be so loose that I actually played very well. Bjorn Borg could have corresponding reactions based on his attitude of anticipated success. When basketball teams come into Pauley Pavilion to play UCLA, having not won there for many years, they might anticipate failure, and this might in turn affect their play. A team like Notre Dame, on the other hand, that has recently had considerable success in Pauley Pavilion, might benefit from the anticipation of success.

Which way the anticipated success or failure will work depends on the athlete's and the team's learning history, and on how they have responded to such situations before. Coaches often express fear about anticipated success, saying that their team is too loose and is looking past the opponent, which can lead to trouble. Similarly, I have heard coaches say that, in playing a superior opponent, their athletes will be loose and ready to play, having essentially nothing to lose.

In general, the coach needs to assess his or her athletes' attitudes on this very carefully from game to game. You as an athlete would do well to do the same, trying to keep yourself on an even keel in approaching all games. Once the coach has determined the team's anticipated outcome, he or she can set about raising or lowering the team's views in much the same way as I described in the section on confidence. Be cautious here also in doing anything designed to bring a team or an athlete down.

One attitude here can have a profound effect on another. If the coach and the athlete have been working with an attitude of *playing for yourself,* trying to do what you can do as well as possible, then the problem of anticipated outcome is automatically minimized. If your customary attitude in approaching an event is to play as well as you can and to improve each time out, and letting the final score take care of itself, then the potentially explosive effect of anticipated outcome becomes defused. The more you maintain your own standard of good play, and the more your coach can separate performing well from winning, the less the anticipated outcome will be a problem. The influence of Coach Wooden in developing attitudes that enabled his teams to run off record winning streaks can in part be attributed to his insistence on this frame of mind.

The third of these attitudes is the most interesting. What roles do *luck, fate, responsibility, and control* play in determining how well you play? As a psychologist, I am fascinated by the fact that some athletes swear they leave everything up to chance and then go out and hustle their brains out, while others talk about "having our destiny in our own hands," and then play as if everything ought to bounce their way. Of course, some athletes do play more in line with their stated beliefs. But the number of inconsistencies among athletes in their beliefs about and responses to luck is astounding.

When we discuss attitudes about luck, fate, and so on, we are really talking about what psychologists call *locus of control*. There are some things in each of our lives that we can control and some things that we can't. Each of us has a particular way of looking at all the things that fall somewhere in between. People tend to see what goes on in their lives as being either under their control or out of their control. Those who see themselves as responsible for everything they do and everything that happens to them can be said to have an *internal locus of control;* people who see things as largely falling outside of their own personal influence can be said to have an *external locus of control.* Obviously, neither group of people is totally right or wrong, and nothing could be proven either way. People bring differing attitudes to their lives, and athletes bring differing attitudes to their sports as readying devices and as explanations of what actually happens to them.

When an athlete trains hard and is committed to doing his or her best in a given competition, it is not unreasonable to expect that the athlete sees the connection between the work and the ultimate performance level attained. But, equally clearly, the skill and work of the opponent, the skill and work of the coaches involved, and the breaks of any particular competition also play a part in determining the outcome, and these are largely out of the individual athlete's control. While the ultimate performance is, objectively speaking, the result of the combined effects of factors the athlete can and cannot control, most athletes do not like to see things that way. The uncertainty of such a situation usually forces them to try to see it one way or the other. So, prior to events, athletes and coaches characteristically have thoughts like "I've worked hard, and if I hustle and do my best today, I'll (we'll) come out on top," or "If things go well today—if I (we) are lucky—if it's supposed to be that way—I'll (we'll) come out on top." Which stance the athlete or coach adopts reflects what prior experience has taught him or her.

For the athlete with an internal locus of control, things are fairly clear: How well he or she does is determined by his or her own efforts. But athletes with external loci of control can fall back on various explanations of both good and bad outcomes. Among these other determinants of the outcome are luck, fate, the breaks, and the hand of God. Which explanation is used is a matter of individual preference.

This attitude centers on responsibility: Just who or what is responsible for the athlete's performance? The stance of this book, and of most coaches I know, is that ultimately each athlete is responsible for how he or she performs, and that the amount of work, intensity, commitment, and so on that the athlete shows will determine his or her performance. Luck determines the outcome of specific events. I do not mean to say here that athletes who see things as being in God's hands or up to fate are being irresponsible; on the contrary, some of the most dedicated athletes I know are deeply religious people who attribute everything to the will of God, even though they themselves work very hard to improve themselves. I have seen athletes who have adopted either of these two stances do very well competitively. How do we reconcile this apparent discrepancy?

We have to look at what purpose the attitude serves for the individual. Generally, athletes who need to remind themselves to hustle do better when they are helped to adopt an internal locus of control. Athletes who might feel too much pressure if they felt that everything were resting on their shoulders tend to do better with an external locus of control, which allows them to shed some of the pressure. The coach who is trying to aid in the readiness of athletes by attending to their attitudinal patterns would do well to follow some simple advice in this confusing and often very personal area: Judge the athlete's attitude by his or her actions, not words.

As I have said, many athletes can say that things are in God's hands even while they act as though everything depended on their own personal readiness. When the final results of the competition are in, they may even change their tune, looking back on their solid preparation as the main factor in promoting their success. The objective reality of the situation is really unimportant. *What's important is that the athlete was able to give him- or herself some comforting explanation beforehand.* The value of the attitude, whether internal or external locus of control, should be judged by the effectiveness with which it aids the athlete in performance readying. In this particular phase of precompetition readying, the coach should take his or her cue from the athlete. If an athlete is talking about luck or fate before a game, fine— don't contradict. Likewise for the athlete who talks about working hard, individual energy, and preparation just prior to the event—just agree. Usually when an athlete talks about these kinds of things before competition, he or she is showing uncertainty or nervousness, and is looking for support. The best stance is simply to give this support, so that the athlete can go on to thinking about the details of what needs to be done in competition. There is no right or wrong; there is only what works best for each athlete. This applies also to coaches, who are equally likely to soften their own pregame anxieties by resorting to one or the other explanation.

All attitudes exist for good reasons, and have something to do with feeling *ready*. Respect and support them, insofar as they serve the goal of top performance. Tolerate the athletes whose attitudes are different from your own. They think their way for a reason, just as you do, so there is little point in trying to convince them otherwise, or in trying to have all of your athletes approach games in exactly the same frame of mind. The bottom line is the athlete's performance, and the words he or she uses to describe how he or she gets there can usually be ignored.

Overview on attitudes

Attitudes form the foundation of everything you do in practice and in competition—the skills, the emotions, and the knowledge of your game. They deserve a good deal of attention.

I have emphasized what the coach can do to affect his or her players' attitude. Now I'd like to look directly at the relationship between coach and athlete. *Relationship* is one of those psychological, "touchy-feely" words that drive some coaches and athletes crazy. Some people think that to talk about *the relationship* is to further corrupt the discipline that is already lacking in the young people of today. Even on the professional level, the hard-nosed coach is being replaced by the one who can establish a relationship with the athletes, and who can motivate them. Is this good? Is it necessary?

No one can really answer these questions. Athletes today are different from athletes of yesterday, but then so is the rest of society. In advocating that coaches try to have a relationship with their athletes, I am stating one of the basic themes of this book, which is one of the themes of our more educated, freer society: There's more going on inside the head than anyone ever thought was the case twenty or fifty or one-hundred years ago, and these psychological factors are very powerful. In fact, the more we study them, the more we find that they are the keys to all behavior. The brain controls everything the body does. Trying to train the body alone is like trying to fix a car without opening the hood. And the best pathway into the athlete's head is the relationship he or she has with the coach.

I am not talking about love or affection. A positive coaching relationship does *not* depend on the coach and athlete liking each other (although it surely helps). More important is reaching some mutual understanding of what's important to each person.

Coach and athlete must work together as a team. Without each other, they are doomed to failure. If the athlete constantly has to figure

Attitudes and Thoughts

out what's on the coach's mind, then he or she can't put all the necessary energy into learning new skills or into competing. Once coach and athlete understand each other, they can proceed to get a great deal accomplished. The coach can teach isolated skills to athletes without much of a relationship, but these alone won't take the team very far in tough competition.

One of the saddest things I have encountered as a sports psychologist is resistance from coaches who seem to think I am saying (1) You have to be a pushover to be a good coach, or (2) You have to be a trained shrink who knows how to get inside people's heads and is willing to spend a lot of time doing so. I'm *not* saying either of these things. You can be tough, and you don't need a lot of time or training to deal with your athletes' attitudes.

The main requirement in establishing a relationship—in fact, all that is required in many cases—is that the coach *attempt* to reach some kind of person-to-person understanding with his or her athletes. Even a clumsy, bungled attempt can do a lot of good. Simply saying, "I want to understand you and I want you to understand me" puts the focus of attention in the right place—on what you are trying to accomplish together. Without such a mutual awareness, the level of competitive success will be limited.

How do you approach establishing a good coach-athlete relationship? One method has worked very well for me: First, talk with each athlete for ten to fifteen minutes before your season, at the very first contacts you have in early practices. (You can spend more time than this if you like, but ten to fifteen minutes will do it.) Find out as many things about the athletes as you can: family, background, school or work activities, likes, dislikes, and so on. And don't be afraid to tell the athlete about yourself: how long you've been coaching, where you played ball, what other things you like or dislike. Then (and this is really the more important step), greet each athlete individually as he or she shows up for every practice or game. Spend ten to thirty seconds (I mean this literally; keep contact under a minute) interacting with the athlete in a friendly way about anything outside of your sport. Anything will do—the weather, something you heard on the radio, a movie you've seen—as long as you are attending to *that athlete only*. This kind of regular, positive, personal attention can work wonders, and it is so easily and quickly done that it's a crime to skip it. People respond to positive attention, the most powerful social reinforcer there is, and it's foolish not to use this to your advantage.

Among other priorities, recall the following few:

1. Be open to learning how your athletes (or your coach) think.

2. For the coach, demonstrate what you want your athlete to do.

3. Always look for individual differences in how attitudes affect performance; never insist that all athletes must have a certain attitude in order to play well.

4. Attitudes have a long cycle, in both being learned and being unlearned, so don't expect quick change. You have to teach or discourage them consistently to have any lasting effect. That's exactly why they need to be a priority and attended to every day. And this long cycle means that you shouldn't try to change any thoughts or attitudes immediately before a competition, even if it's a really bad attitude you observe. Just let it alone, and deal with it between events.

5. Be ready to go outside your sport to find sources of and solutions to attitude problems.

These guidelines are so easy to do, with even the slightest inclination on the part of the coach, that any coach who is not willing to try them, or to go outside the very limited and old-fashioned coaching role of just training body parts to do certain things, is cheating him- or herself and the athletes.

Sport requires two things: arousal and control. The athlete must have arousal to perform with speed, strength, and endurance, and he or she must have control to perform with precision, accuracy, and skill. The arousal component is the freeing, active side of sport, while the control component is the restricting side that is necessary to keep arousal from taking over completely and leading to energetic and unfocused play. Very young children play like this when the teacher lets them loose on the playground—they just run like crazy for a while, like aimless balls of energy. The control that they generally learn turns them from physical motion machines into athletes.

To a large degree, our emotions supply the arousal (See Chapter 2) and our attitudes supply the control. Our thought patterns enable us to use our energy constructively. A main coaching task (or one for the athlete to take on) is to determine which component already exists in each athlete and which is lacking. The goal is to have each component be as high as possible without disrupting the other. If arousal is emphasized to the extreme, it can override all control (the pumped-up, "sky-high" basketball player who commits four turnovers in the first two minutes); and if control is emphasized to the extreme, it can severely limit the amount of energy the athlete can constructively use (the over-cautious tennis player who is concentrating so much on the stroke that he or she moves poorly and with no rhythm and timing). Both are essential and should be emphasized in all athletes; but the individual differences among athletes will determine which you want to emphasize more.

4
LEARNING AND TEACHING IN PRACTICE, PART 1:
Three major steps

Up to this point we have looked at what readying for the individual athlete is all about. We have considered two kinds of psychological functions and their relationships to readying: emotions and attitudes. The main vehicle for the individual use of these psychological functions is described in later chapters on immediate pregame readying and on the specific readying techniques that work best.

But all of this has looked past the single most obvious contributor to the athlete's performance level in competition: practice. It is no secret that practice is very important. Look at how much time coaches and athletes put into practicing, especially when compared to the short amount of time that goes into actual competition. In practice the coach has a chance to help the athlete do things correctly. During competition, it is too late. Practice is the one big readying technique that everyone uses.

The practice field is essentially a classroom where the athlete has the opportunity to learn what he or she will need to know later, and where the coach acts as a teacher, whose job is to try to maximize the learning possibilities for the athlete. It is where the coach tries to stretch the athlete's performance to the limits of his or her potential, in much the same way as an algebra teacher tries to teach formulae or an English teacher tries to teach grammar. The games themselves are the exams, indicators of how much teaching and learning has actually gone on between coach and athlete during practice. More than the specific strategy a coach may choose for a particular game, the amount of learning that has gone on in practice will determine how well the athlete (and the team) will do.

I know: None of this is news. But I am going to focus in the next two chapters on something different from what most books on practice techniques for sport usually focus on. I will discuss the mental side of practice: what goes on inside the athlete's head, and what the coach should know to enable him or her to bring about the best possible learning circumstances.

Practice has always been aimed at teaching the physical behavior that the athlete will need to be able to execute in competition. These are obviously very important and will always be central to any athletic practice. I hope that the first three chapters have made clear to you the influence of psychological factors on athletic success. These chapters are going to look directly at the ways in which practice activities affect these psychological factors, so that you can add this knowledge to what you already know about teaching and learning physical skills.

Whether you pay any attention to them or not, *emotional states and mental attitudes are being learned and taught in practice,* just as surely as are the physical skills everyone is concentrating on. The athlete is not only picking up the physical training, but is also learning what to feel and what to think, based on what the coach responds to positively and negatively. This kind of learning is much less obvious. It's easy for a coach to tell when an athlete is correctly shooting a jump shot or swinging a club. But what the coach can't really see are the internal patterns. The coach can't see that the athlete was swinging the bat incorrectly before and is swinging it correctly now not just because he or she was shown the right physical way of doing it, but also because something has changed inside the athlete's head. Rarely will a change in physical behavior not be accompanied by a change in emotion or attitude.

This is really not so strange as it may sound. The reason that the coach tells the athlete what to do is that he or she knows the ideas will have an effect on the athlete's physical behavior. When a golf coach encourages a golfer to "concentrate on watching the clubhead actually hit the ball," he or she knows that this verbal instruction, *given by the golfer to him- or herself,* can affect the behavior of the head and thereby the swing. What the athlete is thinking about will affect his or her physical performance. The same kind of example can be given for emotional factors affecting the physical behavior. When the golf coach says, "That was right. See how well you hit the ball?" and when the golfer sees the positive result and is happy, both individuals are making it more likely that the golfer will do it again—and doing it again means doing whatever was done *psychologically* as well as physically. The mental and emotional behaviors that went on inside the golfer's head are being learned right alongside the physical behaviors that everyone could see. Many times this is a good thing, but not always, which is one more reason for the coach to pay attention to the psychological as well as the physical in practice.

How can the coach do this without being able to see inside the athlete's head? Capitalize on some basic learning principles that science has uncovered in the last few decades. We know a lot more than we did forty years ago about how we learn things, and about conditions and strategies that promote or retard learning. Most of these strategies are easy to incorporate into existing practice routines.

One of the most basic of these principles is the relationship that social scientists call *stimulus-response*. The coach who is teaching athletes to respond in certain ways to specific situations is already working in this area. Stimulus-response theory simply says that we learn to make responses to certain things that we see or hear or feel (these are the stimuli) in specific ways. For example, the reason it is vital for a baseball team to practice how to move and where to throw the ball with various numbers of baserunners, with different numbers of outs in an inning, and with different scores in different innings is because their success will depend on how well they have learned a specific response to each specific situation. The more they practice under positive learning conditions, the stronger the bond between each stimulus and its response will become, and the more quickly, surely, and accurately the right player will do the right thing.

This kind of example can be applied to a lot of different athletic situations; these chapters are going to focus on what is meant by "under positive learning conditions." Accordingly, you are going to be reading about a number of principles of learning, such as the stimulus-response bond, that will apply to various teaching situations. This chapter will deal with the three main learning-teaching principles that every coach and athlete ought to know: reinforcement, shaping, and modeling. Chapter 5 looks at attention and a number of other specific principles that make use of these three major strategies. Included is a discussion of just how competition depends so heavily on what goes on in practice, with specific suggestions as to how some of the good and bad things you see in your games can be "practiced in" or "practiced out" with the right practice regimen. Finally, I'll tie all of the separate principles together into a tidy package of coaching strategies that can

Figure 4-1. Three Principles of Teaching/Learning.

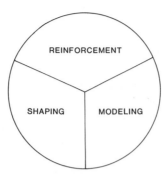

be brought into your own workouts. Because the practice arena is essentially a learning-teaching situation, I am going to address myself primarily to the coach in these chapters. Nevertheless, much of it will pertain equally to you as an athlete, in terms of both dealing effectively with your coach, and planning your own workouts. In fact, since you, the athlete, are most responsible for your own performance, you need to do all you can to maximize your own use of the learning principles.

THE FIRST MAJOR PRINCIPLE
OF LEARNING: REINFORCEMENT

Reinforcement is the most important teaching-learning principle. If a coach has a firm grasp of the uses of reinforcement, even if he or she picks up little else from this book, that coach is still prepared to do a good job of coaching. The effects of using reinforcement properly are that powerful.

What does reinforcement really mean? *Reinforcement is anything that increases the likelihood that the behavior it immediately follows will be repeated. Anything* can be a reinforcer, including words, gestures, feelings, thoughts, physical occurrences, and chance happenings. Whether the reinforcer was meant to act as such has nothing to do with its actual effect. All that matters is whether or not the initial behavior increases in likelihood; if it does, then it has been reinforced.

Let's take an example from a typical coaching situation. As a tennis coach, the behavior you are trying to encourage is that of going to the net after a good first service: You want your athlete to serve and volley more. You have told the player this, but he or she still doesn't do it enough. So this behavior needs to be reinforced. If the player rushes the net and receives reinforcers for doing so—things like praise from the coach, winning the point, or feeling good—then he or she is more likely to increase this behavior in the future. If no reinforcers follow the desired behavior, then it will probably not increase in the future. (In fact, its probability will decrease, as we will see later.) The only way to tell whether something has been an effective reinforcer is to see if the behavior it was intended to increase actually did occur more often. If not, of course, the coach must find another way to reinforce the desired behavior.

The athlete first has to do the desired action before it can be reinforced. Obviously, many behaviors can be suggested verbally or demonstrated, and this is necessary to get the ball rolling. (The other two main principles of learning—shaping and modeling—are techniques for starting new behaviors.) But even suggestion and demonstration do not insure that the athlete will be able to do the thing right at least once, so that you can start the reinforcement process. So the coach is going to have to exercise patience. The more difficult the activity and the less skilled the athlete, the more patience the coach will need. Fortunately, however, many athletic tasks are not that complex and so will occur fairly often. This holds true even for very important skills. Back-checking in hockey, getting good defensive position in basketball, and staying down on a grounder in baseball are all important behaviors that most players will do at least occasionally, even if they do not do them regularly enough or completely enough. Using reinforcement, then, becomes a matter of attending to the athlete enough to see when he or she does the desired behavior, and then reinforcing it in whatever way seems to work best for that athlete. The coach needs to exercise patience in seeking the desired behavior, and creativity in seeking reinforcers. The proof of the pudding, so to speak, is in the tasting: whether or not the behavior increases, and not the coach's belief about what *should* be a reinforcer.

There are three categories of reinforcers: physical, nonphysical, and social. These categories can be thought of as the channels through which the process of reinforcement works. Let's look briefly at each, thinking in terms of things that can be done immediately after a desired behavior occurs.

Physical reinforcers are the most basic. They have their roots in the physical drives and pleasures that we experience. The most fundamental of these are food, water, sleep, and sex, things that meet the basic requirements of our survival. Because they are so basic, they are

Figure 4-2. Three Kinds of Reinforcers.

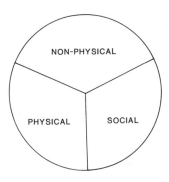

among the most powerful reinforcers one can use. Unfortunately, they are usually not applicable to athletic situations: You can't stop a runner to reinforce a technique by giving him or her a piece of cake or having him or her take a nap. Water and rest, on the other hand, can be used, especially in practice. Because of the exertion in most sports, fatigue and thirst are common. When an athlete or team has been working hard and the coach wants to reinforce that behavior, he or she might call for a rest and a drink. This can have a strong reinforcing effect if it is done before an athlete requests it, but it is also an effective reinforcement technique even when the rest and refreshment come *after* an athlete asks for them. The body learns that the desired behavior will be followed by a very pleasurable reinforcer. This kind of gut-level learning goes on whether the athlete is aware of it or not.

Other physical reinforcers, while less fundamental, are equally effective and much easier to inject into the sporting situation. These are things like physical fun, pats on the back, and the Tommy Lasorda–inspired hug. The term "pat on the back" refers more often to a verbal exchange these days, and that has some advantages; but there is an added advantage to having physical contact actually be part of the reinforcer. The physical dimension adds a more basic, pleasurable physical feeling to the reinforcement, and this always aids in the learning process. It will work best when kept within the bounds of acceptable physical contact; anything that makes either party uncomfortable will only undermine the overall effectiveness of the reinforcement technique. Still, there are times when putting your arm around an athlete while talking to him or her after a good, hard performance can have very strong positive effects, and the coach should always be alert to these kinds of opportunities.

Physical fun is also easy to put into practice as a reinforcer. In baseball, for example, players typically like hitting more than fielding. This gives the coach the option of trying to reinforce good effort in the area of fielding or pitching or base running by giving out extra batting time. Scrimmages are also popular among athletes in many sports (especially compared with "boring" workouts), and they can be used as reinforcers when a team has been applying itself particularly well. Remember, physical reinforcers operate on a gut level, and they don't have to be explained to the athlete for them to work.

Nonphysical reinforcers are things that people typically find rewarding but that don't rely for their power on physical contact or satisfaction. The most obvious example is money. On the professional level, money can be used very effectively as a reward for desired behavior; it is less easily used with amateurs. But substitutes for money can be found. Privileges are a major type of nonphysical reinforcers. Allowing the athlete to avoid some less pleasant aspect of practice can be useful, if it is done explicitly as a reward for some specific action and it is not done in such a way as to favor the athlete. Nonphysical reinforcers are difficult to use during practice sessions, but they should be considered long-term tools, to be applied after workouts or games in which the athlete has conspicuously shown the desired behavior. Arranging time off or special privileges at home, or providing other activities that the athlete enjoys can be useful in reinforcing the behavior of younger athletes, who also respond to in-practice reinforcers; going first in some enjoyable practice activity can really make an impression on some kids. Overall, the area of nonphysical reinforcers is one in which the coach needs to exercise some awareness and creativity to see just what outside things the athlete responds to. When such things can be integrated into the sport, they can help.

The most commonly used reinforcer is the *social reinforcer*. Social reinforcers are positive behaviors, thoughts, and feelings that people show one another, and they are very powerful. The hugging and back patting described under physical reinforcers also apply here as social reinforcers, as do smiles, applause, head nods, and other gestures of approval. These expressions of reinforcement pile up, and have a cumulative positive effect on the athlete's producing the desired behavior(s).

But by far the most common, useful, and versatile social reinforcer is language. All coaches use words as primary teaching tools, describing, exhorting, and otherwise trying to get their athletes to behave in certain ways. Their words also have a reinforcing function, primarily as they constitute praise and approval. They can simply be saying,

"Good," "That's right," "Way to go," or any other short expression, or they can be sitting the athlete down and telling him or her that they are pleased with his or her efforts. Never underestimate the power of giving out these kinds of positive words.

Because words are short, fully under your control, and don't get in the way of practice routines, they are the perfect reinforcers to use in workouts. It is so easy to say, "Right," or "Very good," to an athlete after he or she has done something that you like that it's ridiculous not to say so. Especially when athletes are learning new skills, short, direct encouragement is your best tool, because it gives the athlete immediate feedback on what to do and not do. This brief, verbal praise does not require great feeling, either; studies have shown that simply saying the word "Good" in an even tone of voice each time a person does a certain desired behavior increases the likelihood that the person will do the behavior more often, whether he or she knows it or not. Imagine how useful this can be in conjunction with direct instruction and some tone-of-voice emphasis.

A reinforcer closely tied to language is attention. How much attention the coach pays to an athlete immediately after a given behavior helps to determine whether or not that behavior will increase. Attention is almost always socially reinforcing, even if the person giving the attention is verbally discouraging the behavior. For this reason, the coach needs to make sure to attend to those things he or she wants to see increase, and not to others. In the upcoming section, this distinction will be made clearer.

Reinforcement: how it is used

The three kinds of reinforcers—physical, nonphysical, and social—are the tools the coach can use to reinforce behavior. Which reinforcer you use depends on the situation and the people involved. But there are specific ways that reinforcers work, which I will call *reinforcement techniques*. There are four basic reinforcement techniques; these are the strategies you can use to build positive behavior.

In coaching, there are basically two tasks in utilizing the learning situation: There are good behaviors that you want to encourage, and bad behaviors that you want to discourage. There are, consequently, reinforcement techniques that *increase* the likelihood of the athlete doing what you want him or her to, and techniques that *decrease* the likelihood of the athlete repeating bad behavior. There are two techniques in each category. To illustrate, I am going to carry one athletic teaching situation throughout the four techniques. I'll focus on the relatively simple behavior of lifting a weight, and look at the task from the perspective of the coach who is trying to teach the athlete the proper skills to maximize his or her potential as a weightlifter.

Teaching the right way to do something

Let's begin with the two reinforcement techniques designed to increase behaviors: positive reinforcement and negative reinforcement.

Positive reinforcement is the most powerful of the reinforcement techniques. Using positive reinforcement consists of following a desired behavior with some kind of reward, or *positive reinforcer*, which can be physical, nonphysical, or social. By following the desired behavior with something positive, you link the two things in the athlete's brain, improving the chances that he or she will do the right action again.

I've used the word *reward* in describing positive reinforcers, but I want to caution you against thinking that positive reinforcement is simply a matter of the athlete having earned a reward. Supplying the positive reinforcer has nothing to do with whether or not the athlete deserves it. The idea is rather that supplying a positive reinforcer immediately after the performance of a desired behavior solidifies that behavior in the athlete's mind and body. We are all behaving all the time, doing millions of little things that go largely unnoticed. By positively reinforcing specific behaviors, the coach gives an athlete's mind a signpost, so that the body knows what the correct behavior is. It's not just saying, "Good boy, here's a treat for doing what I like." It's more like saying, "That was it: What you just did, that's what you want to keep doing. You are able to do a lot of different things, but that's the one I want." With positive reinforcement, you are using the athlete's natural preference for anything pleasurable to call to his or her attention what he or she is doing *right*. You are making sure that doing it right is no longer a chance occurrence, but becomes part of the athlete's performance routine. This in turn leaves less time for bad habits. You use positive reinforcement because offering something positive is the best way to get anybody's attention and to get them to do anything.

Let's look at our weightlifter. You are trying to coach him or her to use the proper techniques. Using positive reinforcement means, after some brief instructions, watching closely throughout the lift, and telling the athlete what you have just seen him or her do right. Certainly, some things were wrong and some were right; but the most effective teaching tool, positive reinforcement, is applied to that behavior which you want the athlete to continue doing. You reinforce those, and their frequency will increase.

Some coaches will find this approach difficult at first; their first impulse will be to tell the athlete what has been done wrong, in order to make corrections. This is self-defeating. The negative approach calls the athlete's attention precisely to what you don't want him or her to be attending to. Remember that attention itself is reinforcing, because it focuses the athlete's thought and energy. You want to focus the athlete's thought and energy on what is right. *The more specifically and the more often you can tell the weightlifter what he or she has done right, the more likely it is that he or she will do it right more often.* The opposite is not true: Telling him or her what has been done wrong will not decrease the likelihood that he or she will continue to do this in the future, and it may even reinforce the wrong behavior. What usually happens with the wrong approach is nothing: Nothing new is learned. By reinforcing what's right, you teach the right, and the opportunities to do the wrong must therefore decrease. If it takes the athlete ten seconds to make the complete lift, and through positive reinforcement you increase the amount of time that he or she is doing something right, then there is less time, and behavior, to go wrong. If, on the other hand, you focus on what the athlete is doing wrong and try to decrease that, you have not necessarily given the athlete anything right to do in those ten seconds, even if he or she actually stops doing what you said you didn't like. Positive reinforcement covers both sides of the learning and unlearning at once.*

The positive reinforcement model has many events that naturally feed into it. Team congratulations for a home run hitter, hand slapping

---

*What about telling the athlete both what's right and what's wrong? That can be effective, but it requires much more care and expertise than simply using positive reinforcement. It is hard to be sure that the negative in your communication doesn't get heard more strongly than the positive, because athletes tend to expect criticism from coaches. If you can mix the two types of communication and still have the overall tone of the interaction be positive, fine. In my own coaching and consulting I have found it difficult to do so. The tendency is to say nothing until I see something go wrong, and then to say, "No, not that way. Do it like this." This focuses the athlete on the negative. The good things he or she may have been doing right along have gone unnoticed and unreinforced, while the first bad thing I see gets attention. This is a bad pattern to get into. The coach is much better off waiting until the wrong behavior is *well past* and then giving the athlete some instruction in how to do it right. (This assumes that the behavior is not so destructive that it must be stopped immediately, which is discussed in the section on punishing behaviors.)

in the end zone, and the hugging and patting that goes on after a goal in hockey or soccer all serve as positive reinforcers. This is really, in a way, the problem: The dramatic, obvious, correct behaviors get a lot of positive reinforcement, while all the little things that the athlete does right, that are so vital to overall good performance, go unnoticed and are taught in an atmosphere of "Here's what you're doing wrong." The coach who wants to take full advantage of the power of positive reinforcement in routine workouts has got to be very attentive, and actively look for positive behavior to reinforce. This is hard to do, especially since most coaches have themselves been trained in the method of noticing what's wrong. The tendency is to watch your athletes, hoping that they won't screw up, so that you won't look like a bad coach. But watching for signs of the positive in their performance and in your own coaching works better in the long run. I'm not suggesting for you never to say anything negative; I'm advising you to use the positive as much as possible, because it short cuts a lot of the problems of negative coaching. Even if you can't make positive reinforcement your major technique (because you are a crusty old buzzard who gets the most out of your athletes by staying on them), you are probably already benefiting from some rare positive comments that are contrary to your "image." I can't argue about which actually gets the work accomplished— the yelling about what's going wrong, or the rare but heavily appreciated and sought-after positive comments; I can only say that most of the coaches I have known who have had that kind of "on your back" reputation have, when observed carefully, been seen to mix in a generous portion of caring and positive coaching that somehow slips right past everyone's initial impression but that is appreciated in the end by all the athletes.

The other technique for increasing the probability of a certain behavior is called *negative reinforcement*, but not because it has anything to do with punishment or attending to what's going wrong. It is called negative reinforcement simply because it involves strengthening a desired behavior by *removing* some negative factor that may compete with the desired behavior. Reinforcement of a desired behavior is still the emphasis when using negative reinforcement.

If we think about our weightlifter again, we can see that there are some negative factors that can be removed. Since our lifter is not yet using proper technique (not having learned it yet), he or she finds it a struggle to lift more than, say, 150 pounds. Trying to do so is a struggle involving psychological uncertainty and even doubt, and possibly even physical discomfort and the chance of injury, since the stresses of the lifted weight are being put on the wrong parts of the lifter's body (on the hands and arms instead of on the legs and back). When our lifter does manage to do the lift properly, however, these negative factors disappear, and it is their disappearance (as well as the pleasant feeling of positive reinforcement gotten from the coach and from the achievement itself) that reinforces the behavior that has just occurred. Because the lifter did it right, there is no accompanying psychological discomfort, there is much less strain on the wrong body parts, and there is the feeling of mastery instead of struggle. The lack of the negative factors that the athlete has come to associate with lifting reinforces the learning of the desired behavior. This type of reinforcement can operate alongside of positive reinforcement.

In football, linemen are taught specific blocking techniques. Before they are learned, an athlete may, despite physical superiority, habitually find himself on his or her back at the end of each play, because the opponent has used knowledge of leverage to knock him or her down. To be knocked down, pushed around, and beaten is negative. When the player is shown how to do it right, however, these negative consequences are almost always avoided. This reinforces the correct technique. A goalie in hockey or soccer dislikes having a goal scored on him or her. In teaching him or her to handle breakaways by coming out of the net in order to cut down the shooter's angle, the coach gives the athlete a technique that, when performed correctly, will lessen the occurrence of negative events—that is, goals. All these examples remove something negative as a reinforcer for doing a positive behavior.

Usually, of course, positive and negative reinforcement go hand in hand. When a golfer hits the ball well, the positive feelings and words of praise from others, as well as the absence of both negative feelings and the necessity of hitting the next shot out of the rough, all work together to reinforce the appropriate behavior.

The power of positive and negative reinforcers does not depend on the athlete knowing that he or she is being reinforced; they will work without that. But in the case of negative reinforcement, it is often a good idea to tell the athlete to look for the negative things missing when he or she does it right. Our weightlifter should be told to notice, after a good lift, that there is no stressed feeling in his or her hands, and the football blocker should have it pointed out that he or she has avoided the physical and emotional distress that comes from being bowled over. These things may seem obvious, but they do help to reinforce the desired behavior.

One of the best places to use negative reinforcement is in the conditioning of athletes. Most athletes do not enjoy the physical exercises necessary to build good condition, but see them as a necessary evil. Good condition enables the athlete to avoid being dead tired and having an opponent take advantage of this to beat him or her. Conditioning is a gradual process, and with each successive step it is a good idea to remind the athletes that they are continually removing the possibility of such a negative experience. This is negative reinforcement: reinforcing the desired behavior (conditioning) by removing a negative factor (fatigue and defeat).

Negative reinforcement can also be used more actively. There are always things in practice that athletes do not like to do, and the temporary removal of such chores immediately after the athlete has done something right can serve to reinforce that desired behavior. The idea is not so much to reward the athlete for doing something you like, but to reinforce the athlete's performance of desired behaviors. *It is the behavior you are reinforcing, not the athlete.* The best negative reinforcers are the ones that come as a direct result of the desired behavior: not having sore hands because you lifted correctly, not being in the dirt because you blocked correctly, not being in the rough because you swung correctly. These reinforcers are not as strong as straight positive reinforcers, but they do make a valuable addition to the pattern of reinforcement.

Getting rid of bad habits

Also important in coaching are techniques for lowering the probability of undesired behaviors; these techniques can be used to break bad habits and otherwise to discourage activities that interfere with performing your sport correctly. There are two main techniques for decreasing unwanted behaviors: extinction and punishment.

Behavioral scientists call the process of gradually unlearning negative behavior *extinction*. Extinction consists of gradually decreasing the athlete's use of certain behaviors by changing the reinforcement pattern that led to the learning of the undesired behavior in the first place. In general, by totally removing the positive reinforcers from the situation, so that the athlete does not receive any reward for the behavior, you can gradually cause the behavior itself to disappear. If you think of the slot-machine player in Las Vegas, for example, you can see that, after a great many attempts without the reinforcement of winning money, the player will begin to pull the handle less and less, and ultimately stop altogether. The behavior pattern was learned through the positive reinforcement of winning, at least occasionally, but it will disappear in the absence of reinforcement. This is extinction, and it works much better in the long run than punishment.

The best method of extinction is *ignoring* an undesired behavior, which removes all reinforcement for that behavior. This always leads to extinction, since attention is a positive reinforcer. Remember that an athlete is doing things all the time, most of which go unnoticed. What causes some behaviors to recur is reinforcement. Any behavior that catches the attention of the coach or the athlete is therefore given precedence over any behavior that does not. By calling the athlete's attention to any part of his or her performance, whether it was positive or negative, you are reinforcing that behavior. The technique of ignoring insists that you give absolutely no attention to things that are being done wrong.

Let's think of our weightlifter again. He or she is doing many things correctly and many things incorrectly. The coach will religiously and immediately tell the athlete what has gone right, making sure the athlete knows about it and has at least a momentary opportunity to feel good about it. When the coach sees something go wrong, however, the best thing to do immediately afterward is to ignore it, giving it no reinforcement. Likewise, the baseball coach, even after a bad inning, is better off saying nothing at all than explaining in detail what went wrong.

I know this is easy to say and hard to do; I've faced the dilemma myself as a coach. But it does work.

I am not saying never to tell an athlete what he or she has done wrong. I am simply saying that you should do so at another time, when it can be approached more positively. If you try to point out the mistake immediately, the attention you are giving it only reinforces the unwanted behavior. By waiting, you give the athlete the opportunity to get over the immediate discomfort of having screwed up, since the embarrassment or anxiety or fear at having done poorly is at its peak right after the dirty deed is done, and this makes for a terrible teaching atmosphere. By waiting at least a short period of time, preferably until the athlete is about to try the right behavior again, the coach sidesteps this problem. Let's say your shortstop just booted a ball, having made the novice's mistake of keeping his or her hands up until the last moment and then trying to spear the ball right off the dirt. The inning ends, and he or she walks into the dugout. You've seen it all, know exactly what you want to say, and are mentally livid about the two runs that were allowed to score. What should you do?

Well, in the first place, the athlete certainly knows that he or she screwed up. The athlete saw the ball go through for an error, knows the runs scored, and is probably already thinking about the thousands of times he or she has been told to get the hands down in anticipation of a grounder. (You told him or her just last week for the forty-fifth time, remember?) He or she is probably preparing for your wrath. But the next thing he or she will be doing is batting; can your words about how to play a grounder (or other selected expletives) help at the plate? No, they will only make things worse. By even discussing the misplay, you not only reinforce the behavior by attending to it unnecessarily, but you also prevent the athlete from shifting attention to the most important thing right now, namely, batting. You are much better off simply ignoring the whole incident; just walk to the other end of the dugout and get involved in something else, like encouraging your hitters. If you want to say something to the shortstop, wait until it's time for the team to take the field. After all, that's the time to be thinking about fielding. And even then, tell the shortstop what you want done correctly. Don't say, "How about cleaning up that sloppy play of yours or I'll yank you." Instead, try, "Remember, hands down, hands down," and leave it at that. Unless your shortstop has no conscience at all and couldn't care less about the game (which is highly unlikely), he or she will be chastened for a while. But you will have given him or her something positive to think about: no monumental piece of advice, but a simple reminder of what he or she already knew but simply failed to do. And handling the problem this way also makes it less likely that the athlete will still be kicking him- or herself later in the game, when he or she should be concentrating on the upcoming plays.

Incidentally, the ignoring technique belongs in the repertoire of the athlete as well as the coach. When you as an athlete make a mistake, don't be your own worst enemy. Dwelling on what you did wrong helps nothing. What you should do (and should encourage your teammates to do after they have misplayed) is put it out of your mind as quickly as you can. Think about the next thing you are going to be doing, or take a few moments to go back to your usual pregame readying techniques that you have developed (as outlined in Chapter 7). However you do it, put aside your error and try to think about the right way to proceed. It's that kind of positive rehearsal of the right way and ignoring the wrong ways that leads to overall good play.

Learning and Teaching in Practice, Part 1

It's the *timing* of what you, the coach, do or don't do that is critical. Don't reinforce the bad behavior with attention; ignore it, and later on you can do the reminding and teaching that must be done to correct errors. Keep the two times—immediately after, and any other time (like your next workout)—separate in your mind; use the first for reinforcing good things or ignoring bad ones, and the second for instruction.

Up to now I've been very reasonable, urging you to be the same. I've said you should have the patience of a saint, that you should think about the long-term effects of how you respond to unwanted behaviors, ignore them as totally as you can and reinforce only the positive ones. I've assiduously avoided talking about another time-honored method for decreasing undesired behavior: punishment. Let's think about it now.

First off, let me be clear: *Punishment* works, and it has its place in the coach's arsenal of behavioral techniques designed to shape up the athlete's behavior. It works *in its place,* but that place is very limited, especially when compared with the power of positive reinforcement and ignoring, used in tandem.

Technically, punishment consists of the application of aversive consequences to an unwanted behavior, thereby causing the behavior to decrease and, eventually, to disappear. The aversive consequences can be anything that the athlete finds unpleasant: extra work, being yelled at privately, being yelled at and embarrassed in front of friends, being benched—whatever, as the saying goes, gets the mule's attention. And this is precisely the way punishment can be most effective: when it is used as an immediate attention-getter after a behavior that simply cannot be tolerated. When the athlete does something that is so destructive to his or her own performance, or so disruptive of the team's progress, that it simply must stop as soon as possible, then punishment should be used. It definitively states, "What you just did will not be tolerated. What you just did is out of the bounds of my normal, usual reinforcement patterns in teaching you. Usually I tell you how to do things correctly and I don't harp on mistakes. But this particular behavior goes beyond that, and I won't tolerate it."

Every coach will have a different way of determining what is to be ignored and what is not to be tolerated. In general, dangerous or openly flippant behavior makes every coach's list. If our weightlifter is handling the weights in such a way as to endanger him- or herself, then that behavior should be punished. When you can no longer ignore something, you punish it.

What punishment you use should be based on the situation, the person involved, and your own standards. Anything unpleasant will do. Harsh words, if well placed, are usually enough, and extra work is a favorite among coaches I know. But the most effective punishment is the immediate removal of the athlete from all possible reinforcers and the assignment of some unpleasant, task, such as wind sprints or laps. When you decide to punish something the athlete did, you want it to be clear that that's what you're doing. Immediately having the athlete stop what he or she is doing and run some specified amount does this. It removes the athlete from anything pleasurable, especially continuation of the athletic activities that he or she can see teammates still engaged in. It prevents the athlete from receiving any attention. Laps or sprints serve the same purpose as the *time-out booths* some schools use for misbehaving students; the child is simply removed from contact from his or her peers, and thus from whatever may have been reinforcing the unwanted behavior.

Punishment is often used to counteract unwanted behavior that seems to make no sense, is counterproductive, and serves only to get everyone else's attention. The key to using punishment effectively is directing all attention away from the offending individual. Get the athlete away from the team and away from the situation in which he or she has been acting up as quickly as possible. Don't disrupt the activities of the whole team; it is important to continue, letting the time away from the sport serve as part of the punishment. Be as clear as you can about exactly what specific behavior you are punishing; you're not punishing the athlete's overall behavior, but what he or she said or did, and you want the athlete to know this.

And you must be sure that punishment is different from anything else that you do. Punishment should stand alone as the mark of what cannot be tolerated, and should not be confused with mistakes the athlete is bound to make. This is one reason that I recommend some kind of *time-out* activity as punishment rather than words. Words are used for many different things; laps are not. You don't want to make the athlete have to rely on the strength of your words or the tone of your voice to know when he or she is being punished: He or she may misjudge you, thinking that you are really angry when in fact you are not, or that you're only kidding when you really do want the behavior to stop. The best plan is to combine ignoring with punishing in such a way that there can be no mistake about which is which. When the athlete makes a mistake or misbehaves, you typically ignore it, bringing it up only at a later, more comfortable and reasonable time. But when

Learning and Teaching in Practice, Part 1

he or she does something that cannot be tolerated, you punish it immediately with laps or some other time-out procedure. You do both of these things without words (other than to say, "Knock that off and take a lap") because words mean attention and therefore reinforcement. You want to save your words for those times when you see something you want to reinforce. By leaving words out of your punishing and ignoring of unwanted behaviors, you at the same time increase the power of the words you use to teach.

To be effective, punishment must be used with discretion, and cannot be a major part of your coaching style. If you routinely punish the mistakes that your athletes make, you are defeating the purpose of punishment—namely, to stamp out specific, destructive behaviors.

There are a number of reasons why punishment doesn't work as a routine teaching device (and why, correspondingly, positive reinforcement and ignoring work better). In the first place, when you punish the unwanted behavior, you are not teaching the athlete what you want him or her to do; you are teaching what *not* to do. Punishment merely suppresses behavior; it does not provide the athlete with an alternative. This leaves a vacuum, which will probably be filled again, after a while, by the unwanted behavior. This explains why even sternly punished behaviors show up again and again. After the immediate effect of the punishment wears off, when the athlete finds him- or herself in a similar situation, he or she still hasn't learned what to do. At best, the athlete will do some other, unrelated behavior; only by being very lucky will he or she hit on the right behavior for that situation. At worst, the punished behavior will show up again. Providing an alternate, correct behavior is essential to using punishment positively, but it is difficult to do effectively in the emotionally charged atmosphere of having come down strongly on the athlete.

Also, studies have shown that punishment suppresses unwanted behaviors only as long as the punishing person (you, the coach) and the perceived ability to be punished are present. When a child is spanked or restricted for, say, eating candy before dinner and thereby spoiling his or her appetite, the child probably won't eat before meals as long as there is a chance of being caught and punished. If there is no chance—if the parent (punishing person) is not there—he or she may well eat something.

In the case of the punished athlete, this punishment situation takes the form of a practice-game discrepancy. Let's say a tennis player has a bad habit of hitting backhands very loosely. In practice, the coach yells and screams at the player when this occurs, at times even halting practice and angrily sending the player away, or making him or her run laps. This punishment may well be effective in stamping out the undesired behavior in practice; but during a match, no such punishment is possible. The coach can't go onto the court and yell at the player, or make him or her stop for some wind sprints. Under these conditions, the loose backhand can easily return, without fear of punishment. (No, the delayed punishment of being yelled at after the match does not work—it makes the athlete feel bad but doesn't alter his or her behavior.) And even if the coach can punish the athlete during a game (by benching a player, for example), when does the punishment do more harm than the unwanted behavior? Punishing during games is a troublesome cycle to get into, and can be avoided.

Because the threat of punishment must be present for the unwanted behavior to be inhibited, it requires a great deal of vigilance and energy from the coach. If punishment is your main tool, you always have to be ready to punish, and that much energy can clearly be better spent elsewhere—like in teaching and reinforcing other, positive behaviors. The best reason not to use punishment routinely is this: since it must be unpleasant to be effective, its routine use leads to the need for increasingly more severe punishments. This escalating nature of punishment is a pattern we have all seen; it leads to coaches saying things like, "I've tried everything and he still doesn't concentrate on defense." The coach who yells louder with every mistake a player makes is putting him- or herself on a treadmill to exhaustion, and is undermining the valid, effective use of punishment on those infrequent occasions when some behavior must be stopped immediately.*

By far, the best pattern of reinforcement techniques looks like this: If we assume that your athletes do about half the things they're supposed to do correctly (and this is probably too low), you should be positively reinforcing about fifty percent of the time, ignoring about forty-five percent of the time, and punishing only the other five percent. In fact, since athletes usually hit better than fifty percent of desired behaviors, you will probably want to use even more positive reinforcement, less punishment, and continue to ignore the rest. Use words and attention to reinforce positive behavior; use specific punishments to stamp out destructive and infrequent negative behavior that cannot be tolerated; and ignore everything else, at least until the

---

*Interestingly, very difficult athletes who prod the coach to yell and scream progressively louder often respond only to being benched for a contest or two. For such athletes, benching is the ultimate use of ignoring: They are getting no attention at all.

Learning and Teaching in Practice, Part 1

negative event is safely in the past and cannot be directly reinforced by talking about it. If you think about these three categories, you can learn to use them fully and effectively in practice as well as in competition. The clearer you are about responding in these three different ways to these three different kinds of behaviors, the easier it will be for your athletes to learn what they are supposed to do and not to do.

Figure 4-3.

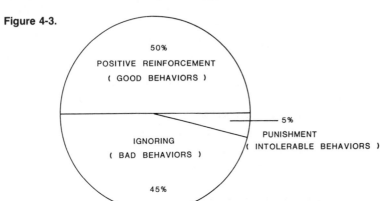

Reinforcement: some guiding principles

Physical reinforcers. Nonphysical reinforcers. Social reinforcers. Positive reinforcers. Negative reinforcers. Ignoring to not reinforce. Punishment. No, there will not be a quiz later. But if these terms aren't clear to you, then either I haven't done a very good job of explaining them or you need to glance again at the particular section you're fuzzy on. I feel strongly about these reinforcement principles that if you don't *own* them, you're less of a coach than you could be.

Whichever of these techniques you may be applying to your athletes, there are some simple facts of human learning that cut across everything else. These have to do with how, when, and where you apply the reinforcers.

There are five factors to keep in mind in using reinforcement effectively:

1. Timing—immediacy of reinforcement. The closer in time the reinforcement comes to the actual occurrence of the behavior, the stronger will be the learning effect. This is true with every kind of learning and for every animal, from jellyfish to human. When one of your athletes does something right, tell him or her about it as quickly as you possibly can. Don't wait until the whole practice session is over or the game is

Learning and Teaching in Practice, Part 1   **99**

history; do it as close to the behavior as you reasonably can. The scientific definition of what goes on during learning talks about pairing stimulus and response with reinforcer, and this simply means that all three things occur at about the same time. If you wait, you will wind up reinforcing the wrong behavior—namely, the athlete's most recent behavior. Even if you tell the athlete what he or she did right a while ago or yesterday or last week, you are taking only partial advantage of the power of positive reinforcement.

2. Consistency. To teach new behavior effectively, you must be as consistent as you possibly can be in reinforcing the positive, ignoring the negative, and punishing the intolerable. Especially at first, when the behavior in question is just being picked up, positive reinforcement needs to come almost every time. Later on, when the good behavior pattern has been partially learned, total reinforcement won't be necessary, and you can periodically tell the athlete that he or she is doing a good job. But in the beginning, reinforcing almost every time works much better. Consistency also means being clear in your own mind about what behaviors you want and don't want, and then communicating this to your athletes the same way each time. It is easiest for the athlete to learn when he or she knows exactly how the coach will respond.

In many situations, consistency is easier to talk about than to achieve. If you as a coach feel the pressure to respond immediately to everything an athlete does or doesn't do with either a positive reinforcer or a punishment, you may not have been consistent throughout a long practice or across a number of sessions. This is another way in which the ignoring technique aids in your coaching. Instead of having to decide instantly whether to say, "Good," or "No, not that way," you are able to say nothing unless you see something good happen. Responding only to the positive gives you time to watch what the athlete is doing, instead of having to point out each little thing that might have gone wrong. By looking at your task as primarily one of applying positives, you make it easier to consistently reinforce what you like. Punishment is used rarely and doesn't interfere with your consistency. Most things are ignored.

3. Respond to effort and behavior, not to performance outcome or people. Remember, the idea is not to reward a person for doing something, but to establish a link between trying to achieve a desired behavior and the reinforcement. Social scientists refer to this as establishing a contingency between behavior and reinforcer: getting the rein-

forcer is *contingent* upon performing (or, in the case of brand new or very difficult behaviors, trying to do so). If you wait until the athlete can perform the new skill at some level of proficiency before you reinforce the behavior, you are defeating the purpose of establishing such a contingency. The idea is first to reinforce the effort, then to reinforce anything the athlete does toward producing the whole behavior pattern. This also applies to psychological behavior. Positive attitudes should be reinforced, and so should emotional states that you feel are helpful. Again, it's not the person you are rewarding; it's a matter of looking for positive behaviors of any kind and reinforcing them, immediately and consistently.

4. **Learning is not entirely cumulative—it has its ups and downs.** If you expect the athlete to perform a new behavior better every single time he or she tries it, you are assuring yourself disappointment. Learning takes an uneven pattern, which steadily climbs overall but which does not necessarily get higher every single time. When you see an athlete make a mistake, after he or she has already given you reason to believe that he or she has learned how to do it right, don't jump down the athlete's throat. What you're seeing is a perfectly normal phenomenon, a part of everyone's learning pattern, and it should be ignored. Only if the problem persists should it be given further attention through reinforcement or punishment. If you see an unwanted behavior, or don't see a desired one, three times within a short span of attempts, then you should give it your attention in practice. If you see it twice, use your discretion, depending on the difficulty of the behavior and the general skill of the athlete.

5. **Reinforcement is critical when first learning new behaviors, but it is also important in *maintaining* such behaviors.** Once a behavior has been learned you needn't reinforce it every time it occurs, but it is wise to reinforce it occasionally. This is called *intermittent reinforcement*. It can be effective once every few times the athlete performs the desired behavior or once every few days, whether or not the athlete has been producing the behavior all the time. You will get a feel for how often each individual athlete needs to have some reinforcement to maintain his or her positive behavior patterns, and you should be alert to individual differences. Some athletes need steady reinforcement or the behaviors begin to disappear, while others need it only once in a great while. If you feel that you have taught an athlete something, but then after a while you notice that he or she is not doing it regularly, you are seeing the effects of not having enough periodic reinforcement to

maintain the behavior. You needn't do anything major; just pick up your reinforcement pace the next time you have your athlete practice the behavior in question.

The more immediately, consistently, and specifically you reinforce desired behaviors while they are being learned, the less you will have to keep giving out goodies for good behavior in the long run. Ideally, toward the end of your season, when the important competitions come, your reinforcement level will be down considerably from what it was earlier. If you do the job well to start with, it stays done with only simple maintenance.

Familiarize yourself with this section thoroughly. Try out the various types of reinforcement so that you can learn how to fit them into your own style and see what works best for you. Your job is to find the right fit. Having visible goals and progress goes hand in hand with using positive reinforcement: The reinforcement keeps the goals and progress visible, and the visibility of the goals and progress make your job as a reinforcing agent much easier. If this sounds like I'm saying, "Emphasize the positive," it should; that's just what I'm saying.

I defined a reinforcer as anything that reinforces. This circular definition, while a pain in the neck for social scientists, is great for coaches: Simply find what works and use that as a reinforcer, instead of deciding ahead of time what "should" be reinforcing for a given athlete. Coaches are among the most practically minded and performance-oriented people I know, and the foundation of the meaning of reinforcement rests squarely on performance. If what you are doing increases the desired behavior in your athletes, keep doing it—it is a reinforcer. If it doesn't, don't try to make sense of it—try something else, until you find what does work for a certain individual or team. If you follow these principles of immediacy, consistency, and the combination of positive reinforcement and ignoring, your athletes will show you the wisdom of your ways.

THE SECOND MAJOR PRINCIPLE OF LEARNING: SHAPING

With some exceptional athletes, all the coach has to do is demonstrate once or twice the right way to do something, and the athlete picks up the new skill immediately. But with most people, you can't teach complex skills by saying, "Here's how the whole thing is done; now you do it." You have to teach the skill in pieces. That's what *shaping* is all about. The more difficult the overall skill is for the athlete, the more vital shaping is to the teaching-learning process.

The term *shaping* is used by behavioral psychologists, who have long realized that teaching skills is not a quick, direct transference of knowledge from one person to another. Rather, it is an ongoing process, a gradual molding of the learner's behavior into a pattern that fits the general *shape* of the desired behavior. It may be helpful for you to think of this teaching-learning process not as the transmitting of information but as the shaping of behavior patterns in your athletes. A sculptor starts with a lump of clay that has a form irrelevant to the desired form; he or she then molds that clay, in successive steps, into the desired pattern. You can think of the small behaviors of your athletes as your clay—undefined patterns that can be changed eventually to fit the shape you want. Instead of sculpting with your hands, you use demonstrations, words, reinforcers, and the techniques described in this book—like shaping.

The essence of shaping is the making of small changes in the athlete's behavior. The goal of shaping is to have the athlete doing the one, larger skill he or she needs to perform well. The sequence is (1) defining the one, ultimate goal behavior (e.g., running a nine-second hundred yards); (2) gradually shaping the pieces of the athlete's behavior in the right direction (ready position, the start, the stride, the breathing); and (3) in the end, having it all melt back into a chain of smaller behaviors, so that the performance is whole and fluid.

It is important to realize that, within the athlete's physical limits, almost any behavior can be shaped with precise enough coaching and strong enough reinforcement. (Our sculptor can build any shape he or she wants, but only in clay; the clay can't be changed to gold, and neither can the coach change an eleven-year-old rightfielder into Reggie Jackson.) It's a matter of getting the athlete to put together small behaviors that his or her body is capable of, which result in the "new" finished product of an overall skill.

Anyone who has seen a complicated animal act has seen the powerful effects of shaping. When a dog walks upstairs on two legs, or a seal plays a tune by honking some horns with its mouth, the effects of shaping are demonstrated. A skilled trainer has worked with the animal for many hours, reinforcing it heavily any time it performed one small behavior that would contribute to the overall performance. The trainer didn't wait for the seal to play "Yankee Doodle" on the horns before reinforcing it; he or she first reinforced it for looking at and smelling the horns, then for touching them, then for honking one, then two, then in a certain order, and so on; until, finally, the audience could hear a seal "miraculously" play a song.

Figure 4-4.

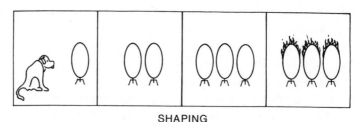

SHAPING

This is painstaking work, but with humans it's not nearly as hard. The dumbest athlete you will ever coach (1) is a thousand times smarter than a seal, (2) is able to understand your words, (3) is motivated to perform well, and (4) knows that he or she is working toward a final goal. He or she can see the links between the steps leading to the ultimate skill, and so each step done correctly represents tangible progress. This is intrinsically self-reinforcing, and motivates the athlete to move on to the next step. By being given these small steps to master the athlete is assured of numerous successes to propel him or her along. Contrast this with the frustration of trying to do a complete performance (for example, a 1½ gainer in diving) all at once, with only the finished product to use as a guide.

Shaping, then, is a *tool* that leads to a step-by-step process in which the athlete builds to the final goal. But it is not just a matter of producing small behaviors "just so," and then having them add up to the one big skill. Shaping involves reinforcing the athlete for any behavior that comes close to the desired one, at every step of the way. When you tell an athlete to hold his or her hands in a certain way to hit the ball better, you are providing a small behavioral step toward the final goal. But the best use of shaping involves reinforcing for coming close to holding the hands correctly, even if he or she doesn't do this small step exactly as you want. With each successive attempt, the athlete will come closer and closer to doing it correctly, and your job in shaping behavior is to reinforce him or her *whenever you see an attempt that comes closer to the desired behavior than did prior attempts.* In this way you will gradually lead the athlete's behavior into the proper overall pattern.

Shaping is a constructive process, directing the athlete toward something specific and positive. As the coach who is using shaping as a teaching technique, your main job is to make the behavior-shaping steps *as small as is necessary to enable the athlete to do something closer to the final goal,* even if the steps seem tiny to you.

How to use shaping as a coaching technique

Let's look at some examples of applying shaping to sports. There are two types of situations in which shaping is a valuable tool. There's the overall skill that looks like one, long behavior (and may even look relatively easy); bowling is a good example. And there's the final behavior that seems to be impossible, like high jumping at a height that is over one's head. In the first case, you use shaping to teach the overall skill because you can see that your athlete never does this overall behavior the same way twice, even though he or she perceives it that way. Not being able to see the smaller pieces involved in producing the overall skill makes him or her unable to make necessary adjustments or to effectively monitor his or her own behavior. In the second case, you use shaping as a way of showing the athlete just what is possible, and how to get there. Let's look at each of these skills, bowling and high jumping, more closely.

To the novice, bowling looks easy, and the casual bowler assesses his or her performance by one thing: How many pins were knocked down? Only slightly more sophisticated is the bowler who judges the shot by where the ball wound up: Did it go where he or she was trying to throw it? He or she is unaware of the many other behaviors that may be affecting each shot, such as the number of steps taken on approach, the speed or size of the steps, the lift put on the ball, the rotation put on the ball, the speed of the stroke, the angle of the arm, the bend in the back, the position of the head, the rotation of the torso, and so on. Becoming a good bowler means becoming a consistent bowler, and paying attention to each small step will eventually pay dividends. It gives the athlete the ability to monitor his or her own performances.

The high jumper also makes use of many small behaviors: the approach patterns, the number of steps, the speed generated, the lift generated, extension of the limbs, body position and flexibility, and so on. Here, as in bowling, the athlete learns what effect each small movement will have on the outcome. Proper technique is important because the jumper will be limited without it. Shaping can be used effectively in both of these situations, and in other sports with similar demands. The use of shaping through small, cumulative steps can be most effectively accomplished by keeping in mind some guidelines.

First is the need for consistent, positive reinforcement. Each small step of progress must be recognized and brought into the athlete's awareness. If you allow small behaviors to pass by unattended, you're not shaping at all. Remember that one of the requirements of using positive reinforcement is that the coach must actively look for small gains to reinforce. Sitting back and noticing only the larger, obvious successes doesn't help much, and it's certainly not shaping. The smaller the steps reinforced, the better, especially in teaching difficult overall skills.* If you have broken something down into pieces and the athlete still doesn't get it, break it down even further. If you've broken down high jumping into approach, jump, over-the-bar technique, and landing, and the athlete still isn't reaching the jump phase in good shape, then go ahead and break down the approach even further into number of steps, hand position, and so on. Get as detailed as is necessary to get to something the athlete can do, and then shape slowly from that point.

In using shaping and reinforcement to work on small behaviors with an athlete, keep your, and the athlete's, attention on just *one small behavior at a time*, to avoid confusion. Don't pick on every little thing; stick to one behavior and shape it. Some coaches, for example, in watching a player take batting practice, will talk about the hands after the first swing, watch a few more cuts and then comment on the stride, and then go on to the position of the head. This can be done effectively only at a high performance level, at the end of a shaping process that has already gotten the athlete doing almost everything well. And even at that high level it may not be effective. The more you focus the athlete's attention on one behavior at a time (usually one per practice session), the easier it is to shape that behavior. You may see other behaviors that need shaping, but it's best to catalogue them in the back of your mind and bring them up later.

As you use the shaping process, what you reinforce will be constantly changing, depending on what the athlete has already learned. At first, you choose a simple *target behavior* and reinforce close approximations of it. Next you reinforce the exact production of the de-

---

*Difficult doesn't mean how objectively difficult a skill is for most people to do; it means how difficult a time the individual athlete has in doing it. In this sense, it is best to use shaping whenever an athlete has trouble doing something, instead of deciding beforehand what skills are difficult enough to demand the use of shaping as a teaching tool.

sired, small behavior. When you move on to the next step, things get a little more complicated. You don't just reinforce every time the athlete gets close to the second behavior; you reinforce the athlete when he or she does the first behavior correctly and then also approximates the second. If the athlete can do small behaviors A, B, C, and D, and you are teaching E, you shape by reinforcing ABCDE, and not E alone. Reinforce the whole chain, once the ABCD pattern has been learned. For example, once a bowler has learned the proper grip and approach and you are teaching him or her how to release the ball, you reinforce only the whole chain—grip, approach, and release—when it is done correctly. If it starts to break down, you go back and reinforce that earlier step. In this way, you keep the focus of the shaping-reinforcing process in one spot: at the cutting edge of the athlete's knowledge and performance ability. The more accurately you can observe where this imaginary line between learned and unlearned skills lies for each athlete, the better able you will be to shape and reinforce just where the athlete needs it.

Ultimately, of course, the small behaviors must be brought together into the larger skill. It is often a good idea to mix the practice of small behaviors with attempts at the overall performance; this integrates the part into the whole. A swimmer may work on a part of his or her stroke, aided by the coach, but competition in which the athlete is periodically asked to put it all together should be mixed in as well.

What it takes to shape effectively— requirements for the coach

Aside from these strategic considerations, the coach needs to be aware of some of the demands shaping will make on him or her. There are three main requirements:

1. Effective shaping requires that the coach have a fairly exact blueprint in mind of what the final skilled behavior should look like, and what the steps are for getting there. He or she needs to know not only what pieces to break the overall behavior into, but also what the best order for teaching will be. Should he or she work on foot placement first, or hand action? A good mental blueprint will make the shaping process easier, because it will enable the coach to be consistent and direct in his or her teaching.

In developing a good mental blueprint, experience and the study of books dealing with physical education and anatomy (kinesiology)

Learning and Teaching in Practice, Part 1   107 are invaluable tools. But they are not the whole story. You need to realize that each athlete is an individual and that no athlete will be able to do things exactly as they are described in books. Your mental blueprint must be flexible enough to allow for such individual differences, and yet it must be firm enough to establish you as a knowledgeable teacher. This is a fine line. It has been my experience that the more zealous and competitive the coach, the less flexible the mental blueprint tends to be. Excessive zeal can lead to demands that the athlete do things a certain way, often impossible for that athlete. Flexiblity and the ability to adjust your methods to individual needs and abilities are vital to using shaping effectively.

2. The coach must combine shaping with positive reinforcement. Positive reinforcement often depends on waiting for a positive behavior to occur and then reinforcing it. Shaping gives you another tool to use, a more active one that allows you to teach what is wanted, instead of feeling as though you must wait patiently. A steady stream of verbal instruction and subsequent positive reinforcement, especially in practice situations, indicates that the coach has been accurate in assessing what the athlete's next step should be, and is making sure to reinforce what he or she likes. (In competition, when performing and not teaching takes precedence, it is usually best to go back to a more passive use of positive reinforcement, since trying to teach and shape can often get in the way of other competitive requirements. See page 236 on reinforcement during games, as well as Chapter 8 on principles of performance during competition.)

3. Shaping requires patience. It is not glamorous and sometimes tedious, and it works only if the steps are properly paced for the athlete. Rushing things defeats the whole purpose of the shaping technique.

I realize that this is easy to say but not so easy to do. You have many things to cover and never enough time to get to everything before competition time comes along. That is a fact of life; the complementary fact of life is that no athlete is ever perfectly prepared. The human limitations of time, energy, and ability determine how much preparation can take place and how much teaching can be absorbed in a given period of time.

I encourage coaches to remind themselves of this fact regularly. Teaching and shaping in small steps, at a pace the athlete can handle, means that you won't cover everything; but cramming things leads only to confusion and half-learned skills, which all too often appear learned but which desert the athlete under the pressure of competition.

Learning and Teaching in Practice, Part 1

It is better to pace yourself according to the athlete's learning limits, and not according to the extensive textbook requirements for fielding a "completely prepared" player. Consider this: In cramming things, the coach is very likely responding more to his or her own anxiety than to the needs of the athletes. The coach covers everything so that he or she can feel that he or she has taught everything that is needed and so cannot be accused of neglecting to cover something, either through ignorance or inexperience. Good coaching means preparing your athletes to do as much as they can in a given competition, not covering everything. You will of course want to have a list of priorities; but how far you get on that list should depend on your teaching ability and your athletes' learning abilities, and not on some predetermined dictum. A coach who says, often in response to criticism, "I taught them how to do that—they just didn't learn it well enough," is probably having to apologize for cramming, for teaching the basketball team how to fastbreak before the players had fully learned how to get defensive rebounds. The team would probably be better off getting the rebounds more consistently and executing the fast break a little less often.

A final word on shaping

Those, then, are the requirements for good shaping. Shaping is a valuable tool, and it belongs in the arsenal of every coach. I'm sure you have noticed that *shaping* is merely a more precise word for much of the teaching that most coaches already do.

I have discussed shaping as it relates to teaching behavioral skills, but it applies equally well to attitudes and emotions. If the coach can influence the athlete on what to think or feel at certain times, and then gradually shape this through small, approximating steps followed by positive reinforcement, the athlete's psychological framework will shape up just as well as his or her physical side. The same requirements apply, with patience being perhaps even more important here than in the teaching of physical skills.

An athlete can also make use of the principles of shaping. In your own workouts, build toward the final performance skills by defining and working on small steps. When you make a little progress, even if you can't do it all perfectly yet, reinforce yourself by doing something you like. Self-teaching is often just as important as expert coaching, even if you are being coached by someone else in formal practices and games. The more you work on things between formal workouts, the quicker you will be able to take the building steps the coach lays out for you in practice, and the more you will both be able to cover in the long run.

THE THIRD MAJOR PRINCIPLE
OF LEARNING: MODELING

Modeling means learning by example. The essence of modeling is demonstrating to the athlete how something should be done. The adage "Monkey see, monkey do" refers to this process: The athlete sees it done right and then does it, as well as he or she can. The word *modeling* refers both to the act of demonstrating a behavior by a model person and to the process by which that behavior is learned by the observer. The coach models a skill, and the athlete learns it through modeling it.

Examples of modeling are all around us. One way that social scientists describe modeling is as the basis of *no trial* learning; it allows us to do certain things fairly well the first time we try them. The first time a person drives a car, for example, he or she usually knows at least the basics and doesn't run completely amuck; most of the learning has occurred by having watched other people drive.* Similarly, how does a doctor doing brain surgery for the first time avoid killing the patient? He or she has observed many similar operations and has learned what to do and what not to do through modeling.

Examples of modeling in sports are equally easy to find. Young athletes are known to pattern themselves after popular heroes, even to the point of walking or wearing their uniforms as the model does. Watch a young football player spike a ball after a touchdown, or a young baseball player break into a distinctive, home run trot. Nobody actively taught them to do these things; they don't require any practice, and they don't contribute to the effectiveness of the athlete's game. They have been learned through simple modeling. Imagine, then, how effective a tool modeling can be when you intentionally demonstrate, practice, and make use of the principles of effective modeling.

Almost all of the social learning that goes on early in a child's life takes place through modeling, and not through direct instruction. Little girls "automatically" learn to sit and talk like their mothers, and young boys learn to move and react like their fathers. This perceiving of an important figure and striving to emulate that figure is the basis of

---

*It doesn't matter whenever the modeler is trying to demonstrate something. All that matters is that the observer watches the person behave.

Learning and Teaching in Practice, Part 1

modeling. In children, it is usually called *identification:* The child identifies with the strong, caring parent figure and (not necessarily consciously) tries to behave in similar ways. More general modeling, of heroes, teachers, and coaches, is an extension of the very basic process of identification.

Identification is so fundamental and begins so early in life that it predates the child's use of language. Modeling, then, works on a non-verbal level, often without the conscious awareness of either the model or the observer. It is basic to our ability to live in society. For this reason, it is an ideal tool to use in the teaching of nonverbal, physical skills. It can be especially helpful in working with less verbal or less intelligent athletes, who may have trouble translating your words into their body movements. Modeling cuts through that complicated verbal communication channel; it seems to operate at a physiologically and mentally more primitive level. That is its great strength.

How to use modeling

It's not enough just to say, "Show your athletes how to do things instead of just telling them," even though this is good advice. Effective use of modeling can be enhanced by an awareness of certain factors that research and coaching experience have shown to affect the power of one's modeling technique. The phenomenon of modeling has been well researched by social scientists who study social learning. This research has uncovered various factors that affect the utility of modeling and that have definite implications for its effective use.

1. The effectiveness of the modeling depends on *how well the model can get and hold the observer's attention.* It doesn't matter whether the model is trying to demonstrate something; all that matters is that the observer be watching—the closer the better. Demanding such attention is less effective than finding ways to make the models you use various and attractive. Rather than doing all the teaching yourself, get others to come in at regular intervals to demonstrate specific techniques. Such a change almost always gets attention, and heightens the learning of that specific skill. Using people whom your athletes respect or find entertaining is a good idea. It's not that you have to "sell" your athletes on paying attention, or "trick" them into attending; you want to maximize the learning that can occur at any given session, and a little variety can help in this.

2. The effectiveness of the modeling depends on the *conse-*

quences of doing the desired behavior for the model. If the model gets obvious rewards from doing this skilled behavior, then your athletes will be more likely to pick up and use that behavior. For this reason, well-recognized and admired models work best. Choose as your models players who win or are all-stars, who have profited from doing what you are trying to teach. Pointing out a technically skilled player whom your athletes don't know, and about whom they can't readily see the positive consequences of doing the behavior, is not that effective. On the other hand, someone who has gone on to higher levels of competition in your sport can be an excellent model. When the college baseball player comes back to the Little League field and demonstrates a certain skill, he or she is a wonderful model, who in effect says, "See how I have gone on to glory by doing this; you can, too." Even if this is not said verbally, the message gets across. Athletes pay attention to and copy successful athletes.

3. The effectiveness of the modeling depends on the *status of the model*. This is slightly different, although in most cases success and status go together. Status is an intangible thing that can't be easily defined or predicted. Some athletes enjoy much success and are very skilled but have little status, while others catch the public eye and are heavily revered. Such reverence helps an athlete work better as a model.

Using professional athletes is a good idea: the more idolized the player, the better. Young athletes can be encouraged to watch games on television or be taken to live competitive events. When doing so, be sure to focus on the specific behaviors you want your athletes to learn. Watching Dr. J. will be fun, but it will be most instructive if you can get your athletes to watch what he does with his hands or his feet, or on defense. Incidentally, organizing outings to view stars also aids in using variety and model-salience to enhance the learning effect.

A warning is in order, however. Professional athletes are notorious for modeling bad habits as well as good ones. For this reason, models should be carefully chosen and specific behaviors emphasized. I can recall one young baseball player taking hitting instruction from his coach, who was working on getting the player's swing more level and compact. After twenty frustrating minutes they took a break, and the boy walked away muttering, "But Reggie Jackson doesn't swing that way. He swings up." The power of a high-status model had just been demonstrated to the coach, and the modeled behavior was unfortunately not good for this athlete.

Learning and Teaching in Practice, Part 1

4. The effectiveness of the modeling depends on the *similarity of the model to the observer,* as perceived by the observer. It is the athlete's perception of the similarity that is important, and not the actual similarity. As long as the athlete sees him- or herself as trying to do the same things as Roger Staubach, or as one day being as good as Staubach, modeling will occur.

Model-observer similarity has implications for another type of modeling as well: the well-known phenomenon of peer group identity. Athletes between the ages of ten and twenty especially strive to do things the same way as respected, successful peers. Young athletes are constantly watching each other, emulating the good (as they see it) and ridiculing the bad. This can be used to advantage by the attentive coach. Point out to the athlete that another player bears watching, especially when he or she does the desired behavior. Don't belabor the point; it works best if you merely point this out, and then don't bring it up again. Instead, praise the model whenever he or she does it correctly. This is guaranteed to get the observer's attention, and will result in positive modeling, especially if you shape and reinforce this athlete when he or she tries to move behaviorally in the desired direction.

The power of model-observer perceived similarity can be used in another way as well. Team leaders make good models, and the natural team leaders are the ones you should have demonstrate things, even if other athletes may actually do the technical aspects of the behavior better (obviously, this is assuming the team leader can do the skill well). Encouraging team leaders to be aware of their role as models can have positive effects. (See Chapters 2 and 3 on team spirit and leadership for a fuller discussion of this.) But if the negative factors (jealousy, intrateam competitiveness) start to outweigh the positive, let peer modeling recede. In such a case, simple positive reinforcement for any athlete whenever he or she does things correctly is the best remedy.

5. The effectiveness of modeling can be improved through *cognitive mediation, the use of words and thoughts to focus the observer's attention properly on what is to be learned.* Even though modeling works essentially nonverbally, talking can help: It leaves less doubt as to what is being demonstrated and what should be modeled. The only trouble with talking during modeling is that some coaches wind up trying to let the words, rather than the physical demonstration, do the work. They'll show how once or twice and then tell how, in detail, ten times. This defeats the purpose of modeling. In using cognitive mediation remember that it is secondary to physical modeling. Talk a little

and show a lot. Use your words only to focus attention where you want it and to reinforce such attention, as well as to reinforce subsequent attempts by the observer. Be the model: don't describe it.

6. The effectiveness of the modeling depends on *the timing of and the opportunity of the observer to actually try the behavior.* (Athletes take note: Here is a way you can increase your own learning through modeling.) As with reinforcement, the sooner the better. After an athlete sees a demonstration, the sooner he or she goes out and tries it, the better the effectiveness of the whole modeling procedure. A good pattern is to combine modeling with practice attempts in fairly rapid alternation. Show how once or twice, let the athlete try, show how again, and let him or her try again, as many times as necessary. The longer you go on with this chain, the shorter each demonstration should be and the longer the practice time.

Some final thoughts on modeling

Each of these factors will enhance the power of your modeling, but they must fit into your own style of coaching. The modeling you use should also be tailored to fit the individual athletes you are coaching. A common mistake is for the coach to model some skill, or use another person as a model, and then to compare the athlete's performance with that of the model. This can be destructive, and lead to statements like, ''No, you're still not doing it right. See how he or she does it? Do it that way.'' The model then becomes a blueprint that must be fit exactly, and that of course is never possible.

A more effective scenario has the coach following the demonstration by shaping the individual's attempts to reproduce the behavior. First you model, and then you immediately begin shaping and positive reinforcement for any behavior that comes close to what the model did: don't wait until the athlete can do it exactly. Modeling can, in some cases, be automatic, no-trial learning, but not usually; almost all the time, shaping and reinforcement are also needed. Don't let the model become a fixed standard that the athlete must measure up to. Modeling is only the first step: continue effective teaching with efforts to have the athlete improve in small steps within his or her own rate of learning, leaving behind the exact actions of the model.

5
LEARNING AND TEACHING IN PRACTICE, PART 2: Attention and other factors

Modeling, shaping, and reinforcement are the three major principles that govern effective teaching and learning, but other factors also play a part. These factors are more specific: the intake of information, the retention of information, and the use of learned information (the behavioral performance that comes with cognitive learning). Let's look at these factors.

Attention: the start of all teaching and learning

When it comes to teaching, it's obvious that nothing at all can happen unless the student pays some attention to what is going on. He or she doesn't necessarily have to be hanging on every word the coach says, but must be paying minimal attention. The greater the degree of attention, the better.

Attention is not an all-or-nothing phenomenon, however; the degree of attention that athletes pay to coaches can be affected by a number of different factors. I'm going to look at those factors, suggesting ways that you can maximize the attention you get from your athletes. There are basically two ways: You can build attention into your practice situations by accommodating natural human limitations on attention; and you can improve the attentive abilities of your athletes.

A good place to begin is with what scientists call the *orienting response*, which is the physiological and mental response of the body to anything that comes into its awareness. It lasts only a few moments, and is what we usually think of as catching someone's attention. When you are driving a car, hear or see another vehicle, and turn your eyes toward it, you are exhibiting an orienting response. This response is a basic physical necessity. We have finely tuned sense organs that are geared to notice things around us. Without such a response, our ancestors would have been eaten by every carnivorous animal in the forest. Once we see something, we can choose to keep attending to it or not, but we cannot control our impulse to look at it in the first place.

The newness of the situation does have a bearing on orienting and attending. Our sense organs and our nervous system are set up specifically to respond to changes around us. When things remain the same, we do not respond, but as soon as something new is introduced into our awareness, we orient and give our attention to that new thing. If I am sitting in a quiet room reading, I am attending to the printed page; if I hear a noise or if the light in the room changes, I will orient to these things, temporarily leaving my book. If it's just a clock chiming or a cloud covering the sun, I will probably go immediately back to my reading. If the new stimulus is very compelling, like an explosion or loss of electric power, I will not be able to continue reading, but will keep attending to what has happened.

We orient to changes in both form and content. If I am listening to someone talk and his or her voice changes (form), I will orient to the change; if he or she is talking about the moon and suddenly brings up grasshoppers, I will orient to this as well (content). All you have to do to get people to pay attention to you is to do something different, the more different the better.

Of course, this refers only to people's initial response. Much more complicated is keeping their attention. Let's look at two main qualities of attention: *selective attention*—what a person chooses to attend to and how well he or she can keep his or her attention there; and *attention span*—how long a person can keep attending. Both of these contribute to what is usually called concentration. If concentration is an issue for you, read these two sections carefully.

Selective attention

This means attending *selectively*. There are things going on around us all the time, but we choose to attend only to some of them. This faculty enables us to put our minds on one thing at a time, selectively, so that we don't have to keep orienting to everything around us.

Returning to the example of reading quietly, we can see that I have chosen to attend to my book. I may look up at a light or a noise, but I almost immediately go back to what I was doing. If I'm attending strongly enough to my book, I may not even look up at any other stimulus unless it is *very* strong. Similarly, an athlete may become so engrossed in what he or she is doing (watching the ball, watching an opponent, thinking about his or her own movements) that nothing else gets inside. Such a condition is very desirable. The more powerful the person's ability to selectively attend where he or she wants to be attending, the better. Whatever the level of the athlete's ability to do so, the fewer outside events that occur around him or her, the easier it will be for the athlete to attend selectively and appropriately.

Another way to describe this would be to talk about distraction, which is a serious problem for some athletes. But I have chosen to discuss this issue from the positive perspective, and I hope you will do the same with your athletes. To talk about distractions is to set up an impossible situation; it's like telling someone, "Now, whatever you do, don't think about an elephant. You know, don't think about the trunk or the big ears or the size . . ." Impossible, right? That's why you should approach this with your athletes in terms of selective attention—how to have your mind go where you want it to—and not in terms of avoiding distractions. Remember the two avenues along which to approach attention issues: building attention into your practices by planning around the attention factors that can't be changed, and building the attention powers of your athletes.

In building attention factors into your practices, there are a number of steps to take:

1. Identify which of the many things being taught and practiced require high selective attention. What things take the most concentration? The better you can identify these things, the better you can plan high attention into your workouts.

2. Do the activities that require high selective attention individually or in small groups. This allows your athletes to focus more easily where they should.

3. Do high selective attention tasks early in practice, when everyone's energy level is high. Later on you can go to more repetitious

types of exercises. Begin your workouts with the things that require the most selective attention. For example, in football practice, work with defensive players on reading keys early, and leave sled work or footwork drills until later. This kind of planning is especially important early in your season, when there is much to be learned.

4. Stick to steady routines. This minimizes the amount of orienting that your athletes must do, and it leaves them freer to use their mental energy to attend to where they should be. You want to provide variety and new things within the practice time for each skill, because that aids in attention-getting; but you want the overall schedule of the workout to be routine. The more everything follows a routine pattern, the less the athletes have to attend to being in the right place at the right time, thinking about pacing themselves, and wondering whether they will be doing a certain thing later.

5. Minimize the potential for distractions during practices. The fewer extraneous activities going on around your athletes, the better. Keep your coaching staff to a minimum, so that only one person needs the attention of the athlete at any one time. In any given exercise, each athlete should have only one coach to whom he or she is responsible. One of the biggest selective attention problems can take the form of well-meaning parents, friends, and relatives of the athlete, whose presence is a real distraction. I'm not saying to exclude all such people; their support is often central to the athlete's overall motivation and commitment to your sport. But occasional closed practices are a good idea, especially if distractions are a problem. Such practices also help foster a sense of team spirit.

Anything you can think of that helps your athletes to attend better is worth doing. I'm always amazed at the amount of attention that athletes pay to things outside their own performance, even during workouts. The coach should be the absolute center of attention in practice; when things start to get too loose and people are looking around, the coach should immediately reassert him- or herself by bringing the team close together for a thirty-second chat about attending, by yelling good and loud, or even by punishing an athlete or two. In fact, inattention is one behavior that can be affected through punishment, and it is very high on my personal list of things that are not to be tolerated—if you have followed these guidelines to make it easier for the athlete to attend, and you're still not getting the attention you want. The one advantage that the strict, ranting and raving, punishing coach has is that the athletes never ignore him or her, and never let their attention wander. Punishment should be immediate, quick, and to the point however; make sure your athletes know you're yelling about their inattention and not about their physical skills.

Teaching your athletes to have better powers of selective attention, so that they can concentrate better in games as well as in practices, is also possible. In the long run, it is just as important to devote some of your time to teaching the fundamentals of selective attention as it is to work on physical fundamentals. This means using some of your practice time; just demanding it or giving it a moment now and then isn't enough.

Teaching selective attention is best done in the modeling-shaping-reinforcing pattern. Describe what you mean and then give your athletes the opportunity to practice the skills, and follow with positive reinforcement. Perhaps the best way to describe this process is to look at an example of teaching selective attention in a specific sport.

A skier consulted me because he had been having a problem with his starts. Many ski races begin with a small bar placed in front of the skier, usually across the ankles. When the race begins, the bar is removed. This skier had been having problems ever since he first encountered this practice; he would look at the bar and wait for it to be removed before he left the gate. Consequently, his starts were often slow and frequently awkward. This cost him valuable time, and his concern about the bad starts had a tendency to bother him all the way through the race.

He actively tried not to look at the bar at all. As he put it, however, "No matter how hard I try to not look at it, I do; and even if I don't, I still try to hop over it at the start." The problem was how to get this skier's eyes and mind elsewhere. The first step was to explain selective attention to this athlete: to expose the impossibility of trying *not* to attend to something, to explain how he had learned to attend to the bar, and to point out that, given the circumstances of his previous "no-look" strategy, he was just responding in the only way possible—attending to the bar.

I instructed him to look as far down the course as he could see while he was waiting to start. Rather than not looking down at his feet, he was to look down the course, to think about that point in the race. If he were to glance down at his feet, that was fine, as long as his eyes and his attention came back to the down-course point. He was to concentrate on the course—not to *not* concentrate on the start. He practiced this on his own a few times, and after two or three races, he reported being so engrossed in his race planning while in the gate that he didn't even think about his starts. They improved dramatically.

I know this sounds simple, and it is. The point is always to get the athlete to attend to something, something real and important to his or her performance.

One final way to improve your athletes' in-competition ability to attend selectively is actually to use distractions as part of your training. (Lefty Driesell, basketball coach at the University of Maryland, publicized his use of this approach a few years ago; he played a recording of screaming fans while his team practiced, to get them ready for hostile crowds.) The idea is to provide purposely the very distractions that you anticipate during competition. This allows the athletes to practice directing their attention where they want it. The best time (perhaps I should say the only time) to use this technique is late in your practice schedule, after the athletes have been well-schooled in what they are supposed to do. It is best not to do this in your last practice before a competition. There should be one quiet, normal practice between the attention-training session and competition, a practice in which the athletes work on the same things they did in the noisy session. This is essential to allow them to bolster through repetition the attentive skills they have worked on.

Don't talk about distractions: talk about what the athlete should attend to.

Attention span

Once the athlete's attention is on something, how long does it stay there? Since most things cannot be taught in the brief time involved in simply orienting to the coach, this is an important learning-teaching variable. It encompasses issues like concentration, mental endurance, mental overload, and mental fatigue. Once again, the best way to approach these issues is from the positive side, through an understanding of what attention span is and how it works.

Three factors affect how long an athlete attends to a given topic or person. The first of these is the athlete him- or herself. There are tremendous individual differences in innate ability to attend to something over a length of time. Any coach who ignores this, and who expects all athletes to be able to sit quietly and attend for more than a few minutes, or throughout a three-hour practice session, is fighting a losing battle. (This is especially true with younger athletes. Usually, the younger the athlete, the shorter the attention span.) You have to plan your teaching session and practice workouts to be short bursts, with about a thirty-minute maximum. Any longer and you lose too many people, no matter how you may rant and rave about paying attention. If you must spend an hour on one thing, take at least a five-minute break in the middle. It is always better to teach something in two separate thirty-minute blocks within a workout than it is to spend sixty minutes in a row.

There are things you can do to improve an individual's attention span as well. The best of these is what I call the *Stop–Start technique*. This involves teaching the athlete to control when he or she *starts* to attend and when he or she *stops* attending. Athletes with short attention spans usually struggle to keep attending longer than they feel able to. This sets up another intention-ability conflict—trying to do something that the mind really isn't able to do. In essence, the athlete shouldn't try, but should instead let him- or herself stop attending, and then let it start up again naturally. The more the athlete practices stopping and starting his or her attention, the less of a struggle it will be in long sessions. Getting rid of the sense of *fighting to attend* is the crux of this technique.

The first step is to have your athletes try to drift in and out of attending. This will teach them how to *control their attention*. They should identify what things (thoughts, attitudes, images) stop them from concentrating. The inner things that control both the stopping and the starting are equally important. If you tell your athletes to figure out how to keep on attending, this won't work. Have them start with the easy step: what stops them after a certain amount of time. It may be thinking about a girlfriend or boyfriend, or about an upcoming event. The more specific they can be about it, the better.

Then during those times when the athlete should be attending, he or she can be on the lookout for the attention-breaking thought. When it does come up, he or she should quickly and quietly think of stopping all thoughts including attending to the coach. (Imagining a stop sign can help with this.) Finally, all thoughts should go back to the coach. Notice that the athlete is not forcing him- or herself to keep attending, but is allowing the intruding thought to be fully recognized and then set aside. Only then does the athlete go back to the coach's words, with a *brand new* span of attention.

The goal is for both coach and athlete to perceive attention span not as an all-or-nothing thing, but as something that naturally fluctuates with a natural rhythm. This should be both respected and worked on. In training a basketball player to shoot, you of course expect periods of good shooting and bad, with practice leading to more of the former. You don't expect the player to hit every shot. You should approach individual attention span similarly. Tolerate some natural fluctuation, and help the individual to work through the Stop-Start technique.

The content that is receiving the athlete's attention—what you are trying to get across—can also affect attention span. The more interesting the topic, the longer the attention span. That's why it's easier to keep attention while talking about hitting than about playing right field, or while working on free style rather than on compulsories in skating or gymnastics. The less exciting your topic, the less time you should spend at one time, and the more breaks you'll need in a long session. Variety is the key. The more you vary the content of what you are talking about, the longer your athletes will be able to give you their attention.

Finally, you can affect attention span by presenting material smartly. Your presentation should be geared toward the natural attention abilities of your audience. Your main tools in planning your presentation are juggling the work–rest ratio, and varying things as much as possible. Teach your athletes that you expect top attention while you are talking, and then give them a break, to let things sink in and to let minds wander. This ebb and flow of attention is a fact that you can't get around; it is even present during competition. Since no one can concentrate one-hundred percent all the time, your athletes need to learn (1) how to approach eighty-five to ninety percent, and (2) when to allow their minds to wander a little. Since this must happen sometime, success often depends on when it happens—not in banishing it completely. This is especially true in games, where the athletes must learn when all of his or her attention is needed, and when to relax a little. Teaching such a controlled, rhythmic approach to attention in practice leads to athletes who find it easy to be most attentive when they should be: when the game is on the line.

As a coach, you would always do well to underestimate the attention span of your athletes, and stop before they tire of you or of the current activity. This prevents the automatic mind wandering that must occur if you go on too long, the kind of mind wandering that is destructive because it is out of the athlete's control. Remember, learning control is the key.

Underestimating attention span and thereby stopping short also works in your favor in another important way: If an athlete is able to think comfortably about something for, say, twenty minutes, and you

Learning and Teaching in Practice, Part 2

talk about it for fifteen, he or she will almost always spend the remaining five minutes thinking about what you've said, which is exactly what you want. The essence of learning is the internalizing of something that was external, the personal *owning* of something that formerly existed only elsewhere (in the coach's head). If, however, you talk for twenty-five minutes, leaving the athlete gasping for some mind-space, he or she won't give your words much more thought. The athlete will be all too eager to look elsewhere, and this can lead to other attitudinal problems.

I'll take my own advice and stop a little short, in the hope that you'll give some thought to what you can do to improve the attention you get from your athletes. Handling attention effectively is a matter of control and planning, not just of demanding it. It is a human faculty, governed by certain principles, and not a faucet that can be turned on and off. Remember, of course, to positively reinforce them when they do attend. Give praise not just for hitting or catching the ball, or for doing what they've been told, but also for looking in the right place at the right time, even if the overall performance was not perfect.

Let's take a look at some other topics that affect learning, specifically in regard to how materials should best be presented. These factors, though discussed separately, do not exist in isolation. After reading this section, spend some time putting it all together in your own mind, to see if any of your current coaching strategies could stand some modification.

Intake of information

How do we take in information?* Basically, we take in everything around us through our senses: sight, hearing, taste, smell, and touch. They are our windows on the world. Of these, sight is clearly the most important, accounting for seventy to eighty percent of what we take in. Hearing comes next, and in athletics the sense of touch is also cricital. A common coaching mistake is to rely too much on hearing—trying to tell your athletes how to do something. Visually showing and physically practicing (sense of touch) are better. In general, nothing should be taught only verbally; everything should include visual demonstration and physical practice, with your words used only as additional

---

*Throughout this section, *information* refers to anything learned: behaviors, ideas, concepts, skills, and so on.

directions. The common coaching lament, "But I told him or her that," is often the result of teaching that relied too heavily on the sense of hearing and not enough on the others.

Learning aids, like printed material or blackboard diagrams, should also be considered here. These rely on sight, but require symbolic thinking as well. (*Symbolic thinking* means being able to translate symbols into concepts.) In fact, using them also requires translating the concept into actions. Because learning aids require such complex mental activity, they should never be relied on exclusively. Their only effective use is as an additional teaching device, not in taking the place of other practice techniques like demonstrating, shaping, and practicing. The coach who sends his or her players home with written diagrams to study, and expects the players to be able to do what's on the paper when they return, is setting everyone up for a disappointment. Written material is best used as a bolstering technique, for study after the specific behaviors have at least been walked through once or twice.

In using learning aids, remember to practice the behaviors you want, not to recite the right answers. The idea of quizzing your athletes, requiring them to give oral or written answers to your questions about what they supposedly have studied, isn't usually of much value; even if you get correct responses, you have no guarantee that your players will do things correctly in competition, when behaviors—not answers—are necessary. If you want to quiz your athletes, put them on the practice field, give them the appropriate situation or play, and have them respond physically. These test results will have much more relationship to what they'll actually do in games.

And stay away from learning aids, especially written material, near competition time. They usually do little good and often get in the way of proper emotional preparation. (See Chapter 6 on pregame readying.)

Finally, remember that individual athletes will differ on these rules of learning. Some will learn particularly well with written or spoken information, while others will find it of no use at all. Study your players and see who responds best to what. Then when you have something important to get across, you can do it effectively.

Complexity of material

Simple skills and simple information can be presented effectively in a number of ways, but more complex material needs to be handled more carefully. How complicated the material is will determine the best way

Learning and Teaching in Practice, Part 2

of approaching it. Attention span is one of the things that suffer in the presence of highly complex material, but there are other considerations as well.

What's the difference between simple and complex things? It's a matter of how many different things one must know or be able to do in order to handle a situation effectively. The equation $2 + 2 = 4$ is a very simple one, whereas

$$x = \frac{y(a+2b) \div 346}{ny}$$

is much more complex. The same thing holds true in sports; running a dash is simpler (not easier—simpler) than doing a parallel bars routine, and reading a putt is more complex than diving for a fumbled football.

But the distinction is not always that clear. Two different kinds of complexity can be found in athletics: *complexity of behaviors*—how complicated the actual physical movements involved in an action are; and *complexity of cues*—how complicated a situation is to recognize or evaluate. These don't always go together. Some behaviors are very complicated but can be done whenever the athlete is ready, without having to worry about finding the right situation in which to do them; on the other hand, there are very complicated situations that tax the mental powers of the athlete but that, when properly identified, call for a relatively simple action. How these two kinds of complexity fit together in a given sport helps to determine how the athlete should be coached.

Table 5-1. Cue and Behavior Complexity.

| | | CUE COMPLEXITY | |
		HIGH	LOW
BEHAVIOR COMPLEXITY	**HIGH**	*Football: middle linebacker* TEACH: Early in practice, in short sessions, with much repetition, in small steps.	*Skating: triple salchow* TEACH: In small steps, either early or in mid-practice, in long sessions.
	LOW	*Baseball: stealing bases* TEACH: Early in practice, without the behavior (running), in longer sessions.	*100-Meter Dash* TEACH: Wherever it best fits, or as a low-complexity "rest" after a more complex task.

This chart shows the possible combinations of high and low complexity of cues and behaviors. It gives an example of an athletic activity that fits into each category, and it gives suggestions as to how such an activity should be coached. For example, an activity that involves both high behavioral complexity and high cue complexity is playing middle linebacker on a football team. The athlete must be ready and able to do any one of a number of different things (run forward, left, or right; strip interference; fade back for pass defense; and so on). This is behavioral complexity. He or she must also be ready and able to recognize many different situations before acting, situations that are further complicated by the offensive team, which is trying to mask each play: This is cue complexity. The linebacker must be able to recognize and respond to many different things, and, when responding, he or she may have to do any one of a number of things. The task is high on both types of complexity.

At the other corner of the chart we see running a 100-meter dash, which is relatively simple on both counts. The runner must respond only to the starter's gun, and he or she will be doing the same thing every time: running as quickly as possible. I'm not saying that either of these things is easy to do, but that the cues for doing it and the behavior pattern itself are less complex than some other things. The other corners of the chart represent activities with mixed complexities: A triple salchow (upper right) is behaviorally complex but is done when the athlete chooses, without first deciphering a complex situation, while stealing a base in baseball requires careful attention to every detail of the pitcher's movements, but breaks into a relatively simple behavior pattern. (I am referring here to running: the sliding that may be necessary at the other end of the procedure is best seen as a separate skill.)

The chart also contains suggestions on how to teach each skill, based on the combination of complexity levels. High/high complexity activities are best worked on early in practice, when everyone's attention is sharp and energy levels are high. Spend a short amount of time in any one session on this kind of activity. Learning high-complexity activities is best done in small steps and with much repetition. These are the kinds of skills that can easily become the things you do at the beginning of almost every practice session, throughout your season.

Stealing bases is high in cue complexity and should also be taught early in a session. But it can be worked on for a longer period of time at once, and without as much repetition during the season. This kind of activity, having a complex mental situation but a simple behavior pattern, can even be practiced without doing the behavior, to save time.

Runners can watch the pitcher, break toward the appropriate base for a step or two, and then stop—running it all the way out is only necessary occasionally in practice.

At what point you teach skills involving low cue complexity is less critical. If, as in the case of the triple salchow (a triple jump on ice), the behavior is complex, you're better off not waiting until the end of practice to work on it, but it doesn't have to be done right at the start, either. The athlete will be able to tolerate longer sessions on this kind of behavior, but small steps (because of the behavioral complexity) are still essential. Activities of low/low complexity can be practiced with fewer constraints, and they make good balancing activities to work on immediately after practicing a complex skill. The chart suggests when and in what overall format to teach certain kinds of skills, leaving the exact approach to your own expertise.

Complexity will affect many of the other learning factors discussed here. It affects the need to shape, the need for repetition, the length of attention span you can expect, and the best information intake modality to use. In general, the more complexity you perceive in the activity you are teaching, the smaller the steps you should take in teaching it, the slower you should go with your athletes, the more you should repeat things, and the fresher the athletes need to be to be able to learn well.

Primacy–recency—the learning curve

Another consideration concerning when to teach certain skills is what is called an *Acquisition Curve*, a relationship between when (in what order) things are best learned. What the curve shows (see Figure 5-1) is

Figure 5-1.

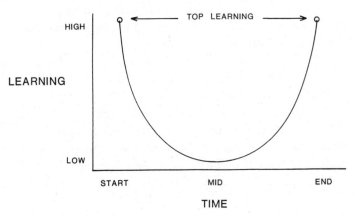

that, when a person is asked to learn a number of things, he or she best learns those that (1) came first, and (2) came last. This is referred to as the principle of Primacy–Recency. (Primacy means first and recency means as close to performance time as possible.) Things taught in the middle of a sequence are the *least* well-learned.

This curve operates over any time period you want to consider. Throughout a whole season, the things you work on early and late will be the most easily learned; and within any one practice session, the first and last few things you do will stick the best. This doesn't necessarily mean that they will be learned the best, because some things are more difficult than others; but if you teach things of equal difficulty throughout a practice, the athletes will retain the early and the late ones best.

It's important to work first or last on things that are difficult, complex, or particularly important to your sport. The first part of practice should involve things that are complex or difficult, because this enables you to take advantage of both the primacy effect and the top energy level of the session. The last thing you do will also have an advantage, but energy levels might be low, somewhat undercutting your teaching effectiveness. The best rule of thumb is to do things that are complex and hard, first; things that are simple but very important, last. Be especially sure to avoid wasting the first twenty to thirty minutes of practice on ordinary things or excessive warming up. Warmups are obviously important, but they need to be done quickly and quietly, without any teaching. This allows the warm-up period to be a readying, prepractice phase, instead of using up the energy of the first practice slot.

Repetition and routine in practice

This is one of the most important of the subtle, intangible, psychological variables that coaches need to attend to. Repetition, routine, regularity, familiarity, structure—whatever you want to call it, it means having things always be the same, or as much the same as is humanly possible. It refers to the atmosphere of order and comfortable predictability that is so vital to athletic training and performance.

Why is routine so important? Aside from the obvious fact that repetition is necessary to physically beat things into athletes' bodies and minds, routine is important from the standpoint of attentional, emotional, and mental energy. An athlete has only so much of these energies. Like physical energy, they are cyclical, and after they are used

Learning and Teaching in Practice, Part 2

up the player needs to rest in order to let them build back up. And they are best applied to one thing at a time. When everything that goes on around an athlete is familiar, he or she needn't use any of this psychological energy to orient him- or herself; all the energy can go into the learning process, where it belongs.

Many coaches don't realize how demanding this process really is. The higher the human mental function, the more psychological energy (attention, in particular) is needed, and learning something new is close to the top of human mental functions. Our minds are what separate us from animals, but the brain does not work without cost. When dealing with something new, it requires tremendous amounts of psychological energy and attention, which is wasted whenever the athlete has to orient to something extraneous or fight distractions. The more everything stays the same, the better the athlete is able to attend to learning or competing. When you don't regulate what goes on before and during a practice or a game, you are putting distractions in your athlete's way.

This is as important in games as in practice. I'll talk specifically about pregame and in-game routines, and about how essential routine is to pregame readying, in Chapters 6 and 9. The same applies to practice. The more the rest of the world stops impinging on the athlete's mind, the better he or she can practice; and the best way to accomplish this is to make the external trappings of your practice situations so ordered, habitual, and routine that the athlete doesn't give them a second thought. This includes the physical setting, the specific faces the athlete sees, the order of doing things, and the overall psychological atmosphere in which you practice. The only extraordinary things that should happen in practice are things that you plan, for a little variety and attention-getting. That's the point: Variety gets attention, so use it only when you want to, and don't let it sneak in unexpectedly to distract the attention of the athlete.

Memory

When you teach your athletes something, you want them to remember it. If they don't remember it, they won't be able to use the information or the skill in competition. Some knowledge of how our memory functions can be useful to you.

There has been a great deal of research on human memory, and it has uncovered a number of points:

1. Short- and long-term memory are different. We use short-term memory, for example, to remember whether we have just gotten the steal sign from the third base coach, while long-term memory comes into play in remembering how to cover a bunt, which was demonstrated last month. It is *not* the case that we always learn something and then gradually lose it over time, or that if we can remember something five minutes later, we will also be able to remember it five years later. The two processes are separate, and can be controlled by the athlete.

Conscious effort can aid in long-term memory, while short-term memory is more automatic. When you are teaching something, the athlete will be likely to remember it for a short period of time almost without effort; but the athlete may or may not remember it later on, in competition. You can increase the likelihood that he or she will remember it longer if you tell the athlete to consciously tell his or her brain something like this: "What you are going to be seeing next is important. Make sure that you store it in your long-term memory, not just your short-term memory, because you will need to remember it later." Then the athlete can take a moment to get his or her long-term memory *attitude* into place. (I assume you have had the experience of telling yourself to be sure to remember something: what you did was click into your long-term memory.)

2. Memory takes place in "chunks," or bits of information. In trying to remember a list of numbers, for example, we don't just remember the whole thing and we don't remember each digit individually. We automatically "chunk" the list of numbers into pieces of manageable length. Chunks of three or four individual bits of information are the easiest to remember: seven is about the maximum for most people to recall easily. (Consider your phone number: just seven digits, conveniently chunked into three- and four-bit pieces.) This can be used in practice situations. In going over plays, you'll notice that situations that come up in competition, or strategies, don't exceed three or four at one time. If there is more to cover, take a break every three or four bits, so that everything can be easily chunked for memory. When you give your athletes material to study, you can suggest to them that they look at three or four things in a sitting and then get up.

Chunking is also aided by the meaning of the information. In remembering the names of the players on your team, for example, an easy way to do it is to name people by position. This puts individual bits of information (the names) into categories, or chunks. In your teaching, you can take advantage of this by dealing with three or four things of a similar nature at a time. When, for example, you go over how to pitch to the opposing team with your pitcher, group the players that he or she will face: lefties, power hitters, and so on. The more you deal with small groups that have some logical criteria breaking them into chunks, the better your athletes will remember what they're supposed to.

3. Even with the use of chunking and the conscious effort to use long-term memory, decay is inevitable. Things are forgotten for three basic reasons: the passage of time, the lack of use of a given piece of stored information, and mental interference (mental operations that get in the way of memory). There's not much you can do about the first of these—time marches on; but the others can be dealt with. When you have taught something about competition that has not come up in a while, it's a good idea to go over it briefly again. Your athletes may still remember it when you bring it up, but they will be much more likely to remember it in competition if you bolster their memories in this way. Things like playing the infield fly rule in baseball, certain special-teams plays in football, and taking a penalty shot in hockey are things that fall into this category, as well as other events that occur infrequently and can also benefit from timely repetition in practice.

Mental interference comes into play in the following manner: Either during the time when the material is first being learned, or as the individual is trying to recall it, something else going on around the individual catches his or her attention, hindering memory. The best way to deal with this is to make sure that you teach things in an uncluttered atmosphere, marked by routine, quiet, and chunking. (This means giving your athletes a few moments, after you have told them something, to sit and think about it, when nothing else is going on. It means taking a little more time to get through a series of things to be taught, but it's worth it in the long run.) Minimizing interference during memory recall is best accomplished by in-game routine and minimal sideline coaching, a point that will be amplified in Chapter 8.

Don't assume that people will remember things. Do all you can to help them, as outlined here and in whatever ways you may come up with. The familiar refrain, "I told them that, why don't they remember it?" may refer to a lack of attention or intelligence on the part of the athlete in question, but it may also be due to less than optimal conditions of learning and recall—conditions that could have been remedied with a little planning by the coach.

Mental rehearsal

Mental rehearsal is something the athlete can do to bolster his or her learning. It belongs in what I have referred to as the *bolster period*, the few moments you give an athlete to think about, remember, and otherwise drive home whatever you have been teaching.

Mental rehearsal parallels behavioral rehearsal, or practice. It consists of seeing yourself doing something in your mind; in other words, rehearsing it mentally before you do it physically. It is a very effective learning technique.

Mental rehearsal will be dealt with more fully as an individual readying technique in Chapter 7. (See Positive Imagery.) It is not only an individual device to be used on the athlete's own time, but something that should be encouraged and planned into practice sessions. Especially early in the learning process, you should schedule into your practices a few minutes here and there where the athlete can sit and mentally rehearse what he or she is being taught. Tell the athlete to sit down, not to talk, and to go over in his or her mind what has just been taught. I've seen coaches use this as a last resort: When an athlete or team has been doing poorly and the coach is exasperated, he or she might stop things and angrily say, "This is ridiculous. Now just shut up, sit down, and *think* about what you're trying to do." The technique this angry coach is using is mental rehearsal. It can be used even more effectively when it is planned into workouts and the anger is left out.

Mental rehearsal is an intermediate step between your demonstrations and the athlete's physical attempts to do the particular skill. Give your athletes time to do so, especially when they have to remember a sequence of behaviors in order to do the overall skill correctly. An additional advantage of using such a bolster period is to get across to the athlete that he or she is responsible for being ready to perform. Too many athletes are told this, but then quickly see that the coach ignores this in practice, sticking only with physical demonstrations and attempts. Injecting ten minutes of thought (spaced out in, say, five two-minute sessions) into a two-hour practice will more than pay for itself in improved attention and mental preparation.

Fun and discipline

This last section on the mental side of practice combines two opposites: fun and discipline. They need each other, or each loses its effectiveness. Fun must be present, especially in young athletes, to balance discipline, and discipline must be present or the fun has no meaning and no direction.

Discipline does not mean yelling, strictness, obedience, or punishment. Discipline means control. The disciplined person is able to use his or her energies in a controlled way, not randomly or sloppily. The disciplined athlete is sharp; his or her attention is where it should be, and his or her actions are precise and assertive. The disciplined athlete plays better because he or she knows what to do to perform well.

Athletes must be shown how to be disciplined. Their natural urges for free play need to be shown avenues along which to channel their energies. It's the difference between completely spontaneous play in the crib and planned purposeful play in the field. In competition, it is more fun when you do well, and this requires some discipline.

The best way to build such discipline is to (1) model it, and (2) reinforce it in your athletes. This means reinforcing your athletes not just when they do well, but also when they pay attention, when they do things under control, and when they show obvious intentions in their actions. This is one of the key factors in determining which Little League players do well and which don't. A ten-year-old outfielder's first impulse after getting the ball with runners on base is to heave it toward the infield, wherever it may land. Through training he or she gradually learns that this is not enough: he or she should think about where to throw it ahead of time, look there, and then throw it to the appropriate person. The athlete learns this by being shaped, by being reinforced first for thinking and then for trying to throw to a specific place. He or she has then been taught a path for channeling his or her energies.

Athletic discipline does not mean enforcing short hair or a rah-rah attitude; these are personal preferences. What it does mean is directed effort and attention.

Discipline may involve punishment, especially in areas where loose play cannot be tolerated. This is precisely what links discipline to fun: If there is a sense of fun among the athletes and coaches, demands for discipline can be much more easily accepted by the athlete. If it's all hard work, then you don't have disciplined play—you have forced labor. The difference shows up in long, tough competitions, where a sense of fun is necessary both to sustain effort and to keep things relaxed.

Putting fun into your practices isn't hard, especially if you yourself enjoy them. Let it show. Enjoy the good plays and the funny, if unproductive, things that are bound to happen. Try some specific tactics as well. Greet the players individually as they show up for practice. Such an initial, positive approach reinforces the player just for showing up. It says, "Good to see you. Glad we both agree that this is fun and worth doing." During practices, occasionally let your athletes do the things they enjoy most. And, after practicing each skill, after each regular practice session, and after the between-game practice period, end on the positive. Finish up with things that are fun, that the athlete can do well, and that will leave him or her with a sense of confidence and enjoyment. Throughout a practice period, but especially at the end, the best feeling for the athlete to have is one of progress through hard work and fun. Aim toward this combination. The feeling is itself reinforcing and energy producing, and the hallmark of a well-coached team.

Linking practice and competition

Just because an athlete learns something in practice doesn't mean that he or she will do it correctly in competition. How can you increase the likelihood that what you do in practice will actually help in competition?

The best strategy is to *make your practices as similar to competition as possible.* Obviously, this is not entirely possible or even desirable; some work must be done separately on parts of skills and on individual techniques. Even so, there are some specific things you can do, within a teaching framework, to increase the probability that learning in practice will transfer to game situations.

1. Pacing and timing are important. Set up your practices so that they are similar to competitive events in the total amount of time they take and in their general rhythm. For example, if a game in your sport usually lasts two hours, practice in two-hour chunks. If you have to go longer, take a break at the two-hour mark. If your competitions are divided into periods, divide your practices similarly. Your athletes will then be learning to gauge the duration of effort required. They will be training in how to pace themselves and what to expect in the way of energy and attentional demands in competition. They will have practiced "being a player" for the exact amount of time that they'll need to be in competition, and, since nobody can be fully alert all the time, this timing is an important skill for athletes, especially young ones, to develop.

Each skill you practice should be paced as it will be in a game. If, as in shooting free throws in basketball or batting in baseball, the athlete will be doing the activity only for a short period of time, but periodically throughout a game, have him or her practice the skill in this way. Of course, you may also want to include longer sessions of free throw or batting practice, but a good portion of such practice should be chunked according to how the skill will be used in competition. There may be some physical utility in shooting fifty free throws or batting for ten minutes, but the athlete is not learning about the rhythm, timing, and psychological demands of having only two shots that must be made, or of having only a few pitches with which to get on base. Once the physical skills have been learned fairly well, these psychological points need some training as well.

2. Give your athletes the experience of being challenged and of producing under pressure. This is often one of the major differences between practices and games: In practice, one does the behaviors repetitively and quietly, while in games there is tension and the thing must be done right the first time. Practice sessions can be broken up by having individuals (or groups, in some sports) try to do things as they would in competition, with people watching and with something riding on their performance. I have seen a top swimming coach periodically use an exercise called a *challenge swim*. In the middle of practice, this coach will stop everyone and single out one swimmer. The athlete will be asked to swim his or her usual distance in whatever time the coach thinks the athlete is ready to achieve by going all out, at this stage of training. If the swimmer makes the time, the whole team gets a break; if not, there are extra laps. Needless to say, team interest is high, voices are raised in support of the swimmer's efforts, and the pressure is on. The learning experience parallels competition and trains the athlete for the kind of psychological challenge that he or she will actually face. The coach can make the time easy or difficult for the athlete, depending on how much pressure he or she thinks it makes sense to put on a given athlete. Team spirit is a pleasant by-product of this exercise, and this approach can be used in any sport. (A runner must do a certain time, a jumper jump a certain distance, a thrower exhibit a certain level of accuracy, a batter make good contact on a certain percentage of pitches, and so on.) You can set up the challenge any way you want to, as long as you make what's being required as similar as possible to what is needed in competition. Athletes usually enjoy this kind of thing in practice: it's more fun than long sessions on behavioral techniques. You also get to deal with victory and defeat, but within the comfortable confines of the practice field.

3. Inject some competition into your practices. This gives you the opportunity to work on things like game sense, poise, and the pressure of competition, but in a protected environment. The fact that it's also fun for the athletes is strictly secondary; the real purpose of using competition in practice is to train your athletes in as many factors that will be in competition as possible.

Aside from the overall strategy of making practice similar to competition, there are some other things you can do to bridge the gap between workouts and games. First, you can increase your athletes' ability to anticipate well in competition by *overlearning*. Go over situations that require reactions again and again, past the point of initial understanding, until the reactions are so automatic that the athlete doesn't even need to think about them. The veteran professional player doesn't have to think about covering the base for a throw or making sure the opponent doesn't drive the baseline: he or she does the right thing automatically. Overlearning can help in this. But consider that overlearning is often boring for the athlete, so do it in a pleasant atmosphere with much positive reinforcement.

As we know, you can enhance learning by giving the athlete a few moments to mentally rehearse what he or she has just learned or is about to try to do, before actually doing it. This step belongs early in the learning process, and should be weeded out as you get close to competition. You don't want your athletes to think in competition, you want them to act; so the closer you get to competition, the more you want to put your athletes into game situations over and over at a rapid pace. The goal (and you should tell your athletes this) is to anticipate, to do your thinking before the play develops, so that when the time comes for action you are ready to act.

Also consider the cycle of competition and practice. Peaks and valleys are natural. Since you are asking your athletes for a lot of energy and attention during practices, you must be sure to give them enough time between practice and competition to let physical, emotional, and attitudinal energy levels build up again. There will be more on this later.

Finally, you need to take into account the individual athlete's competition performance history. Some athletes practice well and play poorly, while others do the opposite. Some do well in competition when they have practiced long and hard, while others seem to do better when they have practiced lightly. It is always to your advantage to recognize these patterns in your athletes and to build them into your workout schedules. In the last practice before a game, for example, you should know who will respond best to being worked hard and who should be asked to do the minimum; who should be told pointedly that it's a big game coming up and who should be sent home after practice as if it were just another workout. The better you know these things, the better you can make what you do in practice fit nicely into what helps your athletes to perform best in competition.

Conclusion

These two chapters have been about funda-*mentals*—the psychological equivalents of the physical basics that you already know are essential to top performance. I hope you can see them as factors to be considered alongside of the physical aspects of teaching and learning your sport.

I have been urging you to try to establish the best possible learning conditions for your athletes. This consists of the basic chain—modeling/shaping/reinforcing-with-positives/practicing—as well as additional learning factors like primacy, recency, and memory aids, as they are applicable. Because not everything is under your control, it is rarely possible to use all of the relevant factors to your advantage in a given practice situation; sometimes two of the factors may even be giving you conflicting advice on how to proceed. But the more you can overcome these handicaps and use these fundamentals to your advantage, the better your athletes will learn what you are teaching. Notice that I don't say the easier it will be for you to teach; I know some of these approaches may take some effort on your part. But I assure you that they are worth it.

The role of the coach is that of an observer, a demonstrator, and a reinforcer. Everything should be geared toward establishing an atmosphere in which the athlete can learn, with the coach a mere aid in this process. The more you can fit your practice routines into a self-learning model, in which the athletes themselves do things that enable them to learn, the better. The coach is not a lecturer or punisher; he or she is a catalyst, someone who makes it easier for the athlete and the important mental and physical knowledge of his or her sport to get together. The measure of success is not how much you have covered or tried to teach, but how much has actually been learned.

There are important differences among athletes regarding mental and physical skills, preferences, and learning modalities. No matter what any book may say about the "best" way to do something, it is only a generalization, and should be subordinated to your observations about each individual athlete. Every coach knows that some athletes do better if they are coddled, others if they are yelled at; some with pep talks and pressure and others with an easygoing approach to competition. The more flexibility the coach can achieve, the better chance he or she has to prepare more individual athletes and the team as a whole. It's a shame to lose a talented athlete just because he or she needs a tender hand and you are a tough coach, just as it's counterproductive not to lean on the athlete who shows you that he or she needs some pushing. The more you can figure out how each athlete learns best, and do what's necessary, the better coach you will be.

Once you have familiarized yourself with these techniques, your main task will be to incorporate these principles into your own approach to coaching. If you can't work them in naturally, they will be of little use to you. These principles are important and they do work, but, as any coach has doubtless told his or her athletes, just knowing what you're supposed to do isn't enough. You must learn how to use them, with energy and control, as you expect your athletes to. And the best way to do so is to practice.

6

COUNTDOWN TO COMPETITION:
The last 48 hours

Your long-range work is over. The weeks and months of practice have been logged, and they have prepared you for competition. There's no more practicing to do; there's only the day or two to wait for the competition itself. You have entered the most critical readying period: the countdown to competition.

Most coaches and athletes agree that this is the toughest time of all. Competitors are emotionally geared to act, not to sit back and wait. The countdown period can thus become one of rising tensions, of having the internal dialogue of your active mind eat away at you, undermining your ability to relax, rest, and otherwise get yourself in top condition to perform.

The countdown period should be a time to get yourself in top condition—physically, emotionally, and mentally—to perform your best when competition actually arrives. It is a time when there is little to do but a great deal to accomplish. This chapter describes a positive approach to dealing with this period; it offers things to do to help yourself get ready, so that you are not merely hoping that starting time will find you ready. Equally important, it also tells you what not to do during the countdown.

This is a critical period in your overall readying. For at least twenty-four hours before your starting time, you are readying, whether you are consciously doing anything about it or not. The question in your mind should not be whether or not to get ready: it should be how to get ready, because the critical readying time of the countdown

139

period will pass whether you are aware of it or not. Ignoring this final opportunity to prepare yourself is just as bad as skipping practice or letting your attention wander during competition.

In structuring your countdown, remember the definition of readying in Chapter 1: Readying procedures (activities, thoughts, or feelings) are the things you do just before the critical activity (in this case, competition) to help you to be in the best position or moving in the best way when you are called on to act. The readying procedures may have little value in and of themselves, but they make the next act (competitive activity) easier. Think of what you do to get ready as being like taking a proper stance in the batter's box, or getting good footing in the blocks before a race. You don't get any points for doing these things, but your performance will improve if you do them. The countdown is an organized way of accomplishing this psychologically.

The goals of your readying are, most importantly, to be feeling exactly the way you usually feel when you play your best: to feel your own personal *feeling* (see Chapter 7); to have all of your attention where it should be, on the game itself; and to feel controlled energy. If you naturally feel these things, your readying will be easy. More commonly, athletes find it easy to feel one or another of these things and have to cultivate the rest. For example, if you are always energetic, then you'll have to work on being in control during your countdown. Do what you need to do, based on your own prior experience and the guidelines offered here.

There are two parallel worlds that can simultaneously affect your countdown: the physical world around you, and the internal world inside you. The physical world is the actual space you are in, what is happening around you, and the physical things you actually do. The internal world is more personal: the thoughts you are having; your feelings, attitudes, hopes, and fears; and the mental images that are flashing in your head. Sometimes these two worlds overlap almost completely, like when you are thinking only about what someone is saying to you; and sometimes they are very distinct, like when you are imagining a possible event in the game while you are just warming up.

It's simpler when the two worlds are coordinated, and that's often the way you want it during competition; but during countdown, this is not always possible. In general, the more control you have over each of these worlds, the better. As you will see in the sample countdown section, the more you can arrange the external world so that it aids your internal countdown, the smoother your readying will go. But of the two countdown worlds, the *internal* one is more important. It is your best tool for getting the most out of yourself once competition begins. Locker rooms and starting times may vary, but you can always control your internal world once you've learned how.

Let's discuss the three concepts that affect everything you do during the countdown: *cycles, rituals,* and *individual techniques*. Then we'll look at the smaller nuts and bolts of the pregame countdown period. As you read through it all, and as specific activities are mentioned, you should be asking yourself one question: "Will this help me to play better?" To some things, your answer will rightfully be, "No," while others may strike you as good ideas. I hope to suggest some new things you can try, as well as to remind you of factors that you know about but are not systematically using. The more things you actually try and the more control you actively take over your countdown readying, the better you will play. That's a promise.

Cycles

Nobody can be ready to perform well every minute of every day. Fluctuations are natural. In readying, the key is *timing* things correctly; you want your fluctuations to be on the upswing when it is time to perform. The cycles of your life do determine your readiness to perform, and the more you can work things out so that competition time finds you up and not down, the better you will play.

Cycle means a pattern with peaks, valleys, and certain amounts of time that come between each peak and valley. The ocean tides are a good example: They are sometimes high, sometimes low, and are always moving from one to the other, over and over, at a predictable speed (see Figure 6-1). A person can no more always be up than the ocean can always stay at high tide. But the ocean's cycle is fixed, whereas people can do something about theirs.

In recent years, some people have seized on the concept of cycles to predict how people will feel or perform on a certain day. They use

Figure 6-1. Ocean Tides: A Natural Cycle.

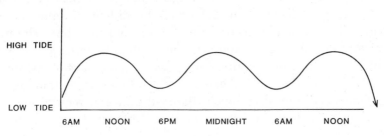

fancy mathematics and scientific-sounding terms like *biorhythms* to explain everything. While the idea of cycles is a sound one, the concept of biorhythms is not. Advocates of biorhythms say that everything is predetermined, based on the day and time you were born; so all you can do is figure out what kind of day you are going to have, but you can't do anything about it. That is ridiculous.

The kind of cycles I'm talking about here don't refer to the "grand scheme" of your whole life; they refer to the last few days, hours, and minutes leading up to competition. They are countdown, or readying, cycles, and they last from about an hour to a few days. The keys to using them to your advantage are (1) to know your own cycles, and (2) to start them at a precise time before competition, so that game time finds you ready to peak. You can use your cycles to improve your readiness, instead of arbitrarily "predicting" what's going to happen.

The three cycles to be aware of in your readying are (1) your physical cycle, (2) your cognitive cycle, and (3) your emotional cycle. While not the only cycles your body moves in, these are the ones that relate most directly to your overall readiness to perform well: the physical condition of your body, the alertness of your mind, and the amount of arousal you are feeling. The more you can cause all three of your body's cycles to be up at game time, the better.

The *physical cycle* is the easiest to recognize and the one that most athletes and coaches automatically observe and do something about. It involves your *physical* readiness to play: energy in your legs, good lung and heart endurance, relaxed but energetic muscles, and so on. All the physical work you do in practicing builds these strengths, and most coaches realize that right before competition you need to rest, so that your physical energy levels can rebuild themselves through the natural body processes of rest, food, and relaxation. If a boxer sparred ten rounds on the morning of a fight, he or she would obviously not be physically ready later that day.

Make sure you stop your physical workouts far enough ahead of a competition to allow the body to regenerate, to become eager for physical activity rather than just tolerating it. Skilled trainers do this automatically, gauging when to cut back on the athlete's training in order to leave him or her physically fit and eager by game time. The more physically demanding the sport, the more time is necessary. Boxing, football, and wrestling require a good two to three days of rest for the athletes to have "live legs" at game time; while soccer, swimming, and basketball need almost as much. Baseball and golf require less. But your own individual cycle is the most important thing to figure out, regardless of your sport. Before each game, see how your body feels, especially your legs, and recall how much rest you've had. A few trials will show what the best amount of off time is for you. Any physical practice you do within your optimal rest time only decreases your readiness. That's why last-minute workouts are almost never a good idea.

The other part of the physical cycle is the warm-up period. Warming up isn't important only for the body's protection from injury; it also wakes up the body, broadcasting the message of upcoming activity to the muscles and nerves. Your physical warm-up period can be relatively short and should never be strenuous, since this detracts from the physical energy you'll need in the upcoming competition. Warmup is the last step in the cycle that is represented in Figure 6-2. You work out hard, then slack off to almost nothing the day before competition. A warmup wakes your body up a little. Then, with the added energy of your built-up rest period, your body is at its physical peak when you want it to be, at game time.

Figure 6-2. The Pregame Cycle.

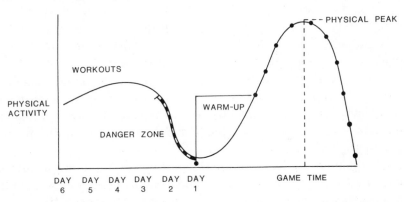

Your *cognitive cycle* follows roughly the same pattern. But while coaches usually do allow their athletes enough time to rest physically, they often don't give athletes enough mental rest. In fact, during the physical *danger zone*, they often heap on the study sessions, with chalk talks, question periods, and the like. This is usually not a good idea; the mind needs rest, too. Without some down time before an event, the athlete's attention and mental alertness will not be at their peak during the event. Mental functions follow the same pattern as the physical. Additionally, as I pointed out in Chapter 3, the learning that goes on right before competition usually amounts to nothing.

Countdown to Competition

The best way to handle the cognitive cycle is to gauge it by the time between the end of physical workouts and the event itself. Whether this time period is one day or three days, use only the first half for skull sessions and study. *Leave the last half of the rest period alone.* You will rarely learn anything new in the second half of this period, and your unconscious mind will be going over what you already know, so further study at this time is usually unnecessary. Mix in your heavy teaching and studying with your normal physical workouts, and follow this with concentrated teaching and review in the first half of the countdown. Halfway through the countdown, stop trying to learn new things; anything you do manage to learn right before a game will almost always harm you more than help you, by taking the place of other thoughts. For instance, when a baseball pitcher has gone over how to pitch to the opposition, and then he or she is given a lesson on the balk rule and pickoff moves just prior to competition, something will suffer. Usually he or she simply won't learn much about the balk rule in that situation, but if he or she does, he or she is in danger of being too aware of that while pitching. (Remember recency?) This can lead to paying too much attention to baserunners, while the opposing hitters get what they like: fat pitches. For cognitive information to be used effectively in competition, it needs to be learned well in advance, so that the mind and the body have time, in practice, to put new things together and really *know* them. Lay off the last-minute cramming.

Finally, there is the *emotional cycle*, the way you feel before and during competition. Feeling right, feeling eager, and having *mental energy* are terms that reflect this cycle. The emotional cycle is the most important and the most variable of the three in determining pregame readiness.

Like the other two, the emotional cycle should follow a pattern of moderate use in routine workouts and a complete rest period, and then peak during the game. Notice that I don't say peak at game time, as I did for the physical cycle; emotional peaking is better saved until later in competition, for critical moments. The emotional rest period is therefore usually longer than the others. It can begin before your physical rest phase, sometimes even days before, and it can continue until one to two hours before competition, depending on the individual. Don't be afraid of emotional flatness in the last practice or two before competition, or even up until one hour before the game. You can get emotionally aroused quickly, and the less emotion you have wasted prior to game time, the more emotional energy you will have in the game. I have seen too many teams get really pumped up in practice, stay excited while they wait for the day of the game, peak at game time, and then struggle in the second half (especially if they are playing a top-notch, well-prepared opponent).

Emotion is an individual thing, much more so than physical and mental learning. You have to experiment with various pregame emotional cycles, seeing which works best for you and then setting up your countdown accordingly. Remember that all three cycles are going on at exactly the same time inside each person. What you do in handling one cycle can interfere with your effective readying in another.

The biggest mistake is to cram information too late in the rest period. It not only messes up the cognitive cycle, but it wreaks havoc on the physical and emotional cycles as well. Whenever you use your powers of attention and intellect, you short-circuit your others. Late studying can lead to *paralysis through analysis.* Instead of moving freely and surely in your sport, your own thoughts paralyze you, and make your movements uncertain and rigid. This will obviously destroy you competitively. The effect on your emotional cycle is even more damaging. Clear thinking and strong feelings do not mix well, and it is vital to have your feelings where you want them in your readying. Your emotions supply you with your energy, and new or complex thoughts undercut this. Do your studying early, and leave the last few hours for physical rest and emotional readying.

One cycle, however, can sometimes aid another. Early in the rest period, studying does give you something constructive to do while you rest physically. Toward the end of the rest period, your physical warm-up works well with your emotional cycle, either getting you up (if that's what you need) or giving you an outlet for pent-up tensions (if that's what you need). In structuring your own countdown period, it is important to learn when and how long it is best for you to warm up.

The point is to learn about yourself. I can't say that everyone should start to warm up at precisely twenty-three minutes before game time, or that you should never study twelve hours before the event. People differ. But now that you are aware of the three cycles, check out how they work in *your* case. The basic principles apply to most people; now apply them intelligently to yourself.

This usually means that you should *identify the one cycle that needs most of your attention, or that is most important to you.* Most athletes find that one or two of the cycles are no problem, and that is particularly tough to handle. I've had athletes tell me that their physical rest and warmup go fine, and that they generally know what they need to know in competition, but that they're never sure about their emotions—they have to struggle to get psyched at the right time. Whichever is the key cycle for you, put some time into trying timing the things you do differently.

Finally, don't fight your cycles. Just because the rest of the team studies at a certain time or warms up at a certain time doesn't mean that that's best for you. Find your own timing sequence for everything you do during countdown. Chapter 7 has some tips for athletes who find their own best countdown cycles and who then have to convince the coach to let them be different. Observe your own cycles, and use them to your advantage.

Remember that you want each of the three cycles to be on the upswing as you finish your final warmups and head into competition; but, precisely because we are talking about cycles (ups and downs), the first part of your rest period is just as important as the last few minutes. You can't get up very high if you never let yourself really wind down—physically, mentally, and emotionally. That's why Chapter 7 has techniques designed to calm you down and clear your mind, as well as ones to help you study and psych you up.

Rituals and routines

The lore of sports is filled with stories about the rituals and routines that athletes have used before competition. Players refuse to wash their socks as long as they are on a hot streak, or have to walk onto the playing field exactly the same way each time, or have to get dressed in a specified order. Superstition and anxiety are usually behind such habits, and athletes have even come to believe that unless they dress or warm up in a certain way, they will lose.

The surprising thing about these kinds of rituals, however, is that they can actually work! Oh, they don't work because of magic or the superstitious reasoning that may have started them in the first place; they help the athlete to be better prepared for competition, because they constitute structured, personal routines, or countdowns. The more familiar everything you do before an event is, the more control you have over your own readying activities. You want all of your attention to be focused on the game at hand, and a personal readying routine of any kind helps your mind to gradually focus more and more on the upcoming event.

The value of any readying ritual is that it acts as an unconscious countdown, an internal readying procedure that keeps reminding you of the impending event. Besides being a confidence-aiding device, it also serves as a *timing device*, allowing you to monitor and control the readying cycles we have just been looking at. You don't have to think, "I'm putting on my socks, so I'll be playing in thirty minutes"; the message is getting through to you physically, cognitively, and emotionally, and the little things you do in your readying routine act as signposts along the way. They allow you to build gradually to your game time readiness.

The great thing about rituals is that they can be anything you want them to be. You can go through a series of thoughts or a series of behaviors, as long as they are things that you can do easily before every contest. Whatever you can find to put your mind and body in the right place for competition is fine. Some people find that walking around in a certain pattern does it, or that doing a certain exercise gets the mind going in the right direction. Whatever it is, make your own personal countdown to competition.

Another advantage in using rituals is that you are certainly doing some things already that can be called a routine. Your personal habits of dressing, warming up, and so on constitute a personal ritual, and the more you stick to it, the more familiar everything will be, making it much easier for you to put your attention and energy into the upcoming event. Remember that anything outside the usual pattern of things requires attention and energy to orient to it and to fit it into what you are doing. The more familiar your readying routines are, the less you have to look around, think about where you are, or in any way respond to your environment, and the more energy and attention you will have to devote to your performance.

The one single ritual that I recommend most frequently to athletes is the *dressing ritual*. Every athlete must put on some sort of special clothing in order to compete: this must be done one piece at a time, and takes longer than a few seconds. Use your undressing and dressing time to really put your mind on the upcoming event. Undress slowly, and put on the necessary uniform for your sport at the same pace. Get undressed and dressed in a particular order, the same way every time, so that it becomes a firm habit. This way, in any situation—in any locker room, day or night, big game or not—you will always have a few minutes that are the same, that are familiar, that are *totally yours*. You can use this time to do whatever mental things are best for you to do before competing. (See Chapter 7.) Coaches should make it a point never to bother their athletes during this dressing period, and neither should teammates. The dressing ritual becomes one of putting on the armor, both physically and mentally: You are donning the equipment to do battle, and simultaneously gearing your mind in the same way. The dressing ritual then becomes like a hallway in time; you pass from all the daily considerations of your world (work, school, family, and so on) into thoughts about the upcoming event alone. The ritual is the hallway between these two worlds, helping you to screen out the larger one and prepare for the more concentrated one, the arena of competition.

Using your dressing time is only one type of ritual; actually, any routine, or collection of small, easy behaviors, can serve as your readying ritual. Do whatever you like, whatever gives you the feeling that you are indeed passing through the kind of hallway or tunnel I've just described, so that when you emerge on the other side your attention is completely on the game. In order for your behavior pattern to qualify as a ritual, it has to meet three criteria: You must do your behaviors the *same amount of time* before each competition, you must do them in exactly the *same order* before each competition, and you must *think about the game* while you are doing them. This will enable you to get your cycles synchronized so that you'll be ready just when you want to be—at game time.

Planning your cycles and using rituals brings your readying process under your own control, so that you can dependably do what helps you to perform better. You will have not merely left to chance what happens to you before competition; you will have purposefully taken yourself through a series of countdown steps that *you* control, and this will give you much more power over your own performance readiness than you would otherwise have. Additionally, these rituals give you something active to do in your readying, so that you are not just waiting for the fateful moment of competition and hoping to be ready. Athletic competition itself requires you to be active and aggressive, energetic and yet controlled, and your readying should be seen in the same way. You don't want to spend a lot of energy in readying, but you can approach it actively and with control if you establish a routine of readying.

A psyching strategy that some coaches use is to purposely change something in the athletes' pregame routines. This is usually done before big games, in order to heighten the team's awareness and excitement. Such a strategy can be useful, but only under specific circumstances. If the team has been doing well for a while, it is risky to make much of a change in their readying procedures. This kind of move is usually better suited to waking up a flat team or really infusing a shot of energy into a squad. Change brings anxiety, especially if you have been rigid about maintaining strict readying patterns all along, so it makes sense to do this only if this what your team needs.

Even more critical to using this strategy positively is the sense that even though things are different before this particular game, they are still under control. Change that in any way gives the athletes the idea that things are different due to reasons beyond the coach's control is bad. This creates the expectation that the competition may be the same way, and that of course undermines confidence and assertiveness on the field. Make whatever changes you have cooked up for your athletes an obvious part of your conscious pregame strategy, and not merely a reaction to the pressures of the day. The key is to make the change an active, controlled one; the weakness and uncertainty of changes brought about by circumstances beyond the coach's control only uses up the athletes' energy and attention. Everything before competition, even changes from ordinary routines, should serve to focus attention more and more on assertively handling the competition.

Routine, familiarity, and structure are great allies in your athletic preparation, because they build the foundation of discipline and control into which the athlete's great energies and natural abilities rightfully fit. So whatever you take away from *Peak Performance*, incorporate it into your routine.

Specific techniques and individual differences

Specific readying techniques can also help you to control your readying. Chapter 7 deals with such techniques in detail, including the use of the *Athletic Performance Improvement Survey* (APIS) to determine just what your own, personal readying procedures should be.

Regardless of which techniques you decide to use, you should keep two general points in mind. First, there is something that I call the pregame *buzz* which comes over athletes before a contest, and it can pose a real threat to proper readying. This buzz is a confused combination of many emotions and thoughts: it is sometimes seen as being psyched up or excited. If it really is pure excitement and eagerness, that's fine; but usually this isn't exactly what's going on inside the athlete. When you are feeling the buzz, you are essentially out of control. You are feeling things in a confused way, as though your feelings were ganging up on you. This is undesirable. It is much better to be feeling only one emotion before you compete. It doesn't really matter what that emotion is; it will vary from athlete to athlete, and this is where your individual APIS and the specific techniques you use will come into play. You need to identify the one emotion you want to feel before a contest and stick to that. The better you can distinguish that one emotion from all the others, the easier your readying will be.

Secondarily, coaches need to be aware of differences among the athletes. Everybody should not be readying in the same way, and one way to divide up your athletes is by the positions they play. Put athletes who perform similar tasks together before the event; then, within that grouping, let them do their individual readying.

Good readying is a matter of controlling the countdown process, but this does not mean that the coach should become a harsh dictator, demanding that everyone on the squad do exactly the same things. On the contrary, breaking things down first by positions and then by individuals allows (and teaches) the athlete to take responsibility for his or her own readying. Because the coach can't get inside the athlete's head anyway, the next best thing is to teach the athlete to do the mental and emotional work necessary for top performance.

The actual countdown and how to structure it

The essence of the countdown is timing; it's not as important that you do specific *things* as it is that you do your things at a specific *time*. Think of yourself as having an *internal clock:* This clock knows that competition will be coming up in a certain amount of time, and it helps you to be ready. Like the countdown on the launching of a rocket ship, the time of action moves closer and closer, but all along the way, at specific times, there are other things to be done. Your own readying countdown also has this quality, but instead of actually watching a real clock tick away the minutes, you mark the passing of time with your own body, through the things you do at various stages of the readying process. The goal is, as always, to have as much controlled energy ready to go at game time as you can.

The countdown procedure is really an elaborate *focusing* technique. With each countdown activity you do, you are telling yourself that you are that much closer to competition. This focuses your attention on your sport step by step, which works much better than trying to get yourself ready all at once during the last few minutes. The countdown allows you to get to the top of your mountain of psychological energy gradually, with each step building on the last. Ultimately, your whole readying procedure will become a smooth, natural process that you can control, like ticking things off a checklist, until you have done the whole job of readying.

The countdown takes place in two separate worlds: the internal world of your mind and the external world of the events around you. You use the external events as *markers* for what's going on inside you. For example, you say to yourself, "I'm warming up now; that means I'll be playing in thirty minutes." More precisely, you are using the timing marker of the external world to tell yourself not only that you'll be playing in thirty minutes, but that you'll be *ready* to play in thirty minutes. This is often the difference between those athletes who are actually ready to go at game time and those who are clock watchers, who can tell you when the game starts but who are not doing the internal work necessary for top performance all the way along the countdown trail. Your countdown is a ritual in which your eyes and ears tell your mind to focus and gear up for action.

What are the markers to use in an actual countdown? There are many, and you may even already have some of your own. Anything that you habitually do at a certain time before competition can be considered a countdown marker, because it serves as a guidepost to your mind, readying it. There are also some events that occur for every athlete before competition and that can therefore be used by anyone as countdown markers. These are the essentials of life and play; in fact, the more central to life the marker is, the better you will be able to use it as a readying device. Here are some countdown markers you can use. The more you make it a point to do them at a specific time before competition, and mold them into a ritual, the better you will be able to control your own readying.

Time—This is the simplest and most obvious countdown marker. It consists of saying to yourself, "In twenty-four hours I will be competing." You can do this at set times before each competition. I recommend using time markers at these intervals: one week (for really big events), twenty-four hours, one hour, about five minutes, and one minute before competition. You shouldn't use all of them, but be consistent about which ones you do use, and try to be doing something specific at each time marker. For the last few minutes this is usually easy. You usually walk onto the field a few minutes before competition begins, and perhaps hear the national anthem or some other such marker. Then there's the immediate readying marker, like getting onto the blocks for a swimmer or lining up for the kickoff. These are automatic, physical countdown markers that have become part of the sport itself. What you want to do is to have the same kind of marking system earlier in the readying process.

Sleep—No matter what else you do, you must at some point sleep for the last time before competition. You can use this as a marker. It is especially effective to try always to wake up at the same amount of time before competition, so that sleep fits naturally into your readying ritual.

Travel—If you have to travel to get to your events, try to do so with the same timing each time. Obviously, different trips take different lengths of time, but you can try to gauge things so that you always arrive at some specified number of hours before the game. Consistency in this can be quite an advantage.

Food—You must also at some point eat for the last time before competition. Make this into a ritual, always finishing this meal at the same amount of time before competition. This countdown marker is as important physically as it is psychologically.

Dressing—I've already described the dressing ritual and the great value it can have as a readying device. Always dressing at a specific time before competition adds to this activity's readying value.

Contact with People—Some athletes can tolerate talking with other people before competition and some cannot. Whichever category you fall into, try to have your contact with teammates, coaches, and others be regular. If solitude is your thing, get off by yourself at about the same time before each event; if you typically do talk with others before a game, stop and start your conversations at about the same time. The overall readying approach leans more toward not talking with others for at least the last few moments before competition, but the most important thing is to be consistent about what you do. Contact with people has great attention-breaking powers; if you're talking, it's hard to be readying internally.

Warming up—Make your warmup times regular. This is as important for physical readying as for psychological. If you've been having trouble up to this point in grasping the significance of the countdown markers, think how important warming up is to you, not just in physically loosening up your body but also in focusing your thoughts and emotions on what you are about to be doing. With practice, all the markers mentioned here can serve the same purpose. After all, putting your body, thoughts, and emotions on what you are about to do is the essence of readying.

Other Personal Rituals—Whatever individual rituals you may have decided on for your own use, be consistent about when you do them.

The Readying Spot—This technique is fully described in Chapter 7 as the most important and useful of all the specific readying techniques. It is included here simply to remind you that whatever you do by way of making a concerted effort to get yourself psychologically ready to perform, do it regularly, at the same amount of time before competition.

Obviously, some of these countdown markers will make more sense to you than others. Pick the ones that do make sense to you, and use them as signposts along the road to readiness. Do these things at consistent times and in a ritual manner, so that they become your whole world prior to competition. Before the game, you want your entire attention to be in one place, on your own readying, and the countdown gets you to this point of total attention in gradual, easy steps.

The ultimate goal of the countdown is to have everything within you merge into one total reality: performance. You merge the cycles within you, your energies, your thoughts, and the small preparatory behaviors you do into one place in your mind. The actual reality of each event will of course be different from all the others, but you want to make the inner world of your own readying as constant as you can. The outer reality of the day of the game itself will merge with the inner reality of your own readying, and you will be ready. Don't trick yourself into believing things that aren't true, just to pump yourself up; rather, let the events of the outer world work for you, and become the fuel for your energies and the countdown markers for your readying. Your own personal way of readying is your most effective weapon in the battle to seize and control the particular challenges of each competitive event.

Summary

The more you use a consistent, step-by-step approach to readying, the more likely you will be to perform at a consistently high level in competition. Your own personal countdown can be relaxing, without many steps or heavy psych-up periods, and that's fine; just be consistent about the way you get loose before a game. What you do doesn't matter as much as when you do it and how consistent you are.

The concepts of ritual, countdown, and readying cycles are all different ways of describing the same thing: the process of focusing your attention and energy before competition. The process described here as countdown ritual is meant to be used as a framework or blueprint for your pregame readying: other specific activities will fit into this larger framework. These other activities include specific individual readying techniques described in the next chapter, as well as the many external events listed in Chapter 8.

The countdown ritual is intended for the readying of athletes and not for the convenience of coaches. Whenever pattern and routine is part of a team's schedule, it is easy for the coach to insist on regimentation. Some of this is of course inevitable (in travel, pep talks, and so on), but the countdown ritual refers to *individual* readying. Allow as much purposeful individual variation as you can in things like warmups, meals, and dressing. The goal is to teach the athletes themselves what a meaningful personal countdown really is, not to force them into one. It is this distinction that separates experienced from inexperienced athletes: The experienced athlete knows how to ready him- or herself and should be left alone to handle it, while the inexperienced athlete needs to be taught the skills of appropriate readying. The outside structure provided by the coach's "rules" for everyone's pregame routine can help the inexperienced athlete in the early stages of his or her competitive life, but there has to be a gradual shift toward a more individual readying routine: otherwise, the athlete will never realize his or her full performance potential. For the coach, this means starting out with imposed structure, while always looking for and encouraging individual athletes to find their own personal pathways to better readying. Teamwide ritual should be used to ensure *minimal* levels of readying, while individualized readying can more nearly approach *maximum* performance levels for each athlete.

The whole countdown ritual follows naturally from an athlete's sense of serious readying. Not that readying means being dour; you simply can't be flip and unaware of what your own readying process means to you and expect to be consistently ready to play well. If you step back and take in the big picture, you'll see that the real challenge of the game starts long before the opening whistle. It starts twenty-four, forty-eight, or even seventy-two hours before that point, at the moment when your formal practice ends and the game itself is physically ahead of you. The countdown period between that point and the opening whistle is the time when you have the most influence over your performance: once the game starts, too many things, most noticeably your opponents, are beyond your control. The countdown period, after the demands of practice are over and before the demands of the game have begun, is the time that is most truly yours. Use it wisely.

7

FOR THE INDIVIDUAL ATHLETE:
Specific readying techniques

Now that you have a better understanding of the general thrust of the readying approach, it's time to start taking control of all the things that can affect your performance. This chapter contains two main kinds of information: (1) how to identify your own individual performance needs through the *Athletic Performance Improvement Survey* (APIS), and (2) techniques for getting yourself ready to play.

THE ATHLETIC PERFORMANCE
IMPROVEMENT SURVEY

First, let's look at the APIS itself. (See Appendix B.) The APIS is a questionnaire, useful in improving athletic performance, that has been used by hundreds of athletes competing at high levels in a variety of organized sports, including football, baseball, swimming, track, and tennis. It is one of the best first steps in identifying and changing one's performance needs. While the focus of the APIS is on the individual athlete, it is equally effective when used with team sports. As a questionnaire, of course, it can only be as helpful to you as the seriousness of the answers you give it.

The best way to approach the APIS is to think of it as a kind of mirror that will reflect back to you your own list of performance needs. You will have to spend time looking closely at it to be able to see the smaller parts of you that are often missed by a quick glance or fleeting thought about why you sometimes do well in your sport. It has already been used by many athletes just like yourself, and is a quick way to scan the many performance areas already discussed in this book.

While the APIS basically covers the information in Chapters 3–6, 8, and 9, it makes those concepts more relevant to you. You will notice that the TRUE/FALSE questions are divided into sections by the small lines at the left-hand margin: you will find that the questions within each section are related, to help you focus on one performance issue at a time. These sections include questions on FAMILIARITY (3–6)—whether you do best in familiar or unfamiliar situations; POSITIVE ELEMENTS (7–8)—the only two elements in the APIS seen as being necessary for almost all people to perform well; SIGNIFICANCE (9–11)—the importance of events to you; SUCCESS/FAILURE (12–16)—how these anticipations affect your performance; WARMUP (17, 18); FEELINGS (19–25, 40, 41); PRACTICE (26–33); OUTSIDE FACTORS (34–36); PRIOR PERFORMANCES (37–39); YOUR MIND (42–47, 65–68)—your mental pluses and minuses; RELATIONS WITH PEOPLE (48–51); PERFORMANCE SPAN, DURATION (52–55); FEEDBACK AND PACING OF ACTIVITY (56, 57); PHYSICAL ABILITIES (58–64); and GENERAL EXTERNAL FACTORS (69–73).

In looking at the APIS, you will notice that not all the questions are asked in quite the same way; this is done for a reason. The survey begins with two general, open-ended questions, which should be answered first. Before you go through the entire survey, your own ideas about your performance will be foremost in your mind. This is what the first two questions are aimed at: Of all things that go on before and during performance, what do you think is important? If you answer these questions first, you will probably include things that are not otherwise dealt with in the survey. If you wait and answer the other questions first, you will be much more likely to stick to the ideas those questions bring up, and you may skip some of your own thoughts about readying. Both are important to your eventual success.

Next come 71 TRUE/FALSE items (3–73), but you will immediately notice that they are not simply TRUE/FALSE. You can also answer each question with a question mark which is meant to be used in two situations: (1) if you are not sure whether the factor in question helps or hinders your performance, or (2) if you feel that the factor is completely irrelevant to your own performance. In the second case, you can probably ignore that factor in later planning of your own readying; but if you have circled a question mark because you're not certain of the best answer, you will do well to put some thought into that item. You may be missing some part of readying that could be very helpful to you, or you may be allowing some factor to interfere with your readying without really knowing it. The question mark answers are often more important than some of the easier answers to other items.

Finally, there are three open-ended items at the end of the survey. These are included because athletes often find that thinking about their answers to some of the other items jogs their memory, and they become aware of factors they forgot to include in the initial readying descriptions.

How to use the APIS

Before you pick up the APIS and start answering the questions, here are some guidelines for making the most out of this experience:

1. Make a copy of the questions as printed here and answer them in writing. Doing them in your head is not very effective.
2. Do it alone, especially the first time you take the APIS: don't be in a hurry to share it with friends, teammates, or your coach. Make sure all the answers are yours. It is probably most important that you not share your answers with your coach until you have had a while to think about them, or even to try out some changes in your personal routine. The emphasis should be on your doing what's necessary for you to perform better. Your coach has probably been taught certain ways of helping most athletes do better, and chances are that he or she is passing these ways on to you. Most likely, you are already trying your coach's way right now: it is probably a sound approach, but not the whole story. Your coach's ideas can sometimes get in the way of your own honest feelings about what helps or doesn't help you to perform well, and it is essential to find your own aids to performance. These aids can then be used along with your coach's ideas to produce the best possible performance. If you let your coach influence your answers in this initial information-gathering phase, you will be cheating both yourself and your coach out of what could be important readying information.
3. Answer the questions in the order that they are given.
4. After you have completed the survey, wait at least one week before reviewing your responses, but be certain that you do review them. It is essential that you review your survey at a later date so that you can bring a fresh point of view to it.

Some of your answers will seem inaccurate, while others will seem more or less important than you thought at the time. Even though you may have put the survey in a drawer for a week, your mind will have been mulling over the readying and performance issues it raised. By allowing this to happen, you avoid having your mood, or events on the day you filled out the survey, determine your answers.

Before I gave athletes instructions to wait a week and review the survey before giving it to me or making any readying changes themselves, I often got back surveys that stated the same theme over and over—in the general questions, in the margins around the TRUE/FALSE items, and so on. One athlete, for example, filled out his survey after a practice session in which his coach had emphasized concentration very heavily, saying that the athlete's main problem was that he didn't concentrate well. This athlete's concern about this concentration problem got in the way of his answers: everything he wrote had to do with concentration. Concentration was a big factor in determining this athlete's performance level, but it certainly was not the only factor. By waiting a week before finalizing your answers, you can avoid this problem.

Next, as you are actually filling out the survey, try to keep these things in mind:

1. Answer the questions for yourself, as an individual athlete. Don't compare your ideas about readying with those of a teammate, or with those of some successful professional athlete, or with what Howard Cosell may have said about psyching up. Find your own way.

2. Answer the questions for the ideal situation. Don't, for example, answer that having contact with people just prior to performing is okay simply because your usual locker room situation makes it impossible to avoid such contact. Assume, in your responses, that you could set up your readying activities any way you wanted to.

3. Take your time! Think about the items without rushing through them. Set aside plenty of time for doing the APIS. It is long, but if you think about these things now, you won't have to be thinking while you're performing. That's the key point in the readying approach: Do the thinking and other hard work *before* you play, so that *while* you perform you can be free of such interference.

4. Let the written items prompt you to think of related items that affect your performance. I tried to think of everything for you in the APIS, but obviously I could never do so without knowing you as well as you know yourself. Allow yourself to make notes in the margins. Oftentimes, these flashes wind up being the most important changes the athlete needs to make.

After filling out the APIS and waiting a week, review your responses. This is the end of your information-gathering phase and the beginning of your planning and action phase. Find the most relevant pieces of information you can, look for patterns in your responses, and step outside yourself to try to get a picture of the overall situation in which you perform best. Doing this requires more than simply rereading your answers of the previous week; be prepared to put some thought into what you'll be doing.

Just as it was important to write your initial responses to the survey, you should have a pencil and paper handy while reviewing your answers. Write down the important elements of your readying, as well as any ideas you may have during the reviewing process. When you're through, you want to have an action plan written out. In doing so, consider the sections of the APIS as units. For example, look at all of your answers to the eight questions about practice (26–33) and ask yourself, "How can I best set up my practice activities to produce the best readying for the best possible performance?" Do this with all the sections.

In trying to make sense of the many answers on your APIS, you will probably find it helpful to let your overall insights fall into two categories: the circumstances *around you* (external world) that lead to good performance, and the feelings or thoughts *within you* (internal world) that do the same. The first category will probably look like a list of things that happen to you before playing, and many of them will seem unchangeable to you. We'll look at that problem in a moment. For now, remember to be idealistic. The second category, your feelings and thoughts, will be discussed in detail later in this chapter.

The final step in the review process is to take your two lists of ideal performance conditions and try to choose from each of them just one crucial statement. This will be hard, but the more you can come up with *one external* and *one internal* condition for yourself, the easier it will be to use the techniques in this chapter in a concentrated, effective way. Usually we think that we have to solve all of our problems at once or we haven't really accomplished anything; on the contrary, the more we can focus our attention on one task at a time, the more likely we are to make headway.

In summary, we can see that the products of the APIS will be:

1. Two lists of important performance conditions (external and internal), some of which will need change because they currently are not right; and

2. Two crucial conditions, one from each list, that are about to receive your immediate attention. The other conditions will be considered secondary performance factors, and will be dealt with later.

Your lists and crucial factors will be only as good as the effort you put into using the APIS. This survey is merely a tool: it won't do the work for you, but it can help you immensely if you're serious about improving your readying.

Making changes—taking control
over external readying conditions

One of the things that makes us different from animals is that we can plan and manipulate our environment. The nonthinking animals with which we share our planet are not able to control things around them as we can; for example, they cannot create artificial climates inside buildings, nor can they plant and harvest food. They are subject to whatever weather comes along, and must continually hunt for food. As an athlete, you face the same choice: You can try to deal with whatever is going on around you as well as you can, or you can take control of your environment, setting it up so that the things that are best for you will be the things that actually happen. In athletes there are four external areas that affect your performance: these areas are best defined by the people who can affect you: (1) your coach, (2) your teammates, (3) other people in your life (friends and family), and (4) you. These people are your social environment, and you need not take them as you find them, at least in relation to your athletic performance. They can help or hinder you, and it is up to you to determine which will be the case.

First and foremost is your coach. It is very possible that your responses to the APIS suggest that a change in your practice routine might be helpful to you, and in trying to make such a change you will have to deal with your coach. A tennis player, for example, might want to devote more attention to the serve, since he or she has realized

For the Individual Athlete

through the APIS that, when serving well, he or she feels confident and tends to play much better. He or she may want to start or end practice with work on serves, whereas the coach usually works on serves in the middle of practice. The player's task is to get the coach to allow this change; this would constitute a change in the player's readying environment.

Similarly, your interactions with your teammates may have caught your attention through the APIS. Perhaps you feel that you would be better able to get ready to play if no one talked to you immediately prior to performance time, but being in the locker room with others conflicts with this need. Your social environment needs a change.

The same kinds of issues can come up with family and friends. If your APIS lists help you to realize that something in your social environment (like chores, studying, or socializing) interferes with your readiness to play well, then you need to make some changes in these areas. Even you yourself can do some external things to improve your readying: getting more sleep, eating well, and so on.

It is always best to start with your crucial factor on the external condition list. If this factor falls in the *self* category of your social environment, the solution can be as simple as more efficiently planning your time to get more sleep, or to practice certain things more often. But changes in the other three areas will require you to deal with other people whom your APIS responses have identified as a problem in your readying. What's the best way to do this?

Guidelines for talking with coaches, teammates, and friends about readying

You need to make up your mind that you are going to talk with these people about your readying. Athletes are often tempted to try to make changes in their routines on their own, without discussing it with those around them. These efforts almost always end poorly, primarily because the other person involved doesn't understand what the athlete is trying to do. Even though at first it may seem to be a difficult and anxiety-arousing task, talking to your coach, teammate, or family is an essential step in the process. It is the first visible step toward progress—the first outward sign to yourself, and to those around you, that you are working at improving your performance. It is usually well-received by coaches and others if it is presented in a positive way. Here are six important guidelines for stating your wishes to others:

1. **Explain, don't complain.** The focus of your words should be on what you want things to be like, not on the problems that exist. It is always easier for another to accept suggestions for change if they are put in a positive, enthusiastic way. Instead of saying, "Coach, here's what's wrong . . ." try to say, "Coach, what I want to do is . . ., and here's why." Then the other person can respond to the new idea you are suggesting instead of having to defend the old ways of doing things.

2. **Show how much work you have already done.** Rather than spouting off about what you want, make sure that the other person knows that you have been working hard on this issue for a couple of weeks. If you're not careful, you can easily sound as though you are presenting a suggestion that you have just thought of. It is important to get across your sincerity, and to communicate your commitment to improving your performance and yourself. Don't hesitate to show the person your APIS as evidence that you have really put a lot of thought into what you are saying. Many athletes have told me that the most important use of the APIS for them was helping to convince someone around them that they were serious about their sport.

3. **Ask for changes as trials, not permanent decisions.** In talking with another about your readying, you should be ready to try some compromises that may be helpful to you. It may not be reasonable for you to demand changes simply because you think they would be helpful; it is very likely that the person you are approaching is doing things as he or she is for good reasons. Your ideas, then, should be presented as possibilities, as changes in the current routine that can be tried for some specified short period of time to see if they are good for you and workable for those around you. Once such a trial period is agreed to, of course, the responsibility is on you to make things work.

The ideal way to use the notion of trial changes is to make some mini-trials yourself, so that you can say to your coach or teammate that you've tried it briefly and gotten good results. For example, I worked with a swimmer who felt that, based on his APIS, he would do better times in races if he were allowed by his coach to warm up less than he usually did immediately before swimming. His coach required all of the swimmers on the team to get loose for a few minutes before getting up on the blocks, but this athlete felt that he would swim faster without such preparation. Instead of arguing with his coach about this, he tried swimming his distances on his own one day, with a friend there to time each trial. When he was able to approach his coach with some evidence that he swam faster without a full warm up, the coach could much more easily agree to a second trial—this time in a meet.

Remember that the important thing is not necesarily to get your coach, teammate, or family member to agree that your new way is right; the goal is to get them to agree to a trial of the new idea. If the idea works in practice, there's no problem; if it doesn't, you can try other ways of improving your performance, knowing that you needn't be hung up on the possible value of some approach that you never got the chance to test out. In either situation, sink or swim, both you and the other person have gained by working together for something positive.

4. Adjust your approach to the specific person involved. If you can present your ideas in a way that you think the person will be most likely to hear them, the better your chances will be for earning a trial. You will probably do well to recognize the fact that your coach is an expert in your sport. But nobody knows more about *you* than you, and the trick is to form a "partnership of experts" with your coach. Keep the focus of what you say on you and your performance, and not on how to make better runners or football players. The latter is your coach's job, not yours; but keep in mind that most coaches are willing to accept information that will give them a legitimate edge on the competition, and that's precisely what improving your performance will do.

When talking with teammates about a change, keep in mind their own goals. It is usually best to state your case in terms of helping the team as a whole, through your own improvement. Make it clear that what you are trying to do is for you, and that you realize that it wouldn't work for everybody. For example, if you feel that you want to try not talking with teammates immediately before performing, make it clear that you're not expecting everybody else to be silent, but simply that you are going to try to get off by yourself and would appreciate their cooperation. On teams where a number of people have tried this type of readying, what naturally evolves is a pregame situation in which some players talk and joke with one another in one area, while another group of athletes prepare silently elsewhere. The point is for each to do what's best for him or her: remember that that's what you're asking for.

In dealing with people who are not directly involved in your athletic endeavors, things can sometimes get more complicated. Playing better may not be their main goal in dealing with you, so in asking for their cooperation you will probably do well to emphasize other things. Communicate to them your need for their support in trying to improve yourself; it is very difficult for anyone to argue with you about trying to become a better person, or to grow in some way. If you are sincere in explaining your goals and motives, things will be much easier. You must also show your willingness to compromise. For example, if you are asking someone you live with to do some household chores for you before a big game, remember to offer your efforts at some point in time to help them. Because many famous coaches and athletes constantly tell us that to excel we must have a singleness of purpose and must put everything else aside to work at our sport, we often forget that not everyone around us shares our goals and will be willing to make things easy for us. It is in your best interests to have people cooperate with you on your readying.

5. **Plan your speech, especially the beginning.** If you anticipate a lukewarm reception to your suggestions, be sure to have a firm grasp in your own mind of what you are asking for. People often find that starting a difficult conversation is the hardest part, and that once things are under way they can usually express themselves clearly. To help yourself get past the initial stumbling block, and to make sure that you do not begin by complaining, begin your conversation with something like this:

"_____, I have given this a lot of thought, and I'd like to ask you to help me make a change that will really help me. . . ." Notice that the focus here is on (1) your thought and effort, (2) the fact that you are asking, not telling, (3) the fact that you are going to suggest a change, and (4) the hope that it will be helpful to you. It is more important to put these things in your own words than to memorize this opening line, but you will do well to include these points in your request.

6. **Rehearse—for real, out loud.** Especially if you are nervous about approaching your coach or some other person about this, the more you rehearse the clearer you will be when the time comes. If possible, rehearse the conversation with a friend. If this is not possible, you might try talking to your mirror or writing out your words. If words come easily to you and if you have an easy, verbal relationship with the person in question, you probably won't need to use this last guideline much. That's fine. But if approaching the person in question does seem hard to you, don't let your anxiety stop you from doing what you need to do to get yourself ready to perform to your utmost. For the same reasons that practicing your sport helps you to play it better, rehearsing your words can help you to communicate better.

If you step back and look at what it means to ask a coach, teammate, or friend to change, you will realize some other things. The success of your attempt will often depend on your conviction, and on the sincerity with which you present yourself. That's why using the

APIS can be so important in helping you to decide in your own mind what needs to be done. Even though asking your coach for a change may seem out of line, keep in mind that your coach is on your side. He or she wants the same thing you do—better performance—but you are the only one who has the time and the "inside information" to work on the details of your readying. Most coaches I know appreciate the athlete who takes his or her sport seriously enough to work at it, both physically and mentally.

In approaching those around you, take charge of the situation and commit yourself to making the circumstances of your preparation as favorable as possible to yourself. Allow yourself to think big about the possibilities, so that you can come as close as possible to arranging the ideal conditions for your performance. Make sure that you start this process with your crucial factor, so that there is no doubt in your mind that what you are working toward is important enough to warrant the time and energy you'll spend bringing it about. And finally, remember that the goal is to set up the perfect external readying conditions for you, as an individual; the fact that some of them may be different from other people's is meaningless and the worst possible reason for not giving them a try.

Making changes—techniques for preparing internal states of mind

In a sense, the internal environment you take into athletic competition is even more important than the external. It is likely that you can arrange your world only to a certain degree, and never in the perfect way. But you can come a lot closer to perfection in building the right internal states of mind; with practice you can learn to develop the right thoughts and feelings without any interference from others, and this will leave you in the best frame of mind to play.

Remember that *internal states of mind* refer basically to two things: *thoughts* and *feelings*. Chapters 2 and 3 explained these in detail, but let me remind you of one point: Words are merely labels that we give to our thoughts and feelings: when our list of words runs out, we still can go on thinking and feeling other things that we may never be able to describe to another person but that can be very important to us. For many athletes, it is precisely this last type of thought or feeling that is the key to maximum performance. Anything that goes on inside of you is an internal state, and the raw material we'll be dealing with in this discussion of readying.

Think of specific, internal readying techniques as the internal equivalent of physical exercises. Just as you go through a routine of physical exercises to prepare your body for athletic performance, use these techniques as exercises for the mind. They are to be used when you have a job to do, and then set aside until you need them again. Once you have practiced these techniques, you will be able to use them in exactly this way.

In reality you will be reading about one main technique and six different ways of using it. The technique is called *The Readying Spot*, and it is the most important part of the Readying Approach to spots.

The Readying Spot

The Readying Spot can be defined as *your place* and *your time* of doing what you need to do to be ready to perform at your best. Notice that the Spot is made up of two elements, place and time. Always use the Spot in a specific place and at a specific time. The Spot requires that you be alone for twenty minutes and that you concentrate on your sport; what you do during the Spot is up to you, but there are a number of things that you should take into account.

Choosing your Readying Spot is the first step: What you need is a place where you can be completely alone for at least twenty minutes. It should be a place where no one will interrupt you, where you can sit or lie comfortably without distraction. It needs to be a place that you have easy access to; ideally, it should be a place that you do not share with anyone, even at other times when you are not using it for readying. And most importantly, it must be a place where you never find yourself in the course of your everyday activities—*it has to be completely different from everything else*, so that when you are in it you are there for readying and never for any other purpose.

All these restrictions may have you saying, "How can I ever find a place like that?" There is usually no need to find an exotic, remote place. In fact, since one of the necessary conditions is that it be easily accessible, it can't be someplace you have to travel far to get to, or have to make elaborate arrangements to have to yourself. The Readying Spot is usually best located somewhere in or around your home, assuming that you can have some privacy for twenty minutes. I usually recommend that people choose some spot in the room where they sleep, a place that's always right there but where they never otherwise would go. For example, if you think about your home you will realize that there are places where you usually walk and where you usually sit or

For the Individual Athlete

lie down. There are also places where you go, sit, or lie down only on certain occasions. Then there are places where you never sit or lie down. For example, I'll be willing to bet that you never sit on the kitchen table or lie down on the bathroom floor. These are extreme examples, but there are certainly other places that you do not use but that could be comfortably used for your Spot. Other places that athletes have used include lying on the floor in the bedroom; sitting on the bed in a position and direction that is never otherwise used (like at the foot of the bed, facing the wall); outside, under a certain tree; and sitting on the floor looking into a closet. I've even had athletes use the Readying Spot successfully sitting in the bathroom. Find a place that's right for you, where you will not be interrupted, where you can be reasonably comfortable, and where you never otherwise have to go.

Choosing the time for your Spot is equally important. You must allow yourself *at least* twenty minutes, since it usually takes five to ten minutes just to get your mind free enough from the business of the day to use the techniques. The time you choose should be one that you can use regularly and daily. The first thing in the morning or the last thing at night are times that have been used with success. Other good times include as soon as you get home from work or school; just before going out to practice your sport; and before or after any given meal. Any time will do as long as you can use it with consistency. You will use your Readying Spot to practice getting yourself into a specific frame of mind, on a regular basis; then you can use the technique just prior to competition for the same purpose.

Be strict about starting and stopping your Readying Spot. When it's time to start, get into the place for your Spot, and when you are finished get up and do something else. Especially at first, you will probably find that you will have trouble getting into your Spot quickly and that after twenty minutes you will not be through. You may find yourself thinking about your mental exercises after your Spot is over, which is not usually a good idea. Be strict about sitting down on time and getting up as soon as you are through with the specific technique you are using. It is even a good idea to use a timer or look at a clock to be sure that you get up after twenty minutes. The time of your Spot should be accessible, regular, and strictly enforced, especially at first.

But why all this emphasis on being alone, on strictly starting and stopping, and on making the Spot "different" from everything else? The reason is simple: To be successful, you must identify your Readying Spot with performance in your sport. The time and the place used for your Spot need to be connected in your thoughts and feelings with basketball, or hockey, or whatever your sport is. It must be set up so that when you are in your Spot, absolutely nothing else intrudes on your thoughts and feelings; you must be free to give one-hundred percent attention to your performance in your sport. That is the key to success, but that condition is very difficult to find in the world around you. There are always demands, responsibilities, or distractions that split your attention into various parts: work, school, family, weather, food, clothes, and so on. The list of things that we have to think about in the course of our day goes on and on, and some people even come to feel that such thoughts run their lives. What the distinctness of the time and place of the Readying Spot does is give you the opportunity to set aside all of those other attention-grabbing items and focus all of your attention on your sport. Without such a concentrated focus, you will be much less effective in your readying. The more you can arrange things so that your Readying Spot is a separate, personal, almost dreamlike experience devoted to your sport, the better it will serve you.

This aspect of the Readying Spot parallels some aspects of meditation, hypnosis, and other self-help techniques. All these methods share the *separateness* of the experience, and they usually involve regularity and quiet time alone as well. The differences come in the mental activities you program your mind to do during each session, and that is what makes the Readying Spot unique: You will be doing specific, sport-related exercises with your thoughts and feelings. Whereas meditation may leave you feeling generally alert and refreshed, it may or may not affect your athletic performance; your Spot, on the other hand, will leave you specifically ready to play your sport better, and that's what this Readying Approach is aimed at.

There is yet another important reason that your Spot needs to be kept separate from your other thoughts, feelings, and activities. In certain of the techniques, you will be dealing with what are usually considered negative emotions: worry, fear, guilt, and so on. You will be using these in order to clear them out of your mind so that you can be free of them when you are playing, or because you have found that feeling certain of these emotions helps you to perform better. Either way, you do not want to have this type of emotion spill over into your other activities. Even though, for example, anger about things may help you to tackle your opponent better, you do not want to be angry when you are dealing with people close to you. For this reason, stop and start your Readying Spot strictly, so that the thoughts and feelings you are using for performance purposes do not find their way into other aspects of your life. The more you can channel these internal states into your sport, the more you will see improvement in your performance. So during the Readying Spot, stay on your sport: before and after your Spot, do other things. In the long run you will find that not thinking about your sport when you are not doing your Spot works to your advantage, since it leaves your mind fresher and more able to concentrate appropriately when it is time for readying. Don't change your whole frame of mind, but focus those thoughts and feelings to their maximum utility at the right times: when you are readying and when it's time to perform.

Let's look at six specific techniques that have proven useful to athletes like yourself. These techniques represent structured exercises that can help improve readying for athletic performance:

1. Relaxation
2. Positive Imagery
3. Negative Imagery (creative worrying)
4. The *Feeling*
5. Attention Clearing and Focusing (for concentration)
6. Planning and Study

Each technique will be described in its own section.

As you read through these techniques, be sure to explore how each one applies to you and your readying needs. Particularly keep in mind your *crucial internal condition* to see if it might be helped by the specific technique you are learning about. The techniques are all different and are intended for various kinds of readying problems, and it is very unlikely that anyone could use all of these techniques beneficially. In fact, each technique can help or hinder your readying; if you are already very relaxed when you play, using the relaxation technique can actually conflict with your proper readying.

Select the technique or techniques that are right for you, based on your own needs as indicated by your APIS, your thinking about your readying, and preliminary trials of some of the techniques. Use the techniques individually, or combine two. Or combine one or more of the techniques with some other personal readying routine that fits your particular needs. The simpler you can keep things, the better, so try to focus on just one technique to start with. Once you have mastered that, go on to others if they seem attractive to you. The more focused your efforts are, the more effective your work will be. Above all, remember that the goal is to identify your most appropriate performance readying strategy and then to practice it to the fullest, whatever combination of textbook techniques and individual rituals it might turn out to be.

TECHNIQUE 1: RELAXATION

Relaxation. Playing relaxed. Running relaxed.

These are words that almost every athlete in any sport has heard over and over, from coaches, professional athletes, television commentators, interested friends, and even from the small voice inside your own head that tells you how to play. Everyone agrees: You must be relaxed to perform well. Because of this, there are many different approaches to relaxation, ranging from hypnosis to whirlpools to the use of drugs. This approach is a self-controlled, progressive relaxation procedure, making use of the principles of the Readying Spot, self-suggestion, and practice. As always, the focus will be not on achieving some perfect state of relaxation, but on finding out what type and level of relaxation works best for you.

Let's think for a moment about why it is so important to be relaxed when competing athletically. Our bodies are set up with muscles to move us around; Our muscles are designed to do two types of things: contract and expand. All of our movements are achieved by the pushing (expanding) and pulling (contracting) of various muscle groups on our bones. When we say that we have some tension in our bodies, what we are saying is that at least some of our muscles are already partially expanded or contracted beyond their point of normal resting. Thus, any movement that we try to make must first overcome some initial resistance just to get to each muscle's normal starting point. This is especially true with more complex and precise movements. The closer our muscles are to a perfect resting state, the easier and quicker the movement. Even more of a problem is posed by the fact that tension is usually characterized by contractions in the muscle—that is, the muscle is tightened. This directly conflicts with any movements that involve expanding muscles, like stretching, reaching, and running, which accounts for the jerky motion that characteristically bothers athletes who cannot relax. The simplest statement one can make about tension is that we have more control over our muscles when they are completely relaxed.

The necessity for relaxation is universal. This does not mean, however, that every athlete should be doing relaxation exercises. On the contrary, if an athlete does not care about a certain competitive event, he or she may in fact be too relaxed to perform well. The ideal is to find the right balance of relaxation and tension for you and your sport. If you are typically more tense than is good for you, then this approach can be useful.

People have spent a great deal of effort in the last forty years to define exactly what tension is. Here we have been looking at tension as a muscular state that is the opposite of relaxation. But energy, anxiety, excitement, arousal, and worry can all be seen as the opposite of relaxation, even though everyone will agree that anxiety and excitement are obviously not the same thing. All of these emotions have one thing in common: They represent a state other than the body's normal equilibrium, and the best word to use in referring to these states is *tension*. It doesn't seem to matter which emotion is the source of the tension; studies have shown that the resulting tension tends to have a particular effect on performance.

As discussed in Chapter 2, the standard way of representing what scientists have found to be the relationship between tension and performance is the inverted-U curve. (See p. 15.) At very low levels of tension, the body is not carrying enough energy to perform well, and performance is lethargic. As the person experiences more tension, the pace and accuracy pick up. This continues until the person reaches a tension level that is perfect for him or her and the activity. Beyond this point, the more tension the person feels, the worse the performance gets. With a great deal of tension, the person will perform erratically, inaccurately, and with many mental errors.

The goal is therefore to find the right level of tension for you and your sport, and then to be able to hit just that level when it's time to compete. You may need to adjust your tension level in either direction. But given the emphasis put on athletic performance in our society—all the pressures, possible rewards, and social implications—most athletes have no trouble in negotiating the first part of the curve, experiencing enough tension to have energy to perform. Most athletes need exercises like the relaxation technique to control, presumably to lower, tension.

Relaxation imagery

This technique can be used immediately prior to competition as well as more generally. It is called *relaxation imagery,* and is simply the use of particular kinds of imagery to bring on a feeling of relaxation. Because the use of imagery is so important to this and the other techniques, let's spend a few minutes thinking about what it is and how it can be used.

Imagery in its basic form is simply a collection of images, or *pictures in the mind.* We all have the ability to imagine certain situations or events that have not actually occurred. One way to do this is to see in our mind's eye movies of events—not necessarily to think about the event but to *see* it happening inside our heads. Try to remember a recent occurrence in vivid detail, by closing your eyes and actually seeing it happen again, in the same amount of time that it originally took. Taking time and looking for detail are important to imagery, for it is usually the vividness of the details that determines the imagery's effect on us.

The images can be of either past or anticipated events, and the distinction between *image-ing* and merely thinking is a critical one. Thinking is usually done in words and can happen much faster than actual events. This imagery technique, on the other hand, depends on the ability to see the appropriate images slowly and carefully, rather than merely letting your mind brush across them. Anyone who has trouble image-ing events in the future—seeing things in your head that you want to occur—would do well to begin by practicing the imagery technique with memories. Try to recall, with your eyes closed and in vivid detail, some event that happened to you long ago and that you have not thought about for a long time. Any event will do, but if you can come up with one that involves your sport, all the better. This image-ing of the past can serve as a practice step, from which you can move into building images of events that have not actually occurred but that may be helpful to you in ways that will soon be described.

Since we take in about eighty percent of our information about the world through our eyes, it is most important to involve your visual sense in any mind work that you do, and this applies also to imagery. But we obviously have other senses that take in information, and these also have a place in the constructive use of imagery. For example, besides seeing yourself performing in a hockey game, you can also imagine hearing the game (the cheering of the crowd, the sound of the skates on the ice, the sound of a puck smacking off the boards), and feeling physically what the game is like (the skates laced around your ankles, the chill of the air rising off the ice, the stick in your hand). There may even be certain smells or tastes that are part of the game for you, like the smell of new equipment or the taste of the water on the bench. All such sensory experiences can contribute to your mind's recreating an actual hockey game, and this is precisely where the power of any imagery technique is born. The more you can recreate the images in your mind, can actually *sense* the event, *see* it happening, hear what is going on, *feel* the physical actions, and otherwise relive or plan the whole experience, the more successful you will be in building a tool that can dramatically change your readying and performance.

Relaxation imagery, as you will discover, focuses primarily on the feelings of your body. The imagery techniques to be discussed later, like positive and negative imagery, will involve more of the visual component. But even though relaxation deals with bodily sensations, it is important to use your other senses as well. The specific instructions will tell you to feel certain things, but seeing or hearing them will add to the imagery's effect.

The relaxation imagery technique consists of a repetition of short phrases in your head. These phrases deal mostly with your bodily sensations, after an initial period of setting the mood with broader imagery. The phrases work as suggestions, in much the same way that the suggestions of a hypnotist work on the mind and body. The important differences are that you will be in control of the procedure and that there will not be a supernatural, trancelike quality to the experience. It will be relaxing, but not magical. If you have never used imagery, self-suggestion, or relaxation phrases before, you will probably feel at first that this technique is awkward. How can you truly relax when you have to open your eyes to read the phrases, when you have to remember to do them twice, and so on? Just bear with this. You will get better and better at using the technique, and you won't have to read everything as you did in the beginning. Some suggestions for increasing the ease with which you can do the exercise, as well as increasing the power of the technique, will also be discussed.

Here, then, is the layout for the Relaxation Imagery Technique.*

1. As always, get into your Readying Spot. This is one technique that requires strict attention to organizing your Spot with full comfort and absolutely no distractions. Arrange for things to be as quiet as possible. As you do the exercise you will begin to drift away from the demands of the real world and into a state of extreme comfort and restfulness. Having to worry about answering the phone, or dealing with any other aspect of your life, will make it impossible for you to allow yourself to lie back and enjoy the relaxation process. This tech-

---

* This procedure and the Relaxation Phrases are a modification of the procedure used by Dr. William Hessell at the UCLA Psychological and Counseling Service, after Elmer Green's (Meninger Clinic) abbreviation of the original process of Autogenic Training developed by Schultz and Luthe, and are reprinted with permission.

nique should be fun and should feel good; if it doesn't, you are doing something wrong. Usually the error can be found in the preliminary setup of the relaxation environment and not in the phrases themselves.

2. Get into a comfortable position, sitting in a chair or lying in such a way that you have full body support. (A backless chair or bench will not do.) Make sure that you are not stiff. As you go through the exercise, allow your body to make any small movements that will help you to feel more comfortable. It is not important that you remain in exactly the same position throughout, but if you have chosen a comfortable position before you begin and have to make only small adjustments as you go along, the relaxation will be deeper.

3. Close your eyes. Imagine or recall, as vividly as possible, a pleasant, relaxing scene. Put all of your energy into the senses of your body in the scene, so that you can feel the relaxation throughout your body. Picture, hear, and feel every detail of the imagery. Some examples of typical scenes are lying on the beach in a warm sun, lying in a warm bath, getting a massage, taking a nap, and relaxing by a mountain lake. Use whatever imagery, either actual or created, helps you to become more relaxed. As always, tailor the specifics of the imagery to you and your likes and dislikes. Do this for about five minutes, or until you are really into the scene.

4. Focus your attention on bodily sensations, and keep the focus of your awareness here during the exercise. Let thoughts simply pass out of your awareness, and get back to the bodily feelings. Don't fight the thoughts—just let them go.

5. Take a deep breath, and for about five to ten seconds tense all the muscles of your body as tightly as you can. Make your hands into fists, tighten the muscles of your arms, neck, face, shoulders, stomach, legs, and feet.

6. Exhale, and relax all of your muscles, feeling the tension in your muscles draining out as you sink back into a comfortable position.

7. Repeat each of the following phrases to yourself twice, or until you begin to feel the bodily sensations that the phrases suggest. Once is not enough.

8. Go slowly! Pause between phrases, and take a full fifteen to twenty minutes to do the exercise. That means waiting fifteen to twenty seconds after you say each phrase to yourself to give your muscles time to respond and relax.

The phrases

I feel quite quiet. . . . I am beginning to feel relaxed. . . . My feet feel heavy and relaxed. . . . My ankles, my knees, and my legs feel heavy, relaxed, and comfortable. . . . The muscles of my stomach, and the whole central portion of my body, feel relaxed, quiet, and smooth. . . . My shoulders, and the muscles of my back, feel smooth, relaxed, and comfortable. . . . My breathing pattern is easy and deep. . . . My neck, my jaws, and my forehead feel relaxed, and comfortable. . . . My whole body feels quiet, comfortable, and relaxed.

I feel quite relaxed. . . . My arms and my hands are heavy and warm. . . . I feel quite quiet. . . . My whole body is relaxed. . . . Relaxed and warm. . . . My hands are warm. . . . Warmth is flowing through my hands, and they are warm. . . . My entire body is relaxed, comfortable, and warm.

If you have tried this relaxation technique, or one like it, you are already aware of its positive effects. Simply sitting back and relaxing is a very pleasurable experience, and one that we often neglect in our busy lives.

Keep a few other points in mind initially; these will help ensure the technique's usefulness and the depth of relaxation you will attain. You may find the first few times you use the technique to be awkward, especially reading the phrases. Using a taped recording of the phrases can be quite helpful. If you make a tape, be sure that you read the phrases slowly and carefully, in a quiet voice, so that the procedure will last a good twenty minutes. You need not use the exact words written here; as long as you know the body parts you are working with, you can use any descriptions of the relaxation process. I, for example, have used words like relaxed, comfortable, and smooth to describe the relaxation state, but you may want to find your own words. Use whatever is soothing to you.

Aside from the initial awkwardness of the words, there is still the problem of learning a new skill. Just as you were not able to play your sport perfectly or to full satisfaction the first few times you tried it, so you may have difficulty with this technique. Just give yourself some time to practice the procedure, and you will find that you get better and better at it.

Whenever you take a deep breath, remember that the exhalation is the important part of the breath as far as relaxation is concerned. Be sure to expel all the air you can, evenly and slowly. As you do the exercise the first few times, see if you can locate particular points of tension in your body and concentrate your efforts there. You can repeat the phrase for that body part more than twice, or you can return to it a number of times through the exercise. You may even want to tense and relax a particularly difficult body part more than once; if so, this should be done at the beginning of the procedure, so as not to disrupt the flow of the progressive feeling of relaxation.

The best way to employ this technique in pregame warmups is to try to find the key phrase or phrases that are particularly effective for you in your Spot. Most athletes find that one or two of the phrases, often corresponding to tension-ridden body parts, always deepen the feeling of relaxation, while most of the phrases merely reinforce this drop in tension. Once you have identified such a phrase, it can be used by itself in situations where using the whole procedure would be inappropriate. I find that the phrase "I feel quite quiet" is the strongest one for me, so I use it frequently throughout the exercise. Repeating this phrase to myself is also helpful just before or during any tension-arousing situation.

I once worked with a swimmer who responded so strongly to the phrase "My hands are warm" that he used it throughout his readying. While limbering up and especially while getting on the blocks, he would repeat this phrase to himself, knowing that this would keep him relaxed and alert. In addition, it served to screen out distractions from spectators and competitors, so that he could concentrate on his race. Anyone who could have seen into his head and known what he was repeating would have thought he was crazy; but the phrase worked very well for him, and his teammates saw him as a solid competitor who was always ready to swim a strong race.

Your key phrase can best be used after you have learned to do the whole procedure, so that the one phrase brings back the relaxed feeling that the entire exercise usually gives you. If you try to use your key phrase before you are sure that you will get the feeling of relaxation, you will have little success, and you will be undermining the long-range usefulness of this exercise.

After you finish doing the relaxation exercise, stay under its spell for a while. Athletes who are in a hurry to jump up and start doing something else are wasting the opportunity to enjoy the relaxed state; but even more importantly, they are undercutting the effect of the relaxation on their overall state of mind. Sit and let the feeling of relaxa-

For the Individual Athlete

tion reinforce you for your efforts. I usually have people sit for at least one minute, letting them leave at that point only if they can't stand it any longer. About one to five minutes is average. I encourage people to stay comfortable, enjoying the feeling for as long as they like. If you have done the exercise more than four times and are still unable to sit and enjoy the final state for one minute, you are probably doing something wrong. Go back and reread the instructions, and make those changes that seem as though they would increase your pleasure.

At the end of the exercise, when you do open your eyes and prepare yourself to get up, you will find that you feel relaxed and refreshed, not groggy. However, if you are sleepy or have fallen asleep during the procedure, don't worry about it. It probably just means that you were overly tired to begin with and needed the sleep. This is assuming, of course, that you didn't just lie down for a snooze. Never fight sleep that comes over you during the phrases; just enjoy it. (What could be more relaxing than sleep?) If this happens to you regularly, perhaps you should rearrange your schedule to get more sleep at the appropriate time. As a matter of fact, this exercise can be used specifically to induce sleep, if that is a problem for you. In that case, do it in bed and not in your Spot.

Occasionally, athletes who have used this exercise have told me that they enjoy it but that they are afraid of using it too much or right before a competition, because they may wind up being too relaxed. They know that they need a certain amount of tension to perform well, and the relaxation technique takes them past this point. My standard response is this: If you have had trouble in the past with too much tension in competition and have messed up your performances because of this, it is almost impossible for you to be too relaxed before a game. Especially at first, when you are experimenting with this technique, your old habit of being tense will still be strong, and when you are in the competitive situation you will respond accordingly—the tension will be there. This tension will be counterbalanced by the overrelaxed feeling you had beforehand, and you will wind up in the best *tension range* for good performance. You will never feel the complete trance-like relaxation you feel in your Spot; the conditions that created that deep state in practice are not present when you are about to perform.

Using this technique prior to competition can only help, assuming that too much tension has been one of your problems. If tension has not been the problem, then doing relaxation exercises will be unlikely to improve performance. If you use it and find it harmful instead of positive, you have probably misjudged your competitive tension level and don't need more relaxation.

On the other hand, after you use this technique a number of times, find it helpful, and begin to make it a regular part of your precompetition readying routine, you may find that your overall tension level has dropped, probably as a result of your success and the relaxed feeling this usually brings. In this circumstance you may in fact want to cut down on your use of the technique by doing it earlier in your pregame countdown to competition (say, sixty minutes before instead of twenty), or by using fewer phrases and taking less time. This will alter the depth of the experience, and leave you more in the mid-range of necessary performance tension. This is a rather advanced approach to using the relaxation technique. If you are reading this section with an eye to doing something about performance tension, don't worry about getting too relaxed.

Do what works for you. Anything can be altered if you find that doing so helps your performance. I'm not as interested in having athletes do these things my way as I am in providing a starting point from which they can intelligently experiment and learn about their readying. It is also essential, especially at first, to repeat the relaxation exercise daily and seriously. You've got to practice this technique. Otherwise you are just wasting your time.

TECHNIQUE 2: POSITIVE IMAGERY

"You gotta believe!"
"I am the greatest!"
"We're number one! We're number one!"

These phrases and others like them can be found nearly everywhere in American sports today. In some cases, a particular individual or team has had a slogan, watchword, or nickname that identified the competitor and gave confidence to players and fans alike. There are other phrases that many athletes and fans use to proclaim their superiority and confidence. All such phrases have one thing in common: They are the verbal descriptions of success and confidence, thinking and feeling positively about competition. Chances are that the phrases above, for example, bring to your mind vivid images of fans yelling, players chanting, and whole groups of people building a unified feeling of positive anticipation. When followed by victory, they represent the high point of athletic struggle: to be the best.

What the phrases say, and what every coach knows, is that in order to succeed you first have to believe that you can. Aside from practicing the physical behaviors necessary for good performance, you must also practice the thoughts and feelings that go along with success. This can be done as a group, or as an individual. Team and fan spirit is a tool for helping individual athletes to feel within themselves that they can compete at their best.

But why depend on others to motivate you and convince you? It would be much more reliable and effective if you could have this positive feeling yourself, and be convinced of your ability so deeply that these other types of support merely add to your own inner feeling of confidence. This positive imagery technique is one of the best ways to build such a feeling and be able to feel it at the critical times: immediately prior to and during competition.

An athlete I consulted with early in my career can serve as an example of the typical use of positive imagery. I was working with a young baseball player who had a great deal of ability, but in recent games he had been having a lot of trouble hitting left-handed pitches. He was still hitting righthanders quite well, and until recently he had done just as well against lefthanders. But now he felt absolutely helpless when facing a lefthander.

I had this athlete begin a program of positive imagery. He spent some time in his Spot visualizing himself hitting well off lefthanders, as he used to. He visualized specific times in the past. But most importantly, he did his best to recall and practice the feeling he had had when facing pitchers. He practiced in his Spot until he could easily produce this feeling of readiness and confidence through imagery. Then he began doing so in the on-deck circle. He used the images to get the right feeling, and then he brought that feeling to bat with him. He was soon hitting lefthanders as well as ever.

Using positive imagery for these purposes is certainly not new. There are books devoted entirely to the power of positive thinking, and there are even sports figures who have described using positive imagery to improve performance. The positive imagery technique to be described here is a specific way of using principles of positive thought and feeling, and it is meant to be part of an overall program of readying. Using this technique in your Spot, and as one part of your overall readying countdown, are two of the considerations that make this approach to positive imagery unique.

Going over positive images of your performance in your mind can be helpful to your actual performance in two ways.* First, the imagery serves as a *mental rehearsal,* a trial run in which you take yourself through your performance without using your body. This rehearsal works for you in much the same way as actual practice does, laying down a blueprint in your mind for the activities you need to do later. It's not just a matter of knowing what to do, although that can certainly be part of the benefit of this technique: what's more important is that you are giving that part of your body which controls everything else, your brain, some practice at guiding your body through the necessary steps. Even without using your body much, the control portions of your brain lay down the track—the nerve impulses, the muscle movements, and so on—that will go into your actual performance.

The principle is similar to the one that was at work when you did the relaxation exercise described earlier. Simply saying to yourself that a certain muscle group would relax relaxed it slightly. It didn't just feel as though it was relaxed, and you weren't fooling yourself, either. It was actually more relaxed after the mental suggestion. Similarly, using positive imagery doesn't trick you into thinking that you'll do well, but actually prepares your body to make the right moves when called upon. (The fact that there is no trickery going on here will be obvious to you when you do the positive imagery technique correctly for the first time, and find that you can't sit still, that your muscles want to move, and, in fact have already begun to move in the ways you are imagining.)

The second way in which positive imagery can be helpful is in building confidence. Instead of filling your mind with problems, worries, and plans, you will be occupying yourself with the way things are supposed to be done. Confidence consists of thinking and feeling that you will do something well, and that is precisely what the positive imagery technique teaches you to do.

At first the gap between your fantasies and your memories of imperfect past performances will be wide. Do not let this initial gap undermine your commitment to this technique. Keeping your mind on the positive doesn't mean that all your negative thoughts will disappear overnight, but they will gradually take up less and less of your sport-related time and finally give way to more constructive thoughts.

---

*Once again, I am including some explanation of how the technique does its job. I think it is extremely important not to feel that these things work magically, or that they will automatically transform you into a superstar. They work for specific reasons that have to do with the ways your mind controls your body's actions, and they depend on application and commitment for their power.

For the Individual Athlete

This process requires regular use of the technique, as well as physical practice of your sport. The idea is to build combined *mental and physical blueprints* for activity: the continued use of the technique and physical practice create a chain of internal-external practice of the right way to do things. When such a chain is established, confidence is one of the pleasant results.

Imagery involves all of your senses, so that you use your mind's eye to put yourself as fully as possible into the imagined situation. You want to see, hear, and feel everything that would actually be happening during a great performance. The better you can do this, the more effective the technique will be.

The positive imagery technique

As always, getting into your Spot is the first step. This is critical.

The technique can be broken down into two parts: *finding* the best positive image for you, and then *applying* it to your next performance. Ideally, step one should have nothing to do with your actual performance: it should be as much fantasy as possible.

What should your positive imagery be? This varies from athlete to athlete. It has to be something absolutely positive, without even a slight tinge of negative feeling or outcome attached to it. Below are some suggestions, all of which have been used successfully by athletes to improve their performance. If you can find your own perfect positive image, so much the better.

1. **The Athletic Performance Improvement Survey.** Many of the questions on the APIS deal with the perfect conditions for you as an athlete. Some of them even ask you to describe your ideal performance situation. If you have done a good job in filling out your APIS, you can now go back and use your own answers to come up with a full description of a perfect performance day for yourself. It might help you to write down all the positive answers on your APIS so that you will remember to cover as many as possible in your imagery scenes. Of course, you will want to focus particularly on your answers to Items 1 and 2, as well as your circled, most important items.

2. **Child's Play.** Chances are that when you go out to play these days it's not the same as it was when you were a child. Now you have to plan ahead to be in the right place at the right time, think about your backhand or jump shot, and you might even worry about not doing

well. Back when you were ten years old, all you did was go out and play like crazy, as often and as hard as time would allow. Maybe you weren't very good (in fact, you're undoubtedly much better now), but that didn't matter. When you played as a ten-year-old you did so freely, unreservedly, eagerly, and with full commitment. While you can obviously never be ten again, the memory of what it felt like to play so openly and fully is still with you. You probably haven't thought about it or felt it lately, but it is still there inside of you, as are all your memories. Your positive images, then, can consist of imagining yourself as a child, feeling as you did then, playing your current sport. It's a wonderful feeling, and if you try it once or twice, you'll know right away whether or not this is the positive imagery format for you.

If this idea appeals to you but you find that you have trouble remembering it for some reason, there are other things you can do. If you have children around, watch them play a few times, especially if they are playing your sport. If you don't have kids around, go and find some at a schoolyard or park. Stick with kids no older than twelve, and try to watch them without being noticed, since children often change their behavior when adults are around. Notice how completely they attack their activities and how utterly pleased they are when they do well (the younger the better for this aspect of positive feeling). You'll probably notice that they fall down a lot from exertion but get right back up again, that their play is punctuated by squeals of excitement, and that while they are playing they do nothing else—they just play. Try to build as many of these characteristics into your imagery as possible. The goal is to feel as much like a child at play as you can, and don't worry about your "knowledge of the game." Don't think; *feel*.

3. Best Past Performance. Recall how you felt during the best performance of your life. It doesn't matter if this performance was in the same sport you are now readying for, as long as you know that it was your best performance. Try to be a good observer. Focus on the setting, the time of day, the people around you, and your activities. Most importantly, focus on how you felt: how your body felt as you moved, and how you felt before the performance and after it. Focus on how good you felt when you were done, the "thrill of victory," as the television people call it. Don't be afraid to relive the experience in all its glory: You are not idly gloating and getting a swelled head; you are purposely working to feel again the inner and outer circumstances that enabled you to do well. Athletes have their best days not by chance but by the perfect coming together of all the various factors that go into performing well, and you are trying to recreate those circumstances for yourself. The more you practice that right feeling for you, the better you will be able to bring it about in competition.

4. Your Ultimate Goal. One of the most common ways of using positive imagery is to fantasize about one's dream game: playing in the Super Bowl, skating at the Olympics, pitching in the World Series, or maybe just making first string on your school team. Whatever you dream about doing, it can be more than simply daydreaming about something that will never happen. If done in the proper way, such mental imagery can be a stepping stone to better performance at any level.

Experience the dream game fantasy as fully as possible. Try to feel, see, and hear everything that would actually be happening at such a performance, just the way you'd like it to be. Picture the people you'd like to have watching you, see yourself making the moves you'd love to make, hear the cheers and congratulations. Go as far as you can with the imagery: Play your postgame TV interview, and picture yourself looking at your trophy or medal. Imagine the great feeling you'd have inside knowing you had done your best and had been successful. It's probably the kind of dreaming you may have done as a child, but as you've grown older you've probably done less of it, letting reality get in the way of your dreams. For this technique to be most effective, you have to let reality go; don't worry about whether you'll ever actually break that world record. Having the feeling of doing it will enable you to use the physical tools you do have to the fullest and get the most out of yourself. And that's really what it's all about.

5. My Hero. If modesty prevents you from using yourself as the ultimate model, there's always your favorite athlete to model yourself after. Finding a hero whom you can dream about can serve the same purpose as imagining yourself succeeding. Allow yourself to fully imagine what it would be like to be your idol. Picture yourself as Ali in the ring, or as O.J. breaking away for a touchdown. Let yourself experience the hard work and the glory, in as much detail as you can, of your favorite athlete. It's not as important to pattern your style or practice program after your idol as it is to feel the exhilaration of success. If you practice this feeling, your own style and workout routine will develop naturally and with the best results. And your idol needn't be someone real: A fictional athlete whom you've read about or seen on a TV show or movie can work just as well. Just imagine as completely as possible what it would be like to be that person.

6. "Magic." "Mr. Clutch." "Orange Crush." "The Steel Curtain." "The Broad Street Bullies." All of these nicknames conjure up images, people, or things that have special characteristics important for competitive success. Once the labels are attached, athletes tend to respond to them, to become even more of a clutch performer or an impassable defender. The names, the mental images they create, and the feelings they inspire can help the athlete to perform at a high level.

Give yourself a *tag*, a label that says who you are and what you can do athletically. You needn't tell anyone about it, but simply use it as part of your positive imagery technique. See yourself as the kind of athlete you'd like to be, picking out the single, vital quality that you want to emphasize in your performance. Picture yourself as that athlete, or even as that inanimate object that describes you. For example, you might name yourself *The Smooth One*, and see yourself gliding smoothly through competition, never getting ruffled or pressing, always under control and moving gracefully toward your goal. Whatever tag you choose, experience yourself mentally that way: you'll be preparing yourself to perform that way when the time comes.

These are a few ideas for building your own positive images, and you can use all, one, or none of these. Just make sure that you come up with a scenario that you can consistently respond to with full, positive

Figure 7-1.

POSITIVE IMAGERY

emotion whenever you get into it. If you use one of these models for your imagery, you are then faced with the task of transferring the positive feeling to your own next performance. When you have done the imagery technique to the point where you are feeling really good, spend a few moments thinking about your next competition, allowing your good feeling to mix with your anticipation of the game at hand. Make sure that the feeling stays strong. If thinking about the game starts to conflict with the good feeling, stop immediately and go back to the

184 *For the Individual Athlete*

images that helped you to feel confident. With any positive imagery technique, it is essential that you create the positive feeling so totally that it doesn't disappear as soon as you think about your next performance. It is usually a good idea to do the positive imagery at least three or four times before thinking at all about your real situation. As with the relaxation technique, if you try to use this technique too soon, the actual game situations can overwhelm the positive effects of the images. Of all the athletes I have worked with, the ones who have had the most trouble benefiting from this type of approach have been those who wanted quick results, who did the relaxation or positive imagery technique only once or twice and then tried to apply it under pressure. They simply won't work that way. For the same reasons your coach has you practice movements in workouts before you even think of trying them in competition, you have to practice your mental and emotional readying as well, in your Readying Spot.

You have to find your own ideas for positive imagery to be successful. Even if you use one of these, you should tailor it with the details of your fantasties of success. You will probably need to experiment with different images, seeing which ones make you feel the best, most confident, most excited, and so on. Keep a mental eye on how you are feeling while you do the technique; you can further aid the process by focusing on your physiological responses to various images. For example, see which images make your body feel relaxed or tense. Note which ones have you feeling full of energy. If you're scientifically minded, you can take your pulse rate before and after your imagery to see which images change your heart activity the most. Whatever measures you pay attention to, remember that you are looking for the keys to your positive imagery readying, and not trying to fit into some textbook pattern of "correct" psyching.

Avoid thinking in words; use visual images to portray the action. See, hear, and feel, but don't talk to yourself. If you find that you have trouble doing this, try to imagine that you are watching a TV or movie screen inside your head. Watch and listen to what is happening. The more you practice, the better you'll become at this. Occasionally you may find that the positive images don't come to you, even after you have experimented with and practiced them. On these occasions, don't try to force things; stop the exercise and try again later. There's nothing worse than trying to force yourself to feel good. This is a perfectly natural occurrence, even for the most self-confident athletes. The goal of this overall approach is not to make you feel certain ways all the time, but to allow you to feel the best way for you at specific times. We all have events in our lives that conflict with positive thoughts and feelings, and it is natural to have doubts. Avoid dwelling on these, and occupy yourself with something that captures your full attention when your positive imagery doesn't go well. When you come back to the technique later, you'll have a much better chance of being able to utilize it correctly.

If your APIS and your self-experimentation have shown that you need to raise your overall level of arousal and activation to perform well, the positive imagery technique can be quite helpful to you. Include in your thoughts a pep talk, or monologue of encouraging, exciting ideas. Imagine your coach or someone else revving you up, or simply do it yourself in your own words. You might try imagining your idolized athlete or coach talking to you, telling you what you need to hear to be great. Allow yourself to move around as you do it. Flexing, stretching, or even getting up and moving around are okay, as long as your attention remains focused on your imagery. You can try moving around in place, so that you needn't open your eyes.

Because it is enjoyable and often activating, the positive imagery technique is a good one to use at the end of your Readying Spot. It should leave you feeling good about your sport and yourself. You might also follow the imagery with some positive reinforcers; think about the honors and congratulations that will come out of the scenes you are imagining. When you are finished with your Spot, do something that you like, to reinforce physically the positive feeling you have gotten from the imagery technique. In short, enjoy the good feeling you have developed, and reward yourself as well as you can.

This technique doesn't have to stay in your Spot, but can follow you into other activities. Once you are good at using your imagery to produce positive feelings and thoughts, you can even use the technique without getting into your Spot—while you are walking or driving around, anytime you are alone and have a few minutes. Using the positive imagery technique in this way (but only after you have mastered it in complete privacy and silence) serves as a good bridge between the artificial setup of your Spot and the real world. By having the images, thoughts, and feelings out in the world, you come a step closer to having them on the playing field. You can do the technique in gradual steps, before practices and then before and during games. At every step, be sure that the imagery is still strong enough to effectively produce the right feelings. That's the reason for taking small steps between your Spot and actual competition.

The final word? Don't be humble. The success of this technique

For the Individual Athlete

depends on your ability to experience fully the great feelings that accompany positive performance. You don't have to go around boasting about yourself to others, but you must have enough mental flexibility to allow yourself to dream, to enjoy the glory of moving, thinking, and winning the way you've always wanted to. Imagine yourself as acclaimed in your sport as you possibly can, with all the honors. Some people call this egotism, but egotism is believing yourself to be the best person in the world and telling others about it. What we are looking at here is the ability to believe in yourself as the best athlete you can possibly be, and to have that satisfaction within yourself, where it counts most. It is true: You can be only as good as you allow yourself to believe.

TECHNIQUE 3: NEGATIVE IMAGERY (CREATIVE WORRYING)

By now you know very well what imagery is, and the previous section described ways of using your mind to practice your sport the way you want to play it—correctly. This section on negative imagery has the same goal as the one on positive imagery: to improve your performance. But negative imagery is not the exact opposite of positive imagery, since it would make no sense to use imagery to rehearse doing things poorly. The focus of the negative imagery technique is on *worrying*. Worrying is a perfectly natural part of life and can easily occur before any big event. While worrying is more of a problem for some athletes than for others, all athletes must deal with it in some way. The negative imagery technique will give you new ways of looking at your anxiety, ways to worry creatively and positively. Its goal is to help you control the forces that influence your performance, instead of being at their mercy.

The negative imagery technique helps athletes deal with their anxiety in two very different ways. For those athletes who need some energy boosting before competition, creative worrying can provide such energy. It can provide nervous stimulation so that you can avoid being flat and unprepared for the rigors of competition, especially in demanding physical sports like wrestling and football.

A much larger percentage of athletes find that anxiety causes problems in their performance. For this group, the negative imagery technique helps to leave you without worries at competition time. It does so by forcing you to crystallize your worries instead of letting them spread throughout your awareness and spoil your readiness to do anything. Rather than fighting *not* to worry (which is what almost all athletes try to do), you will learn to *worry intensely, efficiently, and in a concentrated manner*. By doing so, you will find that your worries won't last, but will burn themselves out in a short, intense burst, leaving you free to concentrate on your task calmly and effectively.

Why? Well, it is a biological fact that intense experiences, whether they are physical exertions or emotional states, do not last very long. Our bodies are constructed to do and feel most things at a moderate level, so that we can do what we need to do (breathe, pump blood, and so on) over time. We also have the capability to perform very intensely for a short period of time, in emergencies. But even in these periods of intense arousal and activity, our bodies are eagerly waiting for the first opportunity to slow down, to get back to the normal equilibrium, or what physiologists call *homeostasis*. This explains why, for example, hot-tempered people who periodically explode will cool down quickly as well. The brief but intense explosion of feelings uses up their anger and leaves them free to go on to other activities without anger following them at a low, nagging level. The same approach can be taken to managing anxiety. The goal is to burn it up quickly with the negative imagery technique, so that low-level, nagging anxiety will not follow you into times and activities where it will harm your performance. The key is to worry with intensity.

There are two variations of negative imagery meant to be used separately, either to lower or to raise anxiety. Choose one or the other, based on your knowledge of yourself and your APIS profile. As always, start by getting into your Readying Spot, and then proceed to the technique outlined below.

The negative imagery technique, goal #1—lowering anxiety

The essence of this technique is to worry: to learn how to stop worrying by learning how to start. You will apply the Stop-Start Technique described in Chapter 5, but this time you'll apply it to anxiety rather than to attention.

You will actively seek out things to worry about, especially as they relate to your performance of your sport. The typical athlete who comes to a consultant because of problems with anxiety reports that he or she just can't get the worries out of his or her mind. If this is true of you, you probably spend a lot of time and energy trying to avoid these worries, and you may even plan your daily activities to lessen the chance that your worries will overtake you. It is almost as if your worries form a big, dark cloud that follows you around wherever you go, invading your awareness whenever it wishes to, and despite your efforts to avoid it. The best way to deal with this problem is to worry intentionally, and that is precisely what you have gotten into your Spot to do.

Get comfortable, close your eyes if you like, and begin to go over in your mind all the things that worry you. Don't just think about them; visualize them and feel yourself in the anxiety-arousing situation. Whatever the feeling of anxiety is like for you, try to feel it as strongly as you can. Some people find that anxiety rests in certain places in their bodies, like the neck or in the pit of the stomach (see the Relaxation Technique), while others experience it more as a sense of confusion and uneasiness in their minds. Whatever the feeling is for you, do whatever is necessary to intensify it. Picture each anxiety-ridden situation in as much detail as you can. When you have stayed with a given situation long enough for your anxiety level to have dropped significantly, move on to another situation. The idea is to keep all of your attention on the anxiety-arousing situations in your life. You should start with sport-related anxieties, of course, but you need not avoid other issues that tend to make you anxious. This technique can be very helpful in many areas of life.

As you worry, solutions may or may not come to you. Either way, *finding solutions to your problems is not the point of the negative imagery technique*, and finding answers to difficult questions should not determine how long you use the technique in each trip to your Spot. Most athletes find that solutions are a pleasant by-product of this technique, as would be true of almost any effort to sit quietly and think about things. But the goal is to make yourself worry, to feel the full brunt of your anxiety so that it will then begin to decrease. Clear thinking and problem solving are the natural follow-ups to intense anxiety, but such clear-headedness rarely occurs when one sits down specifically to solve a problem. That is why the goal of this exercise is to feel as strongly as you can the pressures and worries around you; if you do feel your anxieties effectively, the thinking and problem solving will get done by themselves. Don't let solutions determine the length of your Spot. Stick to twenty to thirty minutes, and stop even if you haven't solved everything.

In using this negative imagery technique, there is also a complementary activity that you should do when you are not in your Readying Spot. Since you are trying to focus intensively all of your anxiety into a small period of time while in your Spot, you have to do everything possible *not* to worry at other times and places. This can be difficult at first, but one way of helping yourself is to write down your anxious thoughts whenever they occur. You are doing this to remind yourself about your Spot, and you are keeping a list of your worries safely written down so that you can give them your full attention in your Spot. When you find yourself worrying in any situation other than your Spot, try to say to yourself something like the following: "I'm worrying about that again. Okay, what I'm going to do is write myself a note about this so that I can worry about it in my next Spot. That way, I'm absolutely certain that I won't forget about it, and I will get my usual quota of worrying about it done. I just won't do it now, since I'm involved in doing other things and I wouldn't be able to give it my full attention now. I definitely will worry about this, but in my next Spot. With a note to myself written down I can't possibly forget. So for now, I'll just put away the note and get back to what I was doing."

The idea of having a quota of worrying may seem funny to you, but most of us do worry on the quota system. For each of us, there is a certain amount of worrying that we expect to do about certain things, and if we don't do it we can get very uncomfortable. That nagging feeling that there's something we've forgotten to worry about or haven't worried about enough can undermine our overall sense of well-being and contribute to poor performances. The mistake most of us make in doing our worrying is thinking that we have to worry about something for a long time. Actually, we'd be much better off worrying very intensely for a short period of time and getting it out of the way. That is precisely what the negative imagery technique and the Readying Spot do; they give you a specific time and place in which to worry effectively. The trick, of course, is to make sure you use it.

It is essential that your use of the negative imagery technique be strictly timed and not allowed to fluctuate according to the seriousness of the problem at hand. At the end of your allotted worrying time, make sure that you engage your mind with something else strong enough to capture your attention. Many athletes find that the positive imagery technique or the relaxation exercise is useful after negative imagery. If you try these combinations, remember to get up physically and mark the boundary between the negative and positive exercises. You can also end your Spot when you finish your negative imagery, but be sure that you do something else active and involving. *Do not use this technique before going to bed* or when you have nothing else to do afterward. If you find that you are still thinking about your worries after you have

For the Individual Athlete

ended your Spot, you are not doing an activity that is involving enough for you. Find something that works: reading, watching television, talking on the phone, or doing something else. You can even practice your sport if you like, but make sure that you have limited your worrying to your Spot.

As with any change in behavior, you will probably find this technique difficult and perhaps unrewarding at first. It will require effort to limit your worrying to the twenty to thirty minutes of your Spot. But with practice, you can. I usually tell athletes not to judge the effectiveness of this negative imagery technique until they have tried it every day for at least a week and have found what activity to use after their Spot. It is precisely the difficulty of doing this time-and-place-limited worrying that makes the technique effective.

Learning to control (stop and start) your anxiety is also basic. Instead of the issue being whether or not to worry—and usually struggling not to—the issue becomes learning how to start and stop an essential life process, namely, worrying. The realization that anxiety is normal and unavoidable, but *controllable*, takes place with time and practice. Most people mistakenly try to use their *stop-worrying* ideas without realizing that the *start-worrying* response is half the battle. Behavioral scientists sometimes refer to this kind of technique as *negative practice*, and it works because trying to do the very thing we've always been struggling not to do teaches us how that thing usually gets started in the first place. As you use this technique, you will gain new insights into how and why you worry, and learn about your own mechanisms for starting to worry. Instead of anxiety being a vague feeling that comes and goes, it becomes a specific sense that you can recognize, produce, and control. You will know how to stop it cold by burning it out intensely and effectively.

The negative imagery technique, goal #2—raising anxiety

This technique is for athletes who are *not* bothered by anxiety, and for whom a certain amount of fear and worry before a contest is helpful in raising their overall tension level high enough to be in the optimum performance range. It is for athletes who are calm enough about their sports performance not to be afraid of doing something that will make them more anxious.

Almost all the athletes for whom this technique has been useful have come to me saying that they need to be psyched up and worried before competition, or they don't perform well because they are flat.

They have rarely had the experience of being so nervous that they didn't do well because they were energized at too high a level for their sport; they are always on the low side, and feel that they can use fear and anxiety as motivating factors. This technique can help you to use anxiety in exactly this way, with you and not circumstances determining when and how much anxiety should be present to reach your optimum performance level. If all of these things don't apply to you, if you are wary of doing something that will raise your level of worrying, or if you feel that you are usually sufficiently aroused by competition itself to ensure not being flat, skip this section. It is meant for the nonworriers among us.

Using this negative imagery technique as a performance motivator does not mean that you will be trying to change your whole personality into that of someone who worries all the time. It is meant to be used strictly in relation to performing your sport, ideally right before competition to get you to the right level of tension. In regularly using your Readying Spot for this type of negative imagery, your goal is to practice worrying so that you can create the proper, worried atmosphere for yourself when competition is at hand. In this respect, it differs from the other type of negative imagery technique, which is intended to have beneficial effects throughout your day and to serve as precompetition readying practice. The more you practice worrying under control, the better you will be able to reach the best tension level for yourself at game time.

To begin using this technique, get into your Spot and do everything you can to worry about your sport. Picture yourself not doing well as vividly as you can. Make yourself dwell on the negative consequences of playing badly. Keep all of your attention on your performance in your sport and don't let yourself worry about other areas of your life.

Since you may not be used to worrying all that much, you might start by imagining yourself having performance problems that others have told you about, or making mistakes that you have seen others make. Allow yourself to get as anxious as you can tolerate being; then stop, and move immediately to some involving activity. Do not follow your negative imagery with relaxation or positive imagery. Especially at first, practice starting and stopping your worrying, so that you learn how to control it both ways. The more times you do this, the better you will learn how to create and control precompetition tension when you really need it. Make sure that you are comfortable with your ability to *stop* the worrying, since confidence in this ability is necessary for you to be able to begin worrying strongly in the first place. The emphasis should be on the feeling of tension you are creating and not on causing or avoiding the actual problems you are picturing. Do everything in your power to increase the physical sensation of tension in your body, up to the level at which you think you can perform your best. To determine this level, try out this exercise immediately prior to practicing your sport, so that you can see precisely how much tension you need to create to be in your top performance range. Do what works for you.

Let me now offer this warning: If at any point in your use of this technique you find that the anxiety you are artificially creating for yourself begins to spread into other areas of your life or into times other than your Readying Spot, stop using it. The mechanism we are discussing here is exactly the opposite of Negative Imagery—Goal 1. Instead of trying to burn out genuinely negative anxiety by focusing intensely on it, here we are trying to use a few intensely felt anxieties as a controlled motivator. But the possibility always exists that once you have started the process of producing anxiety, it will spread, as it naturally does in many athletes. If you find this to be the case, then you are not controlling the stopping and starting of the feeling enough to have it be useful to you immediately before competition, and you are better off not trying to use it at all. Try to find some other motivating techniques from among those described in this book. It makes little sense to trade in your low-anxiety performance for a high-anxiety performance problem, and this technique is powerful enough to do so unless you use it carefully. As an alternative, use positive imagery, pep talks in your head, anger, excitement, or anything else you can think of to raise your tension level. See the next section on the *feeling* for readying ideas.

Overview: using negative imagery sensibly

The negative imagery techniques presented here give you two very effective ways of dealing with anxiety. In a sense, they are too simplistic: There's no reason to think that these few pages on managing anxiety are going to solve all the problems inherent in the very complicated relationship between anxiety and performance. But these techniques do give you at least the basic tools with which to approach your own anxiety.

You needn't be subject to anxiety's effects, since you now have some ways of modulating your anxiety to fit your performance needs.

Let me repeat a few of the most important points to keep in mind. Be sure that you choose one goal at a time, either raising or lowering your anxiety at specific times. Pay a good deal of attention to stopping and starting your worrying; the techniques, activities, or little tricks you find helpful in starting and stopping the intense worrying process are not incidental to your successful use of the techniques; they are crucial to it. Make sure that you limit your worrying to your Spot. Be certain to worry intensely, for a prescribed period of time, with as little carryover of anxiety afterward as is humanly possible. And above all, in whatever way you wind up using these techniques, be certain that you, and not the anxiety, are in control. Learning how to control your anxiety by practicing twenty minutes a day can be the first step toward actually making larger changes in your everyday life, and it will certainly show up in your athletic performance.

TECHNIQUE 4: THE *FEELING* AND HOW TO GET IT

All the techniques up to this point have been designed to help you deal with certain thoughts and feelings common to athletes. Tension, anxiety, relaxation, and other mental states have been discussed. This technique, on the other hand, doesn't deal with any one type of thought or feeling. Here we move from considering feelings common to all athletes to that one personal feeling that is best for you. I call it the *feeling:* your own special way of feeling, different from the way anyone else in the world can ever feel, that prepares you and means that you are ready to do your best in competition. For this reason, many athletes say it's the best feeling in the world.

To make use of the *feeling,* there are two steps: First, you must identify what the *feeling* is for you, and then you must learn how to produce it for yourself when you need it. If you're lucky, as you are reading this you have already begun to think about that perfect feeling you've had on certain occasions when you've performed exceptionally well, and your task will be to learn to reproduce the *feeling* at appropriate times. If you're not one of the lucky athletes who have had a successful experience associated with a particular feeling, then your first task is to figure out what the *feeling* is for you. Either way, what you are about to embark on is the search for and mastery over the single best technique for the production of top athletic performance.

Find the *feeling*

The *feeling* can be absolutely anything: anger, love, hate, anxiety, fear, eagerness, or any feeling, good or bad, that defines your special brand of feeling ready. It can feel wonderful, as though you are so ready for a truly great performance that you can hardly stand it; or it can feel miserable, so that you are afraid to go out and perform, or are sick to your stomach. But it is always distinctive for you.

Usually the *feeling* is a combination of feelings and thoughts that are related to your life, past athletic experiences, and your manner of experiencing the categories of feelings discussed earlier. It is usually very difficult to describe, or even to think about clearly. Athletes who are trying to identify the *feeling* for themselves usually start out very sketchily, saying something like, "Yeah, I think I know what you're asking for, but it's hard to describe just how I felt that time. I can't really give it a name." I would then ask the athlete (as I'm suggesting you do right now) not to worry about naming it, just to describe it as thoroughly as he or she can, in whatever words come closest. Once he or she has done so, I'll often try to give it a name, but one that would be meaningless to anyone but that particular athlete.

For example, I have worked with an athlete who, in trying to identify the *feeling*, went back in his mind to a particular track meet when he was in high school, a day when he performed just about his best ever and on which he felt "great" and "really ready to explode" and "a little nervous about the guy I was racing against." In talking with him, I referred to that feeling in a number of ways: "that high school feeling," "the ready to explode feeling," and the "beat Jackson (the person this athlete had raced against that day) feeling." Even though none of these phrases described exactly the way he had felt that day, the athlete chose the one that came the closest to combining in his memory all the bits and pieces of feelings and thoughts that he had experienced then, and he and I agreed to use that phrase in referring to the *feeling* from that time on. The athlete now had a mental hook on which he could hang all the diverse sensations that were to go into the *feeling* for him, and, most importantly, a tagword that he could now use to call up that *feeling* when he needed it. With practice, he learned to control the *feeling* when he needed to, instead of having to wait for luck and circumstance to bring about his *feeling* again.

The exact phrase the athlete chose to represent the *feeling* is irrelevant. Even the words he used to describe the feeling of the day don't matter very much. By "ready to explode" did he mean ready to explode with anger, eagerness, excitement, or anxiety? Did "great" mean like a great athlete or like his normal self on a particularly great day? Did "beat Jackson" refer to outrunning him or showing him up in some other way? Did it mean that he felt like he knew he could beat him or that he wanted to beat him in the worst way? The actual meaning is less important than the fact that he knew what he meant. Our words can never reflect the exact thoughts and feelings we are having because no one can ever truly share our own personal brands of fear or joy or desire. And this is precisely the problem in discussing the *feeling*, for it is impossible for anyone else to ever know just what it is for *you*.

But there are some strategies for finding your *feeling*. As the track example suggests, one good place to start is to try to remember a past competition in which you performed remarkably well—perhaps your single best performance ever. Ask yourself how you felt that day, what you were thinking, where you were, whom you were with, and anything else you can think of that defines that day and its feelings. Be as thorough as you can be. Don't settle for recalling that you felt good and that you were on the northernmost tennis court and that you were playing good old Charlie. Go into detail, and recall just what "feeling good" was like that day, what there might have been about that court or its surroundings, and just how you felt about Charlie. You are defining a scenario that somehow, for some reason, put you in exactly the frame of mind that let you play your best; isn't it worth some effort to play Sherlock Holmes, to figure out in detail everything about the "scene of the crime"? That's the best way to figure out how it happened, and the first step toward making it happen again.

Another good way of identifying the *feeling* is to review a number of your top performances to see what feelings, thoughts, and circumstances they have in common. Are there consistencies in moods, or physical factors that tend to, for whatever reason, produce top performances? (By the way, in searching for your top performances, don't be afraid to go way back in your memory, even to times when you were very young and physically incapable of performing as well as you do today. You are looking for exceptional performances at any given level of competition, not just your fastest times or highest scores.) Your APIS can be a useful tool in this search, since it asks you to define in detail the conditions under which you perform best. Review all the items and compare them with your top performances, looking for pluses and minuses.

Look for the best readying circumstances, without necessarily trying to figure out why they make you play well. Understanding how and

For the Individual Athlete

why certain feelings and events are linked with top performance will eventually be of value to you, and in many cases this is a necessary step in planning your readying procedures. But in the initial phase, when you are first looking for the determinants of good performance, you may have a tendency to discard some important factors simply because you cannot find reasons why they should actually affect your performance. This is a terrible mistake. If you have gotten this far in this book, you have obviously been thinking a good deal about your performance, and your mind is already used to certain thought patterns linking readying with performance. It will take a conscious effort on your part to break out of these patterns, and to look thoroughly for top performance determinants without first having an easy explanation of how small things can affect your play.

I consulted with an athlete, for example, who had already put a lot of thought into his play and with whom I was trying to identify the *feeling*. In recalling some of his top performances, this tennis player reported laughingly that, following my instructions, he had noted absolutely everything he could about his past top days. "The one thing that I noticed, and which doesn't make any sense to me," he chuckled, "is that I always see myself on those days wearing these old blue tennis shorts that I've had for years. No, actually they're not even tennis shorts but basketball shorts, and I don't usually wear them on the tennis court. I can't see how they could help me play any better, though." Indeed, it is difficult to see how one's shorts could make a difference in one's game, and certainly it would be ridiculous to recommend to all tennis players that they should try wearing old basketball shorts to improve their game. But somehow there was a connection for this athlete, a connection that could be uncovered only by suspending his reasoning power.

With some thought and focused conversation, the tennis player came to realize that wearing those shorts (in combination with some other positive circumstances that needn't be detailed here) did put him in a slightly different mood than wearing his usual "fashion" whites. His images and associations were freer, less structured, and more fun oriented than his tennis uniform would allow. The tennis whites were vaguely connected with the mechanics of his serve, and with all the lessons he had taken, while the old basketball shorts were tied to pick-up games and after school playing around with friends when he was younger. In the presence of some other positive feelings and circumstances, wearing the basketball shorts on the tennis court prepared him to be looser, more athletic, and aggressive in his game, and were associated much less with internal statements like "Keep your wrist locked" and "Play to his backhand." In a sense, he was a different athlete in those shorts, because they recalled a different time and approach to sports. Needless to say, he kept wearing those old shorts, especially when he really wanted to beat someone.

This athlete went outside the game he was playing for help in identifying and reproducing the *feeling*. By suspending the reasoning that says, "I must see a direct link between what I do and how I play or I'm making a fool of myself," he was able to find a feeling that he would never have thought of looking for, and that he could then bring to his tennis game, with or without the shorts. I have found this to be common among high-level athletes who are having trouble in their main sport—they probably are, or have been, engaged in other games in which they do not feel the same pressures that they do in their main sport. In helping these athletes to find the *feeling*, I encourage them to go to other sports, or even to other areas of life, to find times when they have felt just right and have performed exceptionally well. Then they can bring the newly discovered feeling into their main sport's readying. The swimmer, for instance, who gets very nervous before a meet but who can be a great touch football player in a pick-up game with friends, can learn to bring his football *feeling* to the pool with him. I have even seen bright student athletes use the well-prepared "I've got it aced" feeling that has come with taking an easy exam as part of their pregame readying. What's important is the *feeling* that you can identify in any area of life, and using your Spot to practice producing it when you want it.

Don't be afraid to experiment with feelings that may help but that you usually don't like to use. Anger, for example, is a feeling that commonly comes up when athletes talk about a particularly fine performance. "It was a freak thing. The officials made the worst call I've ever seen and I was so mad I could hardly see straight. I did play a really great game after that, though." This is valuable information. Being mad all the time is certainly no way to live, but what if you could get yourself genuinely mad about something before a big competition? It just might help. Recalling something that is guaranteed to make you mad can be a great way to get the *feeling*, after you have practiced it enough in your Spot to be in control of it. This applies to any feeling you might have.

Let me encourage you to experiment with this type of *feeling*, since many athletes are reluctant to do so. They feel that being calm is their main strength in preparing themselves to perform, and the

For the Individual Athlete

thought of trying to feel angry makes no sense to them. I can only say that trial and error is the best way to find the best feeling for yourself, even if you think you already have a good approach. Especially if calmness is your long suit, don't be afraid to try getting revved up; your natural bent toward calmness will never let you get out of control. I worked with a long jumper who insisted that she had to be very calm and friendly to everyone before she jumped, and yet this same jumper had jumped at or near her best distance ever on one or two occasions when she was angry. A few trials quickly showed that, while she certainly couldn't make herself furious all the time, if she did so from time to time before important competitions she jumped very well. Gradually, anger and calmness became intertwined as her *feeling*. Experimentation will help you to find yours.

Do whatever you must, whatever you can think of, but find the *feeling*! The *feeling* is the goal of all of these techniques, and it is the main difference between the experienced athlete and the novice. Sure, there are some pieces of information that an experienced player in any given sport will pick up over time and that new players obviously won't have; but the real difference between the two is that the ones who have played long enough have achieved, through many trials and errors, the knowledge of what they should feel like to do well and how to get there. With careful application and experimentation, using the recall techniques just described, you can greatly accelerate this learning, and give yourself a real edge over your competition.

Using the *feeling*

Once you have done the groundwork necessary to come up with the *feeling*, you are ready to put it into action. Your goal is to bring the *feeling* into being before competition, and the best way to do this is to practice bringing on the *feeling* daily during your Readying Spot. The more you practice, the better. There are two main channels for using the *feeling*: One is through imagery, and the other is in structuring your physical world to maximize the likelihood that you will feel right and play well. Let's look at this physical planning first.

As you go through the recall work necessary to identify the *feeling*, you will undoubtedly find that people, places, and objects form a large part of your memory. Who was with you, what they might have said or done, where you were, and other environmental factors contribute to the way you were feeling at that time, and they will certainly continue to do so each time you compete. It makes sense, then, to arrange as much of your physical and social environment as possible to contribute to your *feeling*. Be as thorough as you can. It is usually not that difficult to arrange to have certain physical objects at hand (like the old basketball shorts, for example), and to have your clothing, equipment, and sometimes even the playing area to your liking. You can also talk to your friends and teammates to have them do (or avoid doing) certain things that will help you to build and maintain the *feeling*. If, for example, your *feeling* is a combination of feeling a little scared, calm, and not all that excited about the competition, you certainly don't want people talking to you beforehand about how excited they are, or giving you a pep talk. Whatever the combination of thoughts and feelings that go into the *feeling*, do all that you can to make the actual reality as perfect as possible.

Of course, many physical realities will be beyond your control, and this is where imagery can come into play. In your daily Spots you will have experimented with enough images to have the perfect scenario in your head, the scene that enables you to produce the *feeling* as strongly as possible. Remember that the scenario that produces the *feeling* is not the same one you might have developed in using the Positive Imagery Technique; it would be the same only if you had found that your *feeling* is best produced by imagining yourself playing perfectly and feeling great. The *feeling* can be good, bad, or otherwise, as long as it's the one you've found to be related to top performance.

Because you are working with imagery, remember that you can override reality. If you know, for example, that you'll get the most productive *feeling* by playing on a certain field at a certain time of day and against a certain opponent, you should use these in your imagery even though in actuality you will be playing elsewhere. Your precompetition Readying Spot in no way has to be linked to the actual situation you find yourself in; in fact, that is the strength of this technique. With enough hard practice and thorough, detailed images, you can produce the *feeling* no matter where you are. Thus, you are heading out to play as much as possible on your home turf: the familiar dressing area and playing field, and the world that makes up your internal thoughts and feelings. The *feeling* becomes your home-court advantage, which does not depend on the circumstances of opponent, time of day, weather conditions, or anything else to put you in the right frame of mind to excel (recall the countdown process).

The *feeling* is by far the single best readying technique that you can use immediately prior to competition. If you don't do anything else mentioned in this book, you should at least practice the *feeling* in daily

Readying Spots, and use the *feeling* before competing. It is especially effective when used in combination with other techniques. The most common combination is to do an attention-clearing exercise (#5) and then to do the *feeling*, leaving yourself attentive and ready to play. But remember that your *feeling* can be anything; find the one that's right for you and use it.

TECHNIQUE 5: ATTENTION CLEARING AND FOCUSING (CONCENTRATION)

The attention-clearing technique is most useful to athletes who have trouble concentrating before and during performances. If you are easily distracted, you can probably benefit from a technique that will help you to stay fully in tune with your sport. Of all the various psychological factors that are discussed by coaches, athletes, and other sports analysts, complete concentration is the most widely agreed upon as a necessity, and for good reason. Unless your attention is focused one-hundred percent on the task at hand, you are not performing at one-hundred percent of your potential. Full attention means precisely *that*: You should be aware of nothing else but what you are doing. Some athletes have described this state in spiritual terms, feeling that God was with them, or that the world seemed to be slowing down around them, or more commonly, that they could see and feel exactly what was happening and what was going to happen next in their game. Complete attention is necessary for any of these states to occur.

In discussing this readying variable, I use the term *attention*, while most athletes and coaches think of it as *concentration*. There are two reasons for this choice. First, *concentration* has come to be too much of a holy watchword for some coaches and athletes; if you are having a concentration problem and are reading this section to do something about it, then you have probably heard many lectures on concentration and mental mistakes. You probably have an emotional reaction to the issue of concentrating. That reaction is just so much excess baggage that you are carrying around needlessly, and you will be able to make much better use of this readying technique if you can set it down and stop worrying about how to make your coach think that you have learned how to concentrate. Concentration has somehow become a yardstick by which athletes are measured as people. It is referred to as an inner strength, like courage or virtue, that you either have or don't. Nothing could be further from the truth, and this brings us to the second reason for using the term *attention*.

In scientific study, *attention* is the correct term for the process by which each person uses his or her senses to perceive the outside world. Many studies of selective attention and attention span have found very little evidence to suggest that the character of the person influences attention very much. Scientists have usually found that the circumstances around the attending task determine to what and how well the person attends. Some of our attending is under our control, but some is not; if you are having trouble concentrating, what you probably mean is that you have the habit of attending more than you'd like to when something happens around you. This has nothing to do with your strength of will or your athletic ability; you are displaying what psychologists call a *learned response*. In a sense, you have learned to be more curious about all that is around you. You have learned this, and you can unlearn it in relation to your sport.

Within the range of attending that is under your control, the most important predisposing factor is your mental *set*. If your mind is truly clear of everything but the game at hand, you will have little trouble putting all your attention on that game when the time comes, even if there are many distractions around you. If, on the other hand, part of your pregame attention is on other things, even things that are partially related to your performance, you will find yourself easily distracted. The best way to improve your control over your attention is to clear away as many distractions as possible.

Distractions can be external (the weather at a football game, the crowd at a swim meet, and so on), or they can be internal. The Readying Spot is a perfect model for cutting down the external distractions; it gives you practice in focusing all your attention on your sport. The attention-clearing technique deals with the *internal* distractions you carry with you into competition: hopes, doubts, fears, and expectations that cause you to respond to events during competition in ways that detract from full, even-tempered attention. The technique does this *not* by having you ignore such internal states, but by teaching you how to clear out this excess baggage before it is time to perform. *You will systematically think and feel your way through a variety of mental scenarios,* so that whatever happens around you during your performance, you will have already cleared your mind of the reactions to those events.

This approach is the opposite of what most athletes try to do when they are preparing to perform. It is very common to see a young athlete

For the Individual Athlete

deliberately trying to distract him- or herself before competition so that he or she won't get too nervous by thinking about the upcoming event. I've seen football players, for example, watching television hours before a game, specifically so that they won't think: "What if we get off to a bad start? What if the coach puts me in against that guy? What if it rains? What if I screw up in front of all my friends? What if . . .?" The list can go on and on. The athlete would be better off learning how to think briefly and efficiently about each of these things well beforehand, since he or she is probably doing so anyway, under the cover of watching John Wayne shoot it out. The athlete who is really not worried about such things doesn't need distraction; he or she will probably just watch the movie, and later turn his or her attention to the performance. The athlete who does tend to think about extraneous things, on the other hand, is only masking anxiety and increasing the likelihood that he or she will prove easily distracted when competition begins. Because it is next to impossible to trick your mind into not scanning for potential disasters, you are better off using this trait to your advantage. You can do this, through the attention-clearing technique, by purposely scanning all of your personal problem areas *when you choose to*, and not when you are trying to attend fully to the game.

Here are the instructions for using the attention-clearing technique. Remember to focus on a specific upcoming event. Keep in mind that worrying is not only okay, but part of the technique.

The attention-clearing and focusing technique

Establish yourself as you would for your usual Readying Spot. The exercise itself can take from five to twenty minutes. Once you are in your Spot, think about the following list of items, in the order given below. Concentrate on each item separately. Imagine the scenes as fully and vividly as you can.

As you do so, allow yourself to become aware of any feelings of tension that arise. When you recognize a source of tension, do whatever you need to do to get rid of this tension. A quick application of relaxation procedures (maybe just your key relaxation phrase) can be very effective, or you can simply close your eyes and breathe very deeply and slowly for ten to fifteen seconds. Concentrate particularly on the exhalation, since letting air escape from your lungs slowly and evenly forces your body to do things that are the exact opposite of what it does when you are nervous. When you are sufficiently calm, proceed to the next item on the list.

As you will notice, the list goes from general to specific things. Take a few minutes to think about the many things that affect you and then put them out of your mind, concentrating fully on the last item: your performance in the upcoming event. Here is the list:

1. Think about the world in general—politics, something you might have read in the newspaper, and so on. Spend a few moments on people and things that have absolutely nothing to do with the upcoming event. Try especially to focus on a person who knows you and likes you regardless of what you do in sports.
2. Think about your sport, its history and its practice all over the world. Where does your performance fit into this grand framework?
3. Think about the coach, teacher, or parent who will be evaluating your performance. Think about the demands he or she makes on you, and the pressures he or she is under. What is expected of you?
4. Think about your best friends among those who will be involved in your next event. What is the personal meaning of this event to them and to you?
5. Think about what the upcoming event is going to be like for you. Visualize yourself in action during the event as vividly as you can. Anticipate as many distracting occurrences as you can. Then see yourself totally ignoring them, fully attentive to your task.
6. Finally, consciously narrow your field of vision to *the ball itself*, just as you would see it in the game. See the texture of it, the seams, and so on.(For other sports, choose some other central object.) This is total, focused attention. Stay with this image for at least three minutes, even if your mind tries to wander.

Remember that, in the final analysis, you have chosen to participate in this event, and that you do have the ability to get into a positive, eager frame of mind for it.

The exercise itself, as you can see, is designed to sweep through your thoughts and feelings, narrowing step by step to the one point where you *want* your attention to go. First you clear your mind, and then you focus it. When you have gone through this exercise, your mind should be more clear and ready for the next step: either another of these techniques or the event itself. Remember, you can change the exercise to best suit your needs for getting ready; this factor—learning

For the Individual Athlete

Figure 7-2.

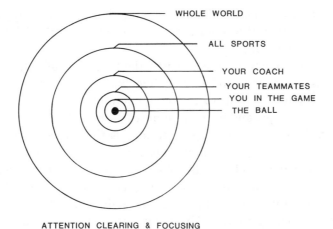

WHOLE WORLD

ALL SPORTS

YOUR COACH

YOUR TEAMMATES

YOU IN THE GAME

THE BALL

ATTENTION CLEARING & FOCUSING

to know and do what *you* need—is the primary determinant of your own success.

Because of the nature of this technique, there are a number of ways that it can be used. Some athletes find that they need to do the attention-clearing exercise only once or twice (during practice times, without a performance event near). When used in this way, it is often an intense experience, in which the athlete does some soul searching about each of the items listed and tries to settle internally some problems. This, of course, takes longer than twenty minutes. Other athletes prefer to use it more as a five-minute mind-clearing ritual. Here the idea is to practice the technique regularly during your Spot so that you become very proficient at it. Then, immediately prior to competition, you can simply and quickly run through the exercise as part of your readying routine.

Probably the best way to use this technique is to combine these two approaches. The first time you try the technique, you will almost certainly find it to be a soul-searching experience that lasts up to an hour and seems to create more problems than it solves. Because of this, try it initially far in advance of competition. Then, when it is more under your control, you can begin to use the shorter exercise before competition. The key is to do the worrying and feel the distractions away from your competition, and then to put these issues away, turning your attention toward your sport.

The attention-clearing technique is the easiest to use in combination with other techniques. While it can be used alone, athletes have often thought of it as a preliminary, "getting ready to get ready" exercise. It can be used as the first part of your Readying Spot, to clear your mind before you start another technique that may actually be the one that is most helpful to your performance. The attention-clearing technique can be a warmup.

There is one technique in particular that many athletes find useful after this warmup exercise: Negative Imagery (Creative Worrying— Goal #1). Pay attention to this combination if you try the attention-clearing technique and find that some of the anxieties and fears brought on by the exercise linger in your mind after the exercise is over. This is definitely to be avoided, and the Negative Imagery technique can help. Having your worries linger is not a bad sign; on the contrary, if that is your response to the attention-clearing technique, then you have probably hit on the underlying problem with your present readying— excessive, floating anxiety. This combination can help you to deal with it.

Whatever use you make of the attention-clearing technique, start in your Readying Spot, as practice. Only after you are aware of the effect the exercise has on you and are comfortable with its use should you try to use it in your precompetition readying. And remember, of course, to do what works for you.

TECHNIQUE 6: PLANNING AND STUDY

This technique deals with what psychologists call cognitions—your thoughts. A certain amount of knowledge and preparation is essential to play a variety of sports well, especially those that involve teamwork and plays. The planning and study technique differs from the others discussed here in that it will not help you to produce a specific product, like a state of mind or a feeling; instead, it consists of seven guidelines that will help you to make better use of the time and energy you put into studying and planning your athletic activities.

The cognitive side of your readying has two parts: getting the knowledge you need to compete well in your sport, and making a plan for your practices and workouts. Here we will focus on getting knowledge into your head, although all of what will be said can be applied to arranging practice situations as well. We will be looking at the common situation in which an athlete sits down to study some material that is essential to good performance in competition. This might be studying plays for basketball or football, or going over strategy for a swimmer, runner, or baseball pitcher, or plotting out specific activities, like skat-

For the Individual Athlete

ing or chess moves. All of these involve mental rehearsal—practicing in your head what you will later be doing with your body.

But before even beginning to study (and before applying the guidelines to be laid out shortly), you should realize that individual differences play an important part in how you should arrange your studying. For example, while some athletes study relevant material in order to feel better about their readiness to perform, others find that they must first feel good about their emotional and physical readiness before they can benefit from studying. Think about your own pattern. Does studying usually help you to feel more ready, and less nervous? If so, then it should be one of the first things that you do as part of your training, and the conditions under which you study are probably not that important. If, on the other hand, you usually can't study much until you have put in a lot of physical work, you should delay your studying until later in your long-term training program. Athletes who tend to feel this way about studying usually have to arrange their study times carefully to avoid distractions.

Even more important is determining the appropriate pattern for your studying. While the Readying Spot is meant to last about twenty minutes, there is often more studying than that to do. In setting up your studying time, you may want to spend longer than usual in your Spot, but you should still get physically ready, arrange not to be disturbed, and do all the other things that define your Spot.

Most important is this: *How much time you should spend studying does not depend on how much studying you have to do.* It should be based on your own individual attention span for the material you are dealing with. Because of our training in school, many of us have come to believe that we "should" be able to sit down and concentrate for at least a couple of hours. To sit down and study for ten minutes would be unheard of. Yet each of us has a different ratio of study time to nonstudy time that will produce the most efficient studying. This study: rest ratio can be arrived at by asking yourself the following two questions: "For how long can I give my *full attention* to this material, before my mind starts to wander?" and "If I study that long each time I study, for how long do I need to rest between study periods?" Finding the ratio that's right for you can be a great aid to keeping your mind on your studying and to having more of what you study stay in your brain.

Many athletes I have worked with on this aspect of readying find it difficult to shake the idea that they have to study for a longer period of time, until they get good and tired. You may find it hard to believe that you can accomplish what you need to by studying for ten minutes at a time. In fact, for most people ten minutes is much too short; twenty to thirty minutes is about the average for most material. The key is to mix in your rest periods so that you feel fresh each time you go back to studying, and are still giving yourself enough time *overall* to cover the material you need to.

I usually suggest that athletes start out with a ratio of twenty minutes studying and ten minutes rest, off-on, off-on, for up to two hours. Adjust your ratio as feels best: If twenty minutes is too short, lengthen it; if ten minutes is too long, shorten it. As a rule of thumb, adjust your study time in ten-minute blocks, and adjust your rest time five minutes or less each time. When you are resting, make sure that you are not still thinking about the material; get up, walk around, and do something mindless if that will help. In spite of the fact that I have had to study a great deal of difficult academic material, I have almost never done any studying for more than two hours at a stretch, at a ratio of about thirty minutes of studying to five minutes of doing something else. As soon as I feel my mind start to tire and wander, I rest for a short time and then go back to my work. The important thing is to experiment until you find the ratio that's best for you.

Figure 7-3. The Study/Rest Ratio.

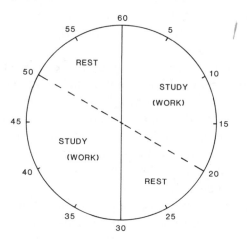

Once you have a feel for your best on-off ratio, and are into your modified Spot, it's time to deal with the material itself. Assuming that you are dealing with knowledge about physical actions, here are some guidelines for you to follow:

1. Start with a mental review or outline of what it is you need to

For the Individual Athlete

know. Don't just plunge into it with no awareness of what should be in your head when you've finished; give yourself an idea of what the goal is: for example, "When I've done all my studying I will know every pass pattern in the playbook." This can help to prevent that "bogged-down-in-the-middle-of-nowhere" feeling later on.

2. Use tools and aids, especially the old standby, paper and pencil. You are not a trained seal that has to learn its act by being thrown fish; you are a human being with the skills of reading and writing, and you can use these skills instead of having to keep everything in your head. In competition, you will probably have to rely only on your brain, but that is not the case when you study. Write down key thoughts. Make a list of things that are not clear to you even after you try to study them, questions that you can ask your coach or teammates later. If you make such a list, you will not be handicapped by the common anxiety of having to remember everything you need to cover. Worrying about whether you'll ever get everything you need into your head is one of the biggest hindrances to effective studying.

3. Be comprehensive; cover everything you think you will need to know. Athletes commonly dislike the mental part of readying, and they try to get away with doing as little as possible. If you do so, you are only kidding yourself. Knowing all your material may not be the most important part of readying, but if you don't know what you need to, your physical practice can take you only so far.

4. Sensorize your thoughts as you study. This means getting your senses and sense organs involved while you study; they are the tools that help you to do your sport. They tell you when to move, how to react to an opponent, and whether you are doing well. The more you get them into your studying, the more your studying will follow you into competition through your body.

Let's look at an example. A football pass receiver studying patterns may say to him- or herself, "On a 12 swing Y-out I go down four yards and break to the right." This is knowledge, and not knowing this will result in many problems on the field. A better way to study it, however, would be to get his or her senses involved in the mental rehearsal: "I'm in the huddle. I've got equipment on and am standing, leaning over, listening to the quarterback. I hear him or her say, 'Okay, let's run 12 swing Y-out, on two. Ready, break.' I clap my hands, turn, and trot slowly to the line of scrimmage. I line up six yards to the left of the tight end, Ed. I look at the coverage, to see where I'll be going. I hear the quarterback say 'Ready, set,' and I take my stance. I hear, 'Hut one, hut two,' and I break off the line. I go straight out for four yards, then I plant my left foot and break to the right. I look back for the ball. I watch the ball come all the way into my hands, I feel it, I tuck it under my arms." Running through the play in this way every time you study it will prevent those dumb mental errors that coaches are always crying about. A swimmer might break down the approach into the blocks, the strategy in the water during the race, and so on. The idea is to feel your way through each part of the physical activity you are studying, rehearsing what your senses will be experiencing when performance time arrives.

5. Do some of your studying, especially of points that seem particularly important to you, aloud. The more sensory channels you involve in any cognitive process, the better you will be able to remember and perform accurately. The combination of thoughts, sights, and sounds—all dealing with the same piece of information—will reinforce the memory of the material.

6. Repeat material in your studying, especially the important points. Going over a particular bit of information can become tedious, but it is often an essential part of learning. Try to spread out your repetitions; instead of studying one thing again and again in one sitting, study it once, go on to other material, and then come back to the original a little later. How much later will depend on you; experiment.

Repetition can also be useful when dealing with material that you do not feel is that hard to learn. The principle here is *overlearning,* or studying the material so thoroughly that you go far past the point of simply being able to recall it successfully. This can help you in two ways: It can increase the ease and quickness with which you recall the material later on, and it can prepare your mind and body to respond automatically under stress, in competition. Your mind operates in many ways that are similar to your body. Just as your coach probably has you practice certain body movements long after the first time that you can do them correctly, you can train your mind to respond automatically by repeating your study of conceptual material.

The effect of stress on your performance cannot be overestimated. Thought processes may represent the highest form of life we know; we are in a sense high-strung, thoroughbred thinking machines, and outside pressure in the form of competitive tension and time pressure can greatly affect the master control for all our activities, namely, the brain. The more you have overlearned important material, the more likely it will be retained and used properly at the critical time.

7. Finish your study sessions by reviewing what you have learned. Many people have a tendency to study until they run out of time and then to think about all the material they didn't have time to cover. This is destructive. When you finish, take a minute or two to go over in your mind all that you have covered. Feel free, as you do this, to pat yourself on the back; you've earned it by studying efficiently. If you feel that you must also look at the negative side (what remains to be done) do so quickly and painlessly. Make a few notes about what you want to remember to start with next time, and leave it at that. This way you won't have to spend energy making sure that you remember what remains to be learned; you can focus on what you have accomplished. If possible, follow your study sessions with something enjoyable, even if only for a few moments. Such positive reinforcement is an important part of learning.

These are the seven guidelines for study and planning. Use them in whatever way works best for you, and be sure to experiment with them until you find the right combination of procedures for you. These guidelines can be used along with another person, like a teammate, to share your studying. This can be very helpful, especially toward the end of your study times, when you have already gotten a good grasp of the material. But it is probably best to study alone at least seventy to eighty percent of the time, since shared studying does increase distractions.

Even though this section has emphasized study and overlearning, *you should not study immediately prior to competition.* In the last few hours of your readying, dealing with conceptual material will only dull you emotionally, and any small gains you may make in learning will be more than outweighed by losses in the area of emotional energy and sharpness. (See Chapter 6 on Cycles.) You must put in your time over-learning your material well in advance of game time, so that you can concentrate on having yourself *emotionally* prepared just before competition. In consulting with football teams, for example, one of the first things I try to get across is that each player will know as much as he is going to about his play assignments a full twenty-four hours before game time, and that no coaches should quiz players after this. That last day needs to be given entirely over to emotional readying. If coach and athlete have the expectation that everything must be learned, and perhaps quizzed, by that twenty-four–hour pregame deadline, it will be accomplished without having to resort to last-minute reviews that may lower the coach's anxiety but do little to improve the player's performance. When competition is near, your body must take over from your brain.

There may, however, be a small group of athletes who benefit from eleventh-hour study. If you feel that one last glance at the playbook helps to calm you before a game, by all means do so. But keep it quick and simple, and don't deal with any new material; briefly review the essentials, and arrange to do it quietly, alone, and without the feeling of being quizzed. When you feel right, you'll play right.

A few final thoughts on the readying techniques

Okay. You've been given some tools for getting yourself psychologically ready to play your best. There have been a lot of suggestions on these last few pages; here are some overriding points to keep in mind in trying to use the techniques:

1. Don't try to use all of the techniques in your readying. Read through them, try them out separately over a period of time, and then sift them down to the one or two that really seem to make a difference in the way you are prepared to play. Be observant and follow your gut feelings about what helps the most.

2. Always keep in mind the two steps that were described in Chapter 1: First *observe* yourself, your readying, and your performance; and then try to *control* as many of the factors related to your performance as you can. Whenever you are trying a technique in the control phase and it's not working right for you, go back and do some more observing to see if you can more precisely tailor the procedure to your own needs.

3. Do it *your* way. In using any of the techniques, don't worry about getting the procedure "right." Feel free to make any changes that help your performance. The suggestions in this book are sound and have been used in competition by high-level athletes, but they are meant to be flexible enough for you to modify them to maximize *your* success with them. Write your own list of readying procedures. Turn yourself loose to experiment. With almost any of these procedures, but especially with the ones containing imagery, it takes only one "right" trial readying and performance to come up with a real performance key. Mistakes, on the other hand, are quickly forgotten and will not affect your progress. If you use this kind of scatter approach, you will know almost immediately when you have hit on something, and you can then stick with that approach. You needn't worry about developing bad habits of readying from just a few trials of any technique. Whatever bad

For the Individual Athlete

readying habits you may already have will be the ones that reassert themselves in the absence of new positive procedures.

4. In planning your individual readying procedures, take into account the unavoidable pressures from outside sources. For example, if you find that positive imagery that excites you and makes you eager to compete is helpful, you may find that having a coach give you a blistering pep talk to psych you up even further will make you too tense to be within your top performance range. It is this range that you are trying to hit in your readying; you are not trying merely to get as high or relaxed or whatever as is humanly possible. In gauging your readying to put you in this range, you should figure into the formula all the things that will happen to you prior to competition, all the people and events that will push your thoughts and feelings in one direction or another. Then you can balance these outside effects with your own personal readying, leaving the cumulative effect well-balanced and in your top performance range.

Of course, an alternate way of dealing with this issue is to avoid these outside effects as much as you can. Ask your coach not to make you attend the pep talk, for example.

5. Even when a technique seems right initially, don't expect immediate results. Regular practice of any technique in your Readying Spot is essential, and all the procedures must be tried out and modified in actual competitive situations at least two or three times before you can expect to see positive results. Don't wait until just before a big competition to use a technique. Use them in less important, more routine competitions, so that you can see how they work and how to incorporate them realistically and effectively into your precompetition readying countdown. Each of the techniques will get progresively more helpful to you the more you use them.

The best advice cannot be given toò often: Find what works best for you. These techniques are not "psycho-gimmicks" designed to magically make you a star; they are the nuts and bolts of getting yourself ready to excel. As such, they represent a challenge to you: With these procedures, you no longer have many of the built-in excuses for less than good performances. Your psychological and emotional preparation need no longer be one of those many things that you cannot control and that you must hope will "go your way." Mental readiness need no longer be seen as mostly luck. Neither your coaches nor your fans nor fate itself is responsible for having you ready inside to perform well, so it is up to you to make the most of your abilities. Get yourself ready!

WHEN THE GAME IS ON

The most important facet of the psychological side of sport is the mental and emotional work you do to prepare yourself for competition. What are the things to do or not to do *during* competition to help yourself to be psychologically ready?

This chapter will look at what goes on in competition, in relation to the psychological factors we've already considered: arousal, energy, control (poise), attention, emotion, and so on. Some things that happen in competition are out of your control, and we'll consider how to respond most effectively to these. Other factors, such as how you act or what you're thinking about, are under your control, and we'll look at the best approach to take with them.

The chapter looks at in-game psychological factors in two ways: First, it discusses five specific in-game problems and how to handle them; then it offers some general suggestions, for both coaches and athletes, about how best to behave and think about the game. The five specific topics are *momentum, mental errors, slow starts and poor finishes, away game problems,* and *what to do after competition,* especially after a poor performance or tough loss.

All my comments will be general in nature, so let me remind you to fit these suggestions into your own ways of playing well. I'll address myself primarily to coaches, but athletes can use these suggestions, too.

Momentum

Momentum: the elusive, powerful spirit of the game, who sits in fickle judgment over all competitors. When you've got it, you can't be stopped; when the other person's got it, it's "hold on for dear life"; the biggest question of all is how to get it on your side.

My training in the social sciences tells me that momentum doesn't really exist, that it's just a figment of the imaginations of all the Howard Cosells out there, whose business it is to try to find words to describe what goes on in sport. I know that no one can measure momentum or predict what it will do, and it would be easy for me to write it off as one of the many postmortem explanations that coaches use to explain a loss. But this would do the term an injustice. Momentum, as something that gives athletes a sense of movement and force, surely does exist. We've all seen games in which a good player never seems to get rolling, and loses to an inferior opponent who gets things going his or her way and then plays confidently enough to win. We've all seen athletes dominate an opponent for half a contest, only to be dominated in turn later on, as if the opponent had drunk some elixir for strength and success. And, perhaps most convincingly, almost every athlete has felt momentum on his or her side, has "known" that he or she could do what he or she wanted and that things would go well.

Okay, then, what is momentum? The best way to answer this question is to forget about the feeling of momentum and focus on a description of what momentum looks like, and what causes it to occur and change.

Momentum appears to be governed by two factors: *success* and *reversal*. Success is always associated with positive things, and momentum is no exception. When an athlete experiences some success or sees it in his or her teammates, momentum is created. When a number of plays go well, or when he or she hits a number of good winning shots, the athlete is likely to experience a sense of momentum (and the opponent is likely to perceive it, too—as a bad sign). Without such successes, the athlete can still feel that he or she is playing well, without establishing momentum.

Reversal also fosters momentum. When things are going poorly and something happens to switch things around to your favor, momentum can be established. Football interceptions, inning-ending double plays, and short-handed goals in hockey can all generate momentum. Often the momentum generated is even greater, and of more lasting competitive value, than the short-term advantage of the reversal itself.

The reversal acts as a lever: It hits your opponent, knocking him or her down, and simultaneously sends you up, flying into the air with energy and confidence.

For coaches and athletes, it's not enough merely to recognize momentum when you see it; the real question is how to do something about it. Basically, there are three things that you would like to be able to do concerning momentum: (1) seize it for your side, (2) keep it once you've gotten it, and (3) deal with it when your opponent has it. Let's look at these three tasks.

Getting momentum on your side in the first place, since both sides start from scratch, is not easy and usually can't be forced. Because success produces momentum, it's usually a good idea to start your competition by trying to do the things that you do best. It is an obvious advantage to get off on the right foot, and trying something new or risky isn't usually the way to do it. Go with your strengths, leaving modification and strategy for later on in the contest.

Reversals can also be used to your advantage. Whenever anything goes your way in competition, emphasize it. The coach who makes a big deal out of a positive reversal is helping his or her athletes to attend to the positive, and to embrace the momentum-generating event wholeheartedly. Especially early in a contest, don't let even a small reversal go unnoticed. Particularly with younger athletes, an atmosphere of "It's our day" or "We're in command" can be established early in a contest through emphasizing everything positive: effort, small outcomes, and reversals.

Obviously, an underlying factor here is confidence. The team with momentum feels confident; but, more importantly, the confident team is always ready to take and use the momentum. Confident athletes find it easy to see every small positive occurrence as evidence that they're rolling. Coaches and athletes can foster confidence through words and actions. (See Chapter 2.) There is always enough fluctuation in a well-matched contest for both sides to see pluses and minuses; the team or athlete that emphasizes the positives is the one more likely to get the momentum. On the other hand, the team that has been coached not to make mistakes has a tendency to see only the mistakes they are making, and they never feel the full force of momentum because their minds have been trained to scan for errors to be avoided. All this, of course, goes back to the discussion of positive teaching and reinforcement.

You might think that once you've gotten the momentum it should be easy to keep it; actually, it's often very difficult. This is because (a) it is highly sought after by your opponent as well, so he or she is fighting to get it all the time; (b) it depends on events, at least some of which are out of your control; and (c) it is naturally transitory, with a short life span and numerous fluctuations.

Even so, there are some *things you can do to keep it*. The best, as always, is positive reinforcement. During a contest, coaches and athletes should try consistently to pat themselves and each other on the back for doing well. Quick, simple expressions of pleasure and appreciation are appropriate, and help the feeling of momentum to spread. The coach who always takes the good things in stride and gripes about the mistakes is decreasing the team's ability to get and keep momentum. (Of course, celebration at an early stage of competition is also to be avoided; the positive reinforcement should be short and businesslike, with everyone's attention immediately turning to the next play to be made.) It's also a good idea to do whatever will keep your string of successes alive; don't just start out using what you think will work best—find what is actually working and stay with it.

In keeping momentum once it's come to you, be careful not to depend on it, or to demand of yourself or your players that it must or should be kept idefinitely. This kind of pressure usually shortens the life of your momentum. Keeping momentum is like riding a wave: You can't make yourself stay up, so you do best to follow the ebb and flow of the wave. Momentum is transitory. When it does come, do an initial, positive, loud emphasis of it; then, rather than keeping your attention on the momentum, revert back to positively reinforcing your own efforts. You get momentum from positive outcomes, but you help to keep it alive by focusing attention on positive performances *in upcoming plays*. Remember the difference!

The fact that momentum fluctuates brings us to the third requirement for handling it effectively: *what to do when your opponent has it*. This is bound to happen, and you can't "will" it away. Occasionally, you may have a contest against an inferior opponent and have things go well from start to finish, but that's certainly the exception. Especially at high levels of competition, when you're competing against quality athletes, momentum in the opponent's hands is a fact of life; in fact, one of the major determinants of who wins championship and playoff games is how well the competitors handle themselves when the opponent is making a surge.

This falls under the general category of *responding to adversity*. The best way to do so is to aim at shortening the length of time your opponent has the momentum. Coaches who demand that their teams immediately grab back the momentum are demanding too much. A more workable approach is to lay low, realizing that your opponent's momentum will naturally decline. Trying to follow a reversal immediately with another reversal in your favor is a bad bet, because momentum is usually too strong at that moment to be pushed aside. You can best shorten bad momentum by deemphasizing that part of the contest. Instead of yelling for somebody to do something right away, ignore the problem as well as you can. Focus instead on specific things you want to do.

The main problem with trying to grab back the momentum immediately is that if it doesn't work, you have wasted so much energy that you may never recover in that contest. Once you say, "This is the big play. We've got to stop them right now and get back the momentum," you are giving yourself and your team an ultimatum. You can do this only so often, or it's meaningless. It's like whipping a horse halfway through the race; it may try to respond right then, but then that's it, and there will be nothing left for the stretch.

It's much better to absorb the blow, mindful that you will soon have an opportunity to deal it back, *after* he or she has spent his or her energy and confidence in this burst of momentum. The best time to try to seize the momentum is not as your opponent is getting up a head of steam, but *just past the peak of his or her energy*. Maintain this kind of attitude: "They are rolling now, and we've got to dig in; but they can't keep this up for long, and then it will be our turn. I'm going to watch closely for any small sign that they've started to falter, and then I'm going to capitalize on that. Instead of trying to stop the snowball coming down the hill, where it's going at full speed, I'm going to regroup a little farther on, where things start to level off and my energy will be most effective. This burst of momentum has gained them a little ground; I can't deny that. What I can do is retrench, to make sure they get no more than this initial thrust."

Perhaps an example will clarify this. You are a soccer coach. Your opponents have been generating a lot of offensive pressure in the last few minutes, and they finally break through for a goal. Should you be yelling for your players to rally, to seize the initiative and take charge, right now? I think not. Your opponents are on the upswing, and it's best to tolerate this with only your usual level of encouragement (a few hand claps and "Let's go" yells). Instead of yelling excessively, you should wait, patiently and alertly, for the slightest easing up of your foe's attack, and the first signs of life from your side. Then get behind this event with all the enthusiasm, energy, and lung power you've got. *Now* is when it will do the most good.

When the Game Is On

This also applies in other sports. In football, don't insist that the defense stop the opponent cold after you've been intercepted; expect a first down or two, and then put forth a big effort of support. In baseball, when your opponents score in the top of an inning, don't insist that the runs be recouped right away; wait an inning or two before putting on a big coaching push. Your athletes will be trying hard to catch up at all times. Don't hamper their long-range effectiveness with an ultimatum.

Of course, in each case, your team will obviously be trying hard to stop the opponent. You expect that. And sometimes they may actually be able to stop the opponent at once. But this effort, even when done well, is almost always limited to being a holding action, while your opponent has the momentum. If you are patient, the same extra effort from your athletes will result in far greater gains, if employed on the downhill side of your foe's momentum peak. That's when you should really encourage them to attack. That's when it will have the *greatest psychological effect* on your players, and that's when it will have a demoralizing effect on your opponent by seizing real momentum for your side.

Go quietly and surely about the business of doing what you want to do, with positive support from coaches and teammates. Real champions are not those who never face adversity or who force it away as if it didn't exist; real champions meet the challenge of a tough opponent without panicking, know that the opponent (if he or she is any good, and he or she must be to be competing at this high a level) will make some yardage and score some points. It's what you do next that will determine your ultimate success.

The issues here are two: *control* and *cycle*. Realize that some things that occur in competition are not under your control, so you shouldn't fight them or downgrade yourself for letting them happen. You can control what you do, not what the opponent does or what the breaks may dictate. If you're kicking yourself in the behind for your failures just because you see your opponent having some success, you are wasting energy that can be better applied to what you are going to do next. Give your opponent credit, and then get back to what you can do. The old saying "God grant me the serenity to accept the things I cannot change, courage to change the things I can, and the wisdom to know the difference" is meant for coaches and athletes alike. Put your energy and attention where it will count, on your upcoming efforts, not on immediately erasing what has just happened.

Cycle is also critical to momentum. Ups and downs in competition are a fact of life. *Momentum will swing back and forth; period.* The important thing to realize is that cycles are units of time; when something goes up, time alone can and will bring it down again. Even if you do nothing, your opponent's momentum will burn itself out, and when it does, it will set the stage for your own upswing.

The mistake that many coaches and athletes make in dealing with momentum is thinking that if they try hard enough, they can keep things moving forward. I don't know of anywhere in life where this is so. Fluctuation is a more feasible goal, and can be accomplished with effort. The trick is to use the down swings (your opponent's momentum cycle) to your advantage. You can do this by (1) expecting adversities and seeing them as a challenge, and (2) timing your momentum-seizing push to coincide with the natural decline of his or her success. Use it as a springboard to catapult you into action. The coach who understands cycles uses them as a guide. The *bad* coach tries to *fight* through everything, all the time, and feels that with enough effort, things should never go the opponent's way; the *good* coach realizes that fluctuation exists, that both sides will have ups and downs, and *allows* for this in his or her planning, so that he or she is not trying to force the athletes against a tide too new and strong to overcome; and the *expert* coach goes one step further—he or she *uses* the natural cycle of momentum to advantage, by pointing out to the athletes when the opponent's crest of momentum has been reached, and that this is the time to strike back, with all the added momentum that will come from the opponent's sudden realization that all is not going as easily as it seemed to be a moment ago.

When it comes to handling momentum, you need to use a mixture of effort and humility. You play hard throughout but your opponent will, too, so you plan that very thing into your approach to the game. Frontrunners who win easily usually do so against inferior competition, and title play often gives them real trouble. Athletes who tend to finish strongly and earn come-from-behind victories are the ones who have really learned these lessons about momentum, and are the toughest of foes—the real competitors.

Mental errors

Mental mistakes: the reason coaches have gray hair, ulcers, and bad dispositions. They can play havoc with your team's overall performance, and they generally make it impossible for some coaches to watch a contest without anxiety. They are the source of that most painful of coaching laments: "We beat ourselves."

When the Game Is On

In this section, we'll look at the specifics of handling mental errors in positive ways, and hope to take this whole problem out of the realm of gut-wrenching worry and self-criticism. Let's identify two different kinds of mental errors and discuss each separately.

The first (*Type A mental errors*) are errors of looseness, lack of application, and inattention. Players look lazy and forget to do things, or do them lackadaisically. They demonstrate lack of order, discipline, and enthusiasm, so that their actions look more like free play than structured competitive effort. Coaches usually identify this problem as athletes being too loose and playing sloppily, maybe even without hustle. The errors they commit are often errors of omission.

Type B mental errors are errors of tension and pressure. In tight situations, athletes forget to do things, don't execute well, or overtry; this results in rushed plays and critical goofs. They look tense and are very self-critical after an error—the opposite of the Type A error. This Type B error is the more common of the two, especially in big games. While the end result of both is the same, the sources are different, and for that reason they require different coaching approaches.

Errors of looseness (Type A) usually come from practices that are too loose. When things are done sloppily in practice, performance in competition often looks the same way. (I am talking about excessive looseness here, not the occasional easy practice that provides fun and release in an otherwise tightly disciplined practice schedule.) Sloppy practice and mental errors of looseness are usually signs that the coach is not in firm enough control of the athletes, and that the athletes themselves need a disciplined, guiding hand to mold them into a competitive frame of mind. If you see these kinds of errors in your team, you'll be doing your athletes a favor by demanding more from them. Even when you are working with young athletes, where the main emphasis is and should be on fun, your athletes will be happier and more effective if you supply enough firm direction to keep them on the task. (See the Fun and Discipline section of Chapter 5.)

There are things you can do in practices and games to avoid mental errors, and there are ways to respond appropriately and effectively to them when they do occur in games. Avoiding Type A mental errors is best done in practices. (See the discussion of concentration and discipline in Chapter 5.) If you devote the first few minutes of each practice session to going over the mental side of your game, Type A mental errors will decrease. Throughout practices, you should repeatedly emphasize where your athletes should be looking, what they should be anticipating, and so on. Frequent skull sessions are helpful. In competition itself, you should do some question-and-answer drills before a game, or during down times. (You of course have to keep this within limits, and this applies only to Type A mental errors, as we shall see.) Anything you can do to put your athletes' attention on things to think about and anticipate is helpful.

Many coaches do overestimate this problem. They see any mental error as a sign of looseness and lack of discipline, and this is not always the case. In fact, most mental errors are Type B, and only teams that are really very loosely coached or who are in the midst of a really down period in their season make Type A errors. Unless your team is always beating itself, you have probably supplied enough discipline, and the errors are not from inattention or lackadaisical attitudes. Make sure that you can see the difference between Type A and Type B errors; when in doubt, it's usually safe to assume that you are dealing with Type B and not Type A.

When Type A mental errors do occur in contests, they need to be dealt with. Since attention is reinforcing, you don't want to jump immediately on the player (recall Chapter 4), but you do want to bring up the error after two or three minutes. Be sure to tell the player what you *want* him or her to do. If things get so loose that many athletes are making Type A errors, you probably have a motivation problem on your hands. (See Chapter 3.)

Type B mental errors are more common and more nerve-wracking. Especially if your team is competitive, the mental errors your athletes will be making are almost sure to be Type B—hurrying, confusion, overtrying, and so on. Type B errors increase in an atmosphere of tension and pressure. In big games, this atmosphere is naturally present, but all too often the coach is the primary contributor to such pressure, and, therefore, to Type B errors. He or she usually makes this deadly contribution in two ways: by demanding perfection, and by using punishment as a main teaching tool. Both of these put more pressure on the athlete who is already trying to do his or her best, and they undermine his or her efforts. You may get by with this approach in lower-level games against inferior opponents, but when you reach the championship games, you will have sealed your own, losing fate. The pressure from you combined with the natural pressure of championship competition will put your athletes beyond their range of optimum performance tension, and you will see Type B mental errors.

Coaches see mental errors as completely different from physical miscues; the old adage is, "Physical mistakes are part of the game, but no one should *ever* commit a mental mistake." To make a mental error

When the Game Is On

is seen as a sign of lack of effort, poor attitude, and bad coaching. *Nothing could be further from the truth.*

Mental errors are *exactly* the same as physical errors and should be handled accordingly. There is no reason to assume that the mind, any more than the body, can do things in the same way over and over without a mistake. The same principles of stimulus and response, practice, reinforcement, and extinction apply to the mind. In fact, because mental functions are more complex than physical ones (the most difficult gymnastics routine does not compare, in terms of evolutionary complexity and order, with the simplest thought), mistakes are *more* likely to occur, and it requires even *more* work to avoid or get rid of them. The higher the mental function, the more it is subject to deterioration and error when emotional interference is present, and that's exactly what pressure does: The pressure of top competition, the threat of punishment, and the insistence on perfection cut right at the underpinnings of good mental attention and execution. Accordingly, mental errors must be treated the same as physical ones, with the principles of reinforcement and ignoring (Chapter 4).

How do you reduce the likelihood of Type B mental errors? Keep things as calm as possible during competition. The less pressure-inducing the atmosphere in the dugout or on the sidelines, the easier it will be for your athletes to deal with the pressure. The coach plays an important role as a model. It's also a good idea *not* to drill athletes on mental points just before or during games if Type B mental errors are a problem. Doing so only increases the pressure and the demand for perfection; it is best to have your skull sessions in practice only, and leave the time of the contest itself for other kinds of readying processes. It is a good idea to plan some looseness into your schedule. Having the last practice before a big game be a loose, fun one, with as little pressure as possible, is a great way to cut down on Type B mental errors. You do not want to use up much mental or physical energy in the last workout before a game; stop short of demanding from your athletes everything they are capable of in the last practice session. Then they will have mental reserves for the competition.

When Type B mental errors do occur, it is essential to fall back on the principles of reinforcement and pressure reduction. During games, Type B errors should always be *ignored;* then give the athlete only encouragement when he or she is ready for the next play. Treat mental errors just as you would physical errors, as outlined in the *ignore* section of Chapter 4.

Excessive Type B errors are usually the coach's fault, for not being able to tolerate a small percentage of them and instead adding more pressure through yelling or in-game mental drilling.* The coach's best ally in dealing with mental errors is patience; ignore during the game what you will work on later, in practice or before the next athletic event. Mental errors can be reduced but can never be eliminated. The old adage should be, "Physical and mental errors are part of the game." The more you demand that they never occur, and the more you jump out of your skin when they do occur, the less likely it is that you will be able to decrease them; in fact, you're probably insuring their return. When you see a mental error, always assume it's a Type B until proven otherwise. It is much easier to undo the damage of mishandling a Type A error than it is to take the pressure *off* after you've mishandled a Type B.

Problems starting and finishing games

Some problems occur at specific points during competition. A team or an individual athlete will regularly start slowly, finish poorly, or make errors at particular points in competition. Here we will look at starting and finishing contests, although most of it will also be applicable to any particular point during competition.

The slow start is a common problem. Athletes look sluggish and fall behind early, or don't take advantage of the opportunities offered them by the opponent. The slow start becomes a pattern, and after a while the athletes just assume they'll start slowly. Where does this problem come from and what can you do about it?

Very often, slow starts result from insufficient readying. Pregame timing is slightly off, so that the competition starts while the athletes are still finishing up their readying. Athletes often experience this as not being ready to play until they are challenged, and the opponent almost has to knock them down before they get rolling.

There are two distinct ways to approach this kind of problem: fighting it and working around it. Most coaches try to correct the problem, doing things that will help their athletes get off more quickly. The best way to do this is to bring your athletes out onto the playing field early, up to an hour earlier than usual. The athletes should also be encouraged to come to the competitive arena early, even if they will be hanging around before they actually get involved in warming up. This

---

*I don't say this about many things, because I feel that the athlete is ultimately responsible for his or her performance. But here the coach usually plays a major role.

When the Game Is On

enables the normal rhythm of their readying to work at its usual pace while starting competition a little later in the readying cycle, so that they are not left at the gate. You don't want to try to change the pace of the athlete's readying, because that's very difficult; you want to change the *timing of the whole cycle,* so that it takes about the same length of time but simply begins earlier. This approach can be augmented by pep talks if you like, but it's the timing change and not the rousing insistence of the coach that makes the difference. In using this approach, be sure to keep an eye out for any individual athlete who responds negatively to the change. (This is quite common.) Overall, it is best to have some athletes report early while others come a little later.

It is natural for you to want your team to put pressure on the opponent as soon as possible, and thereby get a great advantage. But it is dangerous trying to push your athletes or yourself into this role if it doesn't naturally fit. When you take a team that starts slowly and emphasize starting quickly, you often create problems at the other end, late in the contest. Athletes have only so much mental, physical, and emotional energy to use on a given occasion, and when you ask them to use a lot of it early, they can easily burn up too much too soon in the effort to overcome their usual starting inertia. Changing slow starters into fast ones requires relearning both at the start and at the finish, so you can expect your team to fade a bit at the end of the first few contests in which you get them out early. You've got to emphasize the end as well as the beginning.

But even so, the switch may have its drawbacks. Teams usually develop a set character of behaving in certain ways. Often, the best thing for the coach to is not to try to change this character (unless it's absolutely killing you, of course) but to plan around it and use it to your advantage. Starting slowly can be a problem, but it can be seen as an advantage, too: Slow starters easily see themselves as second-half players, who always seem to do better late in competition. Such a self-concept—"I always finish strongly"—is very beneficial, since it supplies confidence and poise at the end of games, when the outcome is usually on the line. No matter what the score is at halftime, the team can feel that its turn is coming up, and they can win. To spend a lot of time and energy trying to change them into a quick-starting team can undermine this.

You can use your team's slow-starting character to your advantage. Play conservatively at the start, planning to keep things relatively even until your athletes get into their stride. Positively reinforce your players for merely staying even for a short while, and, when the waiting period is over, make sure to emphasize that fact with a lot of loud encouragement and anticipation. Most of all, make sure that in emphasizing the quick start, you are not cutting off your nose to spite your face: Don't give away the power of finishing momentum just so that you can feel you have a bunch of eager beaver athletes who are going to demolish the opponent immediately, thereby relieving you of all anxiety about the outcome.

Poor play at the end of competition can be much more damaging, and it should always be attacked with all available means. It usually takes the form of numerous mistakes, sluggishness, tightening up, and the general look of paralysis that comes over a team in the throes of erring when it counts. Fatigue can play a part, and should be dealt with through physical conditioning. But more common is mental and emotional fatigue, the wearing down of the athletes' inner resources due to insufficient readying, the effort already expended, and the pressure of the end of the game. Athletes who deteriorate at the end have usually gone to the whip too often earlier in the contest; they have felt, and have been told by their coaches, that "every play is a critical play," so naturally at the end of a tough struggle, when the plays really *are* critical, they have nothing left inside, no matter how hard they try. Ironically, end-of-game problems can also result from too much coaching emphasis on finishing strongly; when the coach has harped on this issue time after time, mistakes often increase instead of abating.

What you do in practice can make a big difference. Be sure to practice in chunks of time that are roughly equivalent to the length of one of your contests. Within these game-length practice sessions, pinpoint the times that correspond to the times your team is having problems during games. During these times, do things that are easy, fun, and build confidence. It is also a good idea to stop all physical action and do some skull sessions, but the emphasis should be on what the athletes *do* know, so that confidence abounds. You are trying to link up inside the athlete's head (according to his or her internal clock) two things: this particular point in the effort cycle and good feelings. Pairing these two things teaches the athlete to relax and feel good at the necessary time. If your team's problems occur at the end of the game, then this strategy goes hand in hand with the earlier suggestion to end on something positive. That's the best overall approach to improving end-of-game performance through your practices.

What you do in games can also affect things. Don't keep telling your athletes that every out is a big out, or that every possession must result in a score; they'll have nothing left at the end of a contest. If you have been attentive but calm throughout the contest and can remain so at the end, the modeling effect will help your team overcome its finishing jitters.*

There are things you can do to change the flow of your team's competitiveness, but it's important not to fight your team. You may have your own personal preferences for how a team should start or finish, but your team may not be capable of doing things that way. In the long run, emphasizing steady effort, and viewing peaks and valleys as a natural part of the competitive landscape, is the best coaching attitude. When you stress this and positively reinforce good effort whenever it comes, you improve your chances for seeing good play at all times, including starts and finishes.

Playing away from home

Win at home and split on the road—the formula for success. Troubles on the road often confound even the best of teams. Away from home, the team might make critical errors, fade toward the end of contests, or simply play poorly. At home, they are a different group of athletes. Why do teams play better at home, and what can be done to alleviate some of the problems of playing away from home?

Two main problems face the team away from home and contribute to poor play: *unfamiliarity* with the surroundings and *hostility* from the opponents and their fans. Often these two combine to make a powerful deterrent to good play, and when they are added to the fact that the home team is simultaneously benefiting from the familiarity of the surroundings as well as from fan support, they can account for a drastic home-away imbalance. The most important first step to take in addressing these problems is to make sure that your athletes see unfamiliarity and hostility as separate things, and not as one big negative aura that traps them when they play away from home. They are distinct problems that can be handled separately. It is a bad sign when, after a tough road trip, a professional athlete responds inarticulately to the reporter's question, "Why is it so tough to win on the road?" When the athlete's response is general, when he or she talks about the fans and not feeling

---

*I should point out that everything is relative: Being and looking calm doesn't mean looking so relaxed that you are falling asleep. During competition, everyone's level of activity is naturally elevated; overexcitement is the big enemy, and anything that looks remotely like calmness and sureness will stand out as a good example. Additionally, how you look is much more important than how you really feel.

confident and bad breaks and the fatigue of traveling, then it is very unlikely that he or she will be able to do any better the next time out. The more the athlete is able to pinpoint one aspect of the overall problem, the better he or she will be able to do something about it.

Of the factors, *unfamiliarity* is the more important. Hostility is only a secondary factor, especially since most athletes expect the opponent to be hostile. (We *are* talking about competition, aren't we?) Unfamiliarity means simply that things are different and unpredictable when you're away from home, and, as we saw in Chapter 5, familiarity, structure, repetition, and routine make the best atmosphere for good play. But when you're traveling, the streets, the walls around you, the bed you are sleeping in, the arena you are playing in, and even, in the case of long trips, the time of day or the quality of the air may have changed. These things do affect people, especially when they are attempting complex, highly skilled behavior.

When we come to the game itself, the sources of unfamiliarity are three. First, the athletes need to adjust to the physical facilities they'll be playing in: the texture of the grass, the lighting, the temperature, and so on. Everything can make a difference. Second, there are distractions during games. Sounds and sights on the field of play will be different from what the athlete is used to at home. It doesn't matter what the sights and sounds are; if they are different from what you're used to, they can affect you. And third, there are breaks in the readying tempo that athletes use to prepare for competition. The last few hours or moments or days before competition may make demands on the athlete that are not present at home. He or she has to look at and listen to different things (find a clean locker, find a place to sit and think, hear the other team preparing, and so on). All these things add up, and they can break the flow of the athlete's normal pregame readying.

The key to overcoming these problems is simple to state but harder to do: make things as familiar, repetitive, and routine as possible. Always follow the same pregame patterns (with travel and meals, for example) as closely as you can. But because the physical realities of each place are different, there's only so much you can do to make them all seem the same. What you can do is make the internal mental routine the same, so that no matter where you are, you are looking inward and seeing familiar territory.

Making things routine before games is not a new idea. Structured pregame warmups, strict travel schedules, and staying in hotels even before home games all contribute to familiarity and cut down on distractions. They are tools that should be used, as they enable the athlete

When the Game Is On

to put his or her mind where it should be—on his or her own readying. But I like to see teams go even farther on the road to self-imposed familiarity. Ride with the same person each time, bring as many physical reminders of home as you can, and, most importantly, always keep the timing of events the same. The more you stick to a standard countdown of things to do leading up to game time, the better.

Adjusting to the physical characteristics of the arena can be aided by having a workout on the enemy territory—the more, the better. Just make sure you do things as you would on your own practice field. Even if you can't work out, let your athletes see the arena and walk through it as soon as you can. When teams make a cross-town or cross-state bus ride and go directly to the locker room, they are making a mistake. A visual image of the field is critical to the immediate pregame readying that goes on during the dressing period, the final gearing up for battle.

Incidentally, the strategy of trying to make your home arena like the away arena, through physical changes or by artificially creating the noise of hostile fans, is of doubtful value. I've seen some teams use this strategy with success, but I've also seen it flop. I think you're better off having a crisp, easy, confidence-building practice in the familiar surroundings of your home arena before hitting the road. This confidence will last longer than gimmick-induced familiarity.

Routine and familiarity away from home should extend to competition itself. It's a good idea to start all your games in the same way, usually with things that your athletes find comfortable or successful. Football teams that predictably run up the middle to open a game are doing this. Of course, they have to develop a fuller strategy as the game progresses, but starting easily helps. In unfamiliar environments, some energy will always be taken up with orienting, so keeping things routine and simple can really help.

Hostility is a little different, and athletes respond to it in individual ways. Some actually thrive on it, love the challenge of it and the aspect of fighting back. With this kind of athlete, there's probably little you need to do; just help with the familiarity aspect.

But the athlete who responds negatively to hostile environments must pay some attention to the problem. First and foremost, you do not want to fight the feeling. What you want to do is put all of your energy into yourself and your task. Cultivate the feeling of trying to execute well, not of being "against" someone or something. It's like working on a car or building something: Your mind is on the mental blueprints of what you are trying to do, not on fighting against the job. This relates to the concepts of playing within yourself and of playing your game. The more the athlete has a firm sense of what his or her game is, and the more both coaches and athletes emphasize this before away games, the better. Your game is the ultimate "routine."

Experience is obviously a helpful factor in playing in hostile arenas. While you can't prematurely age your athletes, you can accelerate the experience factor in regard to dealing with hostility and bad breaks. I've noticed that teams often do all right away from home until something out of their control goes wrong. You go along playing your game until you get a critical bad call or make a small error. Then the hostile fans and the strangeness of the arena gang up on you.

You can work to avoid this in practices by using *bad-call* or *bad-break* workouts. Put your athletes in game situations and call some critical plays *wrongly*. Let them practice the internal struggle that is bound to go on when, in the midst of trying hard and doing well, a bad bounce or a bad call knocks them down. Then they will be better able in competition to handle the situation appropriately, by looking toward the next play and not the last one. I even encourage players (only during bad-play workouts) to give the particular athlete who has fouled up or who was the immediate victim of a bad break a really hard time, right then. Get on his or her back as hostile fans will, so that he or she learns to cope with it. What you're rehearsing is *internal control* in the face of adversity. (Have the players, not the coach, do the harping. When the coach does it, it's too much like punishment and sets up the expectation that the coach will blow up during games. Especially in hostile settings, this is the exact opposite of what the coach should be doing.) Of course, keep a limit on this player criticism; make it short and sweet, and stop as soon as you see it becoming destructive.

When dealing with away-game problems, the key is keeping your attention on the game itself. Encourage this positively—not by saying, "Forget about it," but by constantly looking at and talking about what's coming next in the contest. In enemy territory, the cooler, more supportive, and more game-oriented the coach is, the better for the team as a whole.

After the game

The game is over. Win or lose, having played well or poorly, both athletes and coaches will have a reaction to what just happened. Usually, the coach says a few things to the athletes about the contest. The final wrap-up on the game is given: where it fits into the scheme of things, and how it relates to the next competition. All the possibilities that existed before the game are now gone; all that's left is the reality of what took place. And sometimes, depending on what transpired, a few well-chosen words can be very important.

What you do after the game is important in setting the tone for the next game. Feelings often run high after a contest, either with the flush of success or with the disappointment of failure, and these feelings can have a lot to do with the attitude the athletes will bring into their next competition. How you as a coach respond to them is critical, primarily because postgame minutes can be periods of very high attention and retention, especially if the athletes are feeling bad. After the game you have a golden opportunity to get something across; don't waste it.

Most importantly, what you must do after the game is distinguish *performance* from *outcome*. Good play usually leads to positive outcomes (winning) and poor performance usually leads to negative outcomes (losing)—but not always. Presumably, in your workouts you have been preaching performance, saying that if your athletes play well they'll do well, but that the main thing is to play to their potential. Winning and losing aren't always under your control; luck and the skill of your opponent can affect them.

If your team plays well, loses, and you let them have it, you are failing to reinforce precisely what you want—good play. If your team plays poorly but wins, and you praise them, then you are reinforcing poor play. In either case, you are teaching your athletes to focus on winning and losing, not on their own performance. Because winning and losing depend on the strength of the opponent, and the breaks, you are teaching them to feel good or bad depending on things out of their control, when the one thing they can and should do something about, their own performance, goes by the boards.

After the game is over, you must show your athletes that you're really serious about having them attend to their own performance. You may say things like that in practice, but if you respond to outcome when the game is over, your cover is blown: Your team will know that you really care only about winning and that your talk about self-improvement is just so much hot air. It's not that you shouldn't care about winning; it's just that your job as coach is to teach your athletes the building blocks that lead to winning, and those building blocks all revolve around their own performance. Their performance is the only thing they can actually do something about, and that's why it must remain the major focus of attention before, during, and after games.

Based on the combinations of good and bad performances and outcomes, there are four types of games, represented in Figure 8-1.

Figure 8-1.

| | PERFORMANCE | |
	PLAYED WELL	PLAYED POORLY
WON	1	3
LOST	2	4

OUTCOME

Each type of game calls for a different response. All the responses are aimed at making it more likely that performance in the next game will improve. Let's look at each type.

Type 1 Games: Good Performance and Winning.—This is the easiest combination to deal with, since things have gone well and your good play has been rewarded. The only thing the coach needs to do is to remember to hand out some praise. Talking specifically about performance is still a good idea here, and pointing out specific good things that athletes did is good practice. Any off-field reinforcers (from buying cokes to giving some practice time off) can be helpful, too, but these are best reserved for really good games. There will always be things that weren't done well, but don't deal with them right after a good game; do your positive reinforcing routine in response to the overall good play. Ignore the mistakes for now, and plan to deal with them later, either in practice or before the next game. The main thing is to let the good feeling of effort and accomplishment sink in immediately after the game.

Type 2 Games: Good Performance but Losing.—Perhaps the hardest thing in sports to deal with is the tough loss. You played well but, in the end, things didn't go your way. How do you then reinforce the good things you've seen, and deal with the naturally lowered emotions of the team to prevent temporary sadness from growing into delibitating discouragement?

There's no set speech that should be given after a tough loss, but there are some elements that do belong in such a speech. First of all, be quick and to the point. Long speeches after tough losses are hard to take, and after the first minute or two the words don't even matter: Each athlete will already have begun dealing with the loss in his or her own way. You've only got sixty to ninety seconds to get your point across, but these seconds are a very high attention period. Make the first thing you say the most important.

Remember to positively reinforce the good play. There won't be a lot of loud praise and backslapping, of course, but a few quiet words of recognition for a good effort can help a lot. It's critical not to let the positive aspects of the performance go unnoticed in the depression over the loss.

Also include some comment about why you are glad your athletes are down. Explain that if they didn't care enough to be down after a tough loss, you wouldn't have much respect for them as competitors. Say that the feeling of being down is natural, but that it doesn't detract from the quality of their performance, which was good.

Finally, and perhaps most importantly, remind your athletes that the feelings will not last. Sadness and anger are natural reactions to loss, and they shouldn't try to fight them off immediately; but after a short while (a day or so) it will naturally wear itself out. At that point, what you have said about their good performance will come to the fore. Telling your athletes that this will happen makes it easier for them to accomplish this vital mental transition. After all, the important thing, once the game is over, is the next game, and it's a good idea to remind your athletes of this. You've been emphasizing "the next play" all along, and now is no time to stop. You don't expect your athletes to be able to blot the loss out of their minds right now, but you do expect them to start looking toward the future in a day or so. Giving them this expectation will make it easier for them to do so. As long as your athletes can see your own disappointment, your own appreciation of their good efforts, and your own awareness that this is not the end, they will bounce back. These three elements can turn the tough loss into a team-strengthening event, binding the players and coaches together both emotionally and in competitive effort.

Type 3 Games: Poor Performance but Winning.—This is a dangerous combination. Effort and attention haven't been good, but the team is reinforced by winning anyway. Sloppy, self-defeating habits are learned this way, and athletes are not finding out what it takes to win the tough games. The danger is that the team will rest on its laurels and good record, but fade when faced with top competition. When you screw up but still feel good about it, you're learning to fail when it really counts.

The coach has to make sure that the team sees the performance-outcome discrepancy here, as immediately as possible. If this is already true (if the team is down after the win because they know they played poorly), then you needn't do much more than quickly say the obvious: "We played poorly and were lucky to win." More commonly, athletes, especially young ones, are up after a win, despite their poor play. In this case, you may want to hit them hard to bring them down to earth.

In your postgame speech you should ignore the outcome and talk about performances. Be specific about what you will need to improve in order to win against tougher competition. You'll never be able to do away with some of the team's good feelings, but that's as it should be. Some good feeling, even after an undeserved victory, builds confidence; what you want to avoid is overconfidence. You don't have to rant and rave to accomplish this, as long as you are genuinely and specifically not pleased after the game. The team will see this and know that they haven't been great. Especially if you have adopted a policy of really praising what you like, your lack of praise after a bad win will stick out like a sore thumb, bringing your athletes down to earth and teaching them that it really is performance that counts.

Type 4 Games: Poor Performance and Losing.—You've just played a bad game and been beaten, maybe even badly. What should you do? The answer depends on the reaction of the athletes. Usually athletes know when they've been soundly beaten and they don't like it. Silence, harsh words, and bursts of anger are common and appropriate. In this atmosphere, the best approach is an amplification of the ignore technique. The coach should say next to nothing, beyond suggesting that everyone go home and think about what needs to be done better the next time. Don't pick out specific errors, and don't rant and rave. There is nothing, neither performance nor outcome, that you want to reinforce, and any attention is reinforcing. You don't need to make your athletes or yourself feel any worse than they already do. Just send them away, and deal with the specific problems at your next workout. Your athletes are probably already chewing on themselves; adding to it, you make the loss too significant. Lingering memories of past blunders don't make for good performance, and what you do now will determine just how much the athletes are thinking about this later on in the season, when they should be concentrating on the next play or the next game. The ignore technique is ideal (1) for not reinforcing bad things,

When the Game Is On

and (2) for minimizing the chances of negative carryover. Your next practice is the time to iron out specific problems.

This assumes that your athletes already know they've goofed and feel bad about it. If they don't, you've got real problems, because if you don't dislike playing poorly and losing, you have no business in an achievement-oriented, competitive area like athletics. In such cases, a fiery lecture can be very appropriate. It is still best to stick to performance issues, to make sure that they know you are blowing up because they played poorly, not just because of the final score. Even the most effective of these speeches will not reach every athlete, but they should be aimed at the team leaders, who will carry the message to their peers long after you've stopped yelling. You can't make your athletes care or try harder or do better, but you can get their own leaders to do so, by reminding them of the pain of poor performance. Remember, however, that this is good strategy only when your athletes aren't already kicking themselves; if they are (and look carefully because, being human, they probably are), simply sign off and get on to the next game.

With each type of game, you've got to take your cue from the team itself. After being with a group of athletes for weeks or months, you will have definite evidence of what they will respond to; use your postgame words accordingly. The overall goals of reinforcing what you like, ignoring what you don't like, and punishing the intolerable still apply. In this context, good performance (not necessarily outcome) is what you want, poor performance and outcomes are what you don't want, and only flip, uncaring responses to poor performance warrant punishment.

The athletes themselves should have *internal standards* that they are trying to meet in their performance; nothing else really matters. There is the external standard of the score (saying, "You won," or "You lost"), and the internal standard inside the athlete. The coach stands between these two as a teacher and interpreter. His or her goal is to show the athletes that the important standard is "You played well," or "You played poorly." Ultimately, the athlete doesn't need the external standard of the coach to tell him or her when he or she has done well or poorly; he or she knows it inside. The pitfall that must be fought all along this road of work and self-improvement is having the athlete learn that the standard to apply to him- or herself is *win-lose.* Win-lose has to be secondary to *play well-play poorly,* or improvement will be limited. The coach's response to the real situations, games, will determine which of the two standards the athlete takes more to heart.

Overall in-game strategies
for coaches and athletes

Aside from dealing with these issues, each coach and each athlete has one overall attitude that he or she carries into competition: a sense of what competition means, what he or she is trying to do, and, perhaps most importantly, how to conduct him- or herself during the game. Your overall approach to the game will determine your effectiveness as a coach or an athlete; your style and your personal manner weaves in and out of the peaks and valleys, the successes and failures, and the strategic decisions, providing you and those around you with a sense of your individual brand of competitiveness.

This sense affects everything else, and that's why it bears looking at here. This section discusses, first for coaches and then for athletes, some thoughts and behaviors that can help you in competition, by making it easier to respond appropriately to the events of the game and to perform as you want to—successfully.

First, the coach: Everyone wants to be a good *game* coach, and everyone has his or her own style of doing so. Here are some general principles you may want to incorporate into your style:

1. You've got to model what you know will help your athletes; this means providing an example of confidence, concentration, and poise. The model you present to your athletes is the single most important part of your in-game contribution. Practice and strategy sessions have played their part, and now what's important is how you conduct yourself through the ups and downs of the game. Your athletes will take their cue from you: If you respond to adversity with self-assurance, they will, too; if you yell and scream, or do anything that smacks of disappointment or panic, this will also spread. I like to think of the model coach as being consistent, positive, and sure of him- or herself. He or she shares a sense of confidence with the athletes; they do not panic in tough situations, but keep working hard, always retaining their balance and concentration. They can come back after low points, because their coach has not looked grim-faced or beaten because of the toughness and setbacks of early competition. The model coach mentally and emotionally keeps his or her feet in all situations, setting the tone for the team. You may not like what you're seeing in a game, but, however bad it is, you've got to deal with it confidently, or your athletes will probably not be able to do so on their own.

2. Remember your positive reinforcement. Slap some backs when

things go right, especially little things early in the contest. The more you can set a tone of optimism and hope, the better.

3. Focus your attention more on performance than on strategy when dealing with your players. Of course, you've got to be thinking all the time and making the right moves; but when you deliver your strategy to the athlete, do so surely and with the emphasis on execution. Let the thinking stay in your head, so that theirs can be free to execute properly. Keep this distinction clear, and aim everything you say to them at their own performance.

4. Similarly, focus yourself and your athletes on their performance, not on the opponent. If you outwardly worry about the opponent's momentum, the hostile environment, or the specific problems your opponent is presenting you with, you are distracting your own athletes from the proper focus of their attention: their own efforts and performance. Talk almost exclusively about what "we" are going to do now, and keep your thoughts about the opponent's strengths and weaknesses in your head.

5. Your main focus has to be on your team, not on yourself. This sounds obvious, but many coaches find it difficult to do, because of either their outgoing personalities or their concerns about how they look to the athletes, fans, and so on. During the game, this can be deadly.

An example of this occurred in the NCAA basketball championship game between Marquette and North Carolina State a few years back; the coach in in question, Al McGuire, tells this one on himself. In the second half of what was a close game, a call went against McGuire and Marquette. A fiery show of anger and histrionics by McGuire ensued, resulting in technical fouls and an even bigger deficit in the score, which eventually proved to be too much for the team to overcome. McGuire says that he lost this game, but that's probably an overly harsh judgment. What he did do, however, was take the game out of the players' hands and put all the focus on himself. Even in less dramatic circumstances, this usually has negative consequences. If you feel a constant need to be active, to force yourself into the game through a lot of yelling and strategic moves, you are training your athletes to wait for someone else (namely, you) to do things. This undermines their energy. The athletes have to make things happen; the coach merely gives a few basic directions periodically. The players are the ones who must feel aggressive. The loud or emotional coach can subvert this, unless he or she is very careful.

I see many advantages to what I call *minimal coaching*. During the game, you remain relatively calm. (You don't have to be a stone, just less excitable than you are at other times.) You have the attitude of having done your job, and now you are handing the ball to your team, whose job it is to show energy and control.

Ultimately, the energy must be with the athletes. On game days, athletes are usually excited, nervous, and eager; they have a lot of physical and mental energy flowing through them (especially in big games). What they need is some point around which to focus that energy. The quiet spot becomes the center around which all of the athletes' energies flow; the athletes can really let loose, forget their inhibitions, and go beyond themselves in effort and energy, because they know that the quiet spot will always be there as a stable foundation, a home base where the competitive storm does not reach. They don't have to think, because they know that someone is quietly and surely doing all the thinking that the team needs; consequently, they can put all of their energy into their efforts and all of their concentration into particular plays. That quiet spot is the coach, the one spot of planful sanity in the otherwise crazy world of desire and effort. Without this spot to fall back on, the athletes themselves always have to keep a small part of their minds in reserve, to make sure that they are in control, are planning what to do next, and can see the big picture.

Think about Super Bowl competition; the two teams that have done the best over the years are the Dallas Cowboys and the Pittsburgh Steelers, both of whom have steady, competent coaches to do the thinking and planning, and both of whom let their players play the game. The coaches almost always seem calm and in command. Even the legendary Vince Lombardi, renowned for his emotional intensity, wasn't nearly the bear during games that he was in practice. The difference, even if it's just a little, is enough to get through to athletes, who take up the emotional slack and play with increased energy, while relying on the coach to do his or her job. This is what being a team is all about, having certain people perform separate functions. When the coach tries to do too much, the players can become too passive; and when the coach loses his or her cool in the heat of battle, he or she fails to fulfill the necessary role as the rock, the supportive foundation around which the individual athletes can extend themselves. That's what leadership under fire is all about.

Now what about you as an athlete? Your coach is going to be trying to do everything he or she can to help you, but the game comes

When the Game Is On

down to you. How can you best handle yourself in competition? Since your job is more important than your coach's, five guidelines aren't enough; there are six (some of which were just applied to your coach as well):

1. Focus all of your attention on yourself instead of on your opponent. You can't do anything about who your opponent is or what he or she is trying to do; you can only do your best. Once your opponent has gotten you thinking about him- or herself, about his or her strengths, style and so on, you have lost the first round in the battle. Your mind has been distracted from what you are trying to do on the field. Don't let this happen. Put your head into your own efforts as much as you possibly can.

2. Don't think too much about strategy, either. While you're thinking you're not acting, and your opponent probably is. I know of a basketball player who loved to catch a couple of his opponents talking to each other about strategy during a game. This guy would then loudly say, "They're in trouble—we've got 'em thinking." When an athlete stops to think, he or she is dead. Leave the strategy and the thinking to your coach; that's his or her job. Confine your thoughts to simple anticipations of what may happen on the very next play, and to your own efforts. Figuring longer-range strategy while you're playing is only for the most experienced of athletes. One reason why there are fewer and fewer player-coaches in sports today is that each job suffers when one tries to do both. Do your job in competition, and let the coach do his or hers.

3. Don't wait for your coach to pat you on the back when you do something well; pat yourself on the back, and do the same for your teammates. Inside your head, say, "Nice play," or "Good move" when you've done something well. This kind of internal positive reinforcement is just as important as what you get from the coach.

Even more important in properly reinforcing yourself during competition is using the ignore technique. When you foul up, don't kick yourself about it forever. Start thinking about the next play as soon as you can. You can think of this as having two coaches inside your head—a good coach and a bad coach. The good coach says, "Way to go" when you do well and encourages you to think about the next play when you've screwed up; the bad coach says nothing when you do well and jumps down your throat when you make an error. Don't let the bad coach win. Tell him or her to shut up, and listen to the good coach. This is not just a matter of making yourself feel better; you will actually play better if you listen to your good coach than if you let your bad coach run you into the ground.

4. Anticipate. During the brief lulls in play, think about what may happen next, and about what you are going to do in response. Too many athletes, especially younger ones, simply relax at these points, believing that this is the time to rest and that there's nothing they need to do. Nothing could be further from the truth. These are precisely the times when you should be thinking about your upcoming moves. If you wait until the play develops, it's already too late. One of the main differences between successful professional athletes and other athletes is that the pros are always aware of the situation and what they may be called on to do next. This also helps to keep your mind on the game, making it less likely that anything will distract you.

5. Which brings us to the next guideline: In competition, you want the focus of your attention to be as narrow as you can make it—on the game itself. You want to look at competition as your total occupation, so that you are always thinking about what to do next. Your coach will insist that you concentrate, and may even help you to do so, but it is your responsibility to keep your mind on what you're doing. If this is a problem for you, be sure to read Chapter 7 on Specific Individual Techniques very carefully to find the one that will help you to concentrate.

6. Finally, remember to *play*. I have referred to your "job" and what you "have to" do in competition, but it's equally important not to lose sight of the fact that you are playing a game. You started out playing this game for fun, and it should still be fun for you. As you've improved and gone on to higher levels of competition, more work and more pressure have been involved, but unless there's still at least a small feeling of enjoyment in it for you, you will never reach the top, no matter how hard you work. You need two things to keep at your best, energy and control, and the longer you play, the more your coaches will emphasize your being in control and not making mistakes. You have to remember that this is only half of the formula. The other half, energy, is just as important: it comes from your eagerness to play, to attack the game with all the intensity you did when you were a child, when you couldn't wait to get out of school so that you could pick up the ball and go. Don't let this become just a fond memory. Remind

yourself of that feeling before competition; it will help you to relax and play with nerve and spirit.

Conclusion

These guidelines will help both coaches and athletes to fill their roles better. Let me encourage you to try these things out and to pick and choose, discarding whatever doesn't work for you. The athletes and coaches around you will differ in their abilities to make use of these suggestions, so don't try to force them, or yourself, into a fixed pattern. Not everyone can be as cool as Tom Landry, as heady as Lenny Wilkens, or as eager as Pete Rose; but then you don't have to be. There are many pathways to success, and trying the strategies in this chapter will help you to broaden your approach.

CHECKLIST FOR COACHES AND ATHLETES

Emotions. Attitudes. Reinforcement. Practice. Momentum. The Readying Spot. Final countdown.

These issues and many others have been presented as parts of the readying process. I hope that you feel you have a better handle on these problems now, and perhaps one or two of the techniques are already finding their way into your planning. Trying to use all of what's been said would be impossible, and some of the material will undoubtedly fade from your memory.

This chapter consists of an outline of the factors we have been considering, and some added thoughts about how the sport you play may interact with your own abilities to determine your proper readying approach. This outline is offered as a preseason checklist that coaches and athletes can use to help them survey the whole area of preparation and performance. Reviewing it at the beginning of a period of practice and preparation—whether that period is a full professional season or a summer's worth of social golf or readying for one major competition—can help you to plan better. You will recall the pluses and minuses of past plans, practices, and competitions, with the opportunity to do things differently this time.

This outline is suggested for preseason use because that's when your planning needs to begin. All too often coaches map out the physical preparation of their athletes in great detail ahead of time, while mental and emotional factors come into the coach's awareness only after (1) the physical necessities have been covered, (2) competition has begun, or (3) (and this is the worst possible time) psychological problems and mental errors have begun to appear. Coaches often try to apply some quick, magical technique in midstream, but proper integration of psychological learning principles into the athlete's long-term physical preparation would have worked much better. The earlier you plan your practices to cover physical *and* mental preparation, the better.

Use this checklist in conjunction with the *Athletic Performance Improvement Survey*, and pick out the crucial factors you want to do something about. Then refer to the techniques offered here.

Factors that determine competitive performance

All of the factors pertaining to performance can be classified. In understanding how a person will perform a task, there are four main elements to consider:

1. Information about the task—what is the task, how long is it, how familiar is it, when is it, what does it demand from you?
2. Information about the person—who will do the task, what are this person's abilities and characteristics in anything he or she does?
3. What has the person done in the past regarding this task— how has he or she prepared for the task, how has he or she performed on this task before, and so on?
4. What were the readying activities done just before the task?

These four elements form the basis of the four Major Factor Areas to be discussed here. The first two elements are fairly obvious. They represent information that has nothing to do with time; they are characteristics of the task (like length and equipment) and the person (like strength and intelligence) that are true of the task or the person at any time.

The other two elements, however, do involve time. What the person does with the task has a life span, starting with the very first thing he or she did in preparing for the task and lasting through the performance. Thus, a swimmer competing in a specific Olympic event at a specific time has a history going all the way back to his or her first learning how to swim. Let's break this life span into two parts: (1) all task-person information from Day 1 to performance time, and (2) the immediate task-person interaction, or what goes on immediately prior to and during the performance. We can apply the four Major Factor

Areas to the performance of our Olympic swimmer:

Factor Area 1. What are the relevant characteristics of the task?

Factor Area 2. What are the relevant characteristics of our swimmer?

Factor Area 3. What swimming-related things has our swimmer done up to this particular performance?

Factor Area 4. What has our swimmer done *immediately* prior to and during his or her performance?

These questions are general, and every coach or athlete would answer them differently. Use this checklist as you see fit, incorporating the appropriate techniques and strategies described in Chapters 2–7.

Major Factor Area 1—task characteristics

What things are characteristic of your task, as compared to other tasks, regardless of who is performing it? The answers to this question comprise Factor Area One. Fully understanding the dimensions of the task at hand can serve as a strong foundation on which to build a readying program. Simply saying that your task is "football" or "chess" is not enough; a linebacker's task is different from that of a wide receiver. Let's look closely at the smaller pieces of activity that make up the overall task, so that your readying can be precise.

Tasks differ from one another in the following dimensions:

1. Physical requirements: Of the many ways the body can behave, what does your task require? How much movement? How much speed? How much quickness? Does it require strength? Endurance? How much precision does it require?

Some further notes on *speed* and *quickness* may be in order here. Speed is not only speed of foot; coaches and sports analysts speak of hand speed in a boxer, or of overall speed in sports like wrestling or batting a baseball. In these instances, the word *speed* refers to how rapidly some specific action can be performed (like how quickly a hitter can get the bat through the strike zone) and not to running speed. You may want to break your sport down into two or more kinds of necessary speed and rate the need for each. Apply the concept of *speed* wherever it seems to apply.

244   *Checklist for Coaches and Athletes*

But speed is not the same thing as quickness, which usually describes how quickly you can respond to something that happens during competition. Quickness often requires anticipation. A goalie, for example, may not be able to run very quickly, but quick reactions are vital. The same can be said of the requirements for a baseball infielder or a tennis player who likes to rush the net. Distance runners and swimmers, on the other hand, fall at the other end of the spectrum, since they need very little quickness to excel. In thinking about your sport's demand for quickness, consider overall quickness separately from the need for quickness in certain body parts or in a small area. (For example, the overall quickness required of a goalie is different from the hand quickness of a baseball catcher with a "live" pitcher on the mound.)

2. Mental requirements: What mental operations does your task entail? Does it require high intelligence or a good memory? Does it require verbal ability or spatial ability? Does it pose problems? Does it require specific information? Try to give as much attention to the mental requirements of your sport as you give to the physical. Intelligence, memory, and problem-solving abilities are different mental abilities, as speed, strength, and endurance are different physical abilities. Fitting the athlete to the sport on these mental dimensions is very important.

Great intelligence and exceptional memory are not required by most sports; problem solving, on the other hand, often is. A soccer player, for example, needs to size up a complicated spatial arrangement of players, the field, and the ball, and decide how best to take advantage of it. This kind of "headiness," or game sense, is helpful in many games, and is often required by one position in a sport more than by another. Baseball infielders, for example, who frequently handle the ball in tightly timed situations, generally need more of this quality than do outfielders. While problem-solving ability is a plus in any sport, at certain positions it is a must. If your sport requires it, don't assume that it will take care of itself.

3. Complexity: Is your task a quick, simple one or more complex? Does it require making sense of complicated cues, signals, keys or other bits of information? Are the activities themselves simple or complex and varied?

Perhaps the simplest kind of sport is the sprint. The athlete needs to respond to only one cue, the starter's gun, and needs to do only one thing: run as quickly as possible. Other sports have increasingly complex cues and behaviors. Middle linebackers in football must respond to many cues that are often disguised by the opponent. In addition, he or she must respond to these cues in many different ways, depending on what they say. He or she may run left or right, up or back, make a tackle or defend against a pass. This position is complex both in what the athlete has to attend to and in what he has to do. Golf, on the other hand, can be complex in its cues (the lie, the wind, the texture of the green), but simple in its action—the golfer ties to do one thing, to hit the ball where he or she wants to. (I do not mean to suggest that this is easy to do, only that there is one action at a time, with plenty of time to prepare oneself.) Simple-cue–complex-action sports are gymnastics and figure skating. The cues are fixed (the arena, the ice, and so on), and the competitor is simply told when to start. Then a series of complex behaviors follows, with little response to externals along the way.

The complexity of cues and behaviors can distinguish which sports a given athlete may be good at; this should be considered in planning and practice. Refer to the section on attention in Chapter 4 to help you with your planning.

4. Feedback patterns: Does your task provide you with information about how you are doing as you're doing it? How regularly? How can you use this information while competing?

5. Action-reaction continuum: Is your activity self-initiated, or does it begin in response to what someone else does? Is it mixed? Bowling and golf are examples of totally self-initiated sports; hitting a baseball or playing goalie in soccer or hockey forces the athlete to react. The self-initiated/reactive difference will often determine which of two sports or positions a particular athlete will be better at. The offensive and defensive lines in football are two positions in which this is a consideration. Although both positions require strength, agility, and quickness, the offensive players have planned, self-run plays to execute, while the defensive players must react to whatever happens to them. The distinction between offensive receivers and defensive backs is a similar one. The coach should choose, from a large group of physically similar players, the ones who temperamentally are better suited to attack or defend, to act or react, and make the position assignments accordingly.

6. Duration: How long does your task last? How long do the different parts of the overall task last? Is the duration constant, or can you make it shorter or longer, faster- or slower-paced?

7. Person contact: To what extent does your task involve contact with people? Are the activities competitive? Cooperative? Strictly individual? How many people are involved? How do these contacts with people affect you?

Checklist for Coaches and Athletes

8. Significance: Is the task itself important? Is it fun?

9. Specific characteristics: What other characteristics of your task are important to performance? What are unique?

10. Other characteristics: Anything else you can observe about your task?

Major Factor Area 2—personal characteristics

What things are characteristic of you as an individual, regardless of what task you might be asked to do? Countless psychology books and psychiatric methods have dealt with the personality of the individual, the long-standing characteristics of persons, so the last word on this issue will not be found here. But in-depth psychological analysis is not the goal of this approach. Think instead about those characteristics that might *directly* influence your performance. Most of these have already been covered in some detail, so I will simply list them here. Refer to the appropriate chapter and section for each. In Major Factor Area 2 we are considering characteristics of people that take a lot of time and energy to change. We are looking at these factors not so much in order to change or control them, but to be aware of each person's qualities, for purposes of (1) matching that athlete with the right sport or position, and (2) planning the practice or precompetition situation to take advantage of the person's strengths and downplay his or her weakness.

1. Physical characteristics: What are your physical abilities and liabilities? What are your abilities as far as size, movement, and strength? What specific physical activities are you particularly good or bad at? Can you affect these physical qualities? How?

2. Mental characteristics: What are your mental abilities and liabilities? How do you rate your intelligence, memory, verbal skills, spatial relations, and problem-solving abilities? Do you have specific knowledge that can be used to your advantage? How do you best take in information?

3. Emotional characteristics: What is your general emotional makeup? How much flexibility do you show emotionally? Do you have access to specific emotional states of mind? Have you had much practice at controlling and using your emotions?

4. Interactional style: What is your usual mode of dealing with people? Do you prefer situations that are competitive, cooperative, or

individual? Do you have particular interactional behaviors or skills that can be capitalized on, or ones that could be disadvantageous? What can you do about them?

5. Attention focusing: What are your abilities regarding attention focusing and concentration? How long is your attention span for various subjects, especially for aspects of your sport?

6. Early Development Set: In relation to your sport or to sports in general, what is your history of watching, planning, dreaming, and so on, to participate in that activity? Do you have specific images about your sport? How early did these images and dreams start? When did they peak, or start to decline? Can you still recall them; do they help you to prepare for competition?

7. Discipline: What are your attitudes toward and ability to control your own activities—physically, mentally, emotionally, and in terms of concentration? Do you have abilities or problems with exercising control in specific areas? To what extent do you see yourself as responsible for your own performance?

8. Other personal characteristics: Anything else that can be observed about yourself that is related to performance issues?

Major Factor Area 3—task–person history: prior performance and practice

This and the next Major Factor Area consider a specific person and a specific task *together*, and therefore deal not with overall abilities but with the person's activities regarding the task (for example, you as a tennis player). Area 3 can be broken down into two major categories, with further subcategories:

1. Prior performance: What is your history of performing your specific task or sport, on those occasions when you were actually in a performance situation and not just practicing? Issues to be considered here include:

 1. Time and amount of performance: How experienced are you as a performer of this task? How many actual performances have you had, and over what period of time? Is this a plus or a minus for you?
 2. Reinforcement for performance: What factors contribute to your wanting to perform? Which contributed to good or bad performance in the past? Have you been positively rein-

forced for performing? Have you been punished for not performing or for performing poorly? What specific reinforcers, either from others or from you, have been operating in the past?

3. Long-term performance cycle: How frequently have performances occurred in the past? How frequently have good performances occurred in the past? What has been your optimum between-performances rest period?

4. Social environment: How much support from family, friends, and others have you received for performing this activity? For performing well? Is the social situation conducive to effort and achievement in this area?

2. Practice: What is your history of practicing this task? How, when, where, and why have you practiced? Specifically:

1. Time and amount: How much have you practiced, and over what period of time?

2. Reinforcement for practicing: What factors contribute to your wanting to practice, or to practice hard? Which factors contributed to practicing well or poorly in the past? Were you rewarded for practicing, or punished for not practicing? What specific reinforcers, at what specific practice points, were operating?

3. Long-term performance cycle: How does your practice schedule relate to your performance schedule? Where in your long-term performance cycle have practices been used heavily or been cut back, and with what success?

4. Effort pattern: What pattern of effort has produced your best performances in the past? Have you gone on to perform better when you have practiced steadily, or when vacations from practice have been mixed in? What is the best ratio of practice to vacations for you?

5. Whole and partial learning: How do you respond to practicing parts of the overall performance activity? Do you tend to perform better after practicing specific skills or after practicing the whole performance? How can these two approaches be mixed appropriately?

6. Structure: Do you respond better to practice that is highly structured, or loose? What are the effects of regularity, planning, repetition, and comprehensive scheduling on you? How can these issues best be handled?

7. Person contact: Do you respond better to practice activities involving other people or to those in which you are on your

own? Are competitive or cooperative practice situations more helpful?

8. Social environment: Are your practice activities supported by family, friends, and others? Do other performers support your practice efforts? Is the overall social situation conducive to your spending time and energy on necessary practice? How much practice can you tolerate before other social commitments begin to suffer, which then detract from the positive aspects of practice?

9. Motivation: Are you motivated to practice? What are the sources of this motivation? Is the motivation sufficient to overcome the inevitable tedium of practice?

10. Attitude: Do you practice with a positive attitude, commitment, and energy? Is this necessary for you to perform well later?

11. Coaching: What role does your coach or teacher play in determining the practice regimen? What activities and attitudes form helpful coaching techniques for you? How can your coach help in your psychological readying?

12. Other practice issues: What other issues are relevant to your practice schedules?

Major Factor Area 4—immediate task–person performance conditions: the last 48 hours

We can now turn to the immediate performance conditions to see how they can affect performance. These conditions (thoughts, feelings, location, activities, and so on at the time of or immediately prior to your performance) will be broken down into two types: *internal conditions*, and *external, or more general, conditions*. Remember as you read these lists that neither certain feelings nor certain situations will always be associated with good performance for all athletes or on all tasks; rather, the question to be asked is how feeling X or Y usually affects *your* performance on a given task. Focus on conditions during or just before competition.

Unlike the discussion of Major Factor Area 2, we will be looking at transitory states: thoughts, feelings, and external conditions that can be arranged to put the athlete into the readiest state. Major Factor Area 4 considers the combination of the way that the individual athlete feels right now, and what the other performing conditions are. These things can often be changed, or at least emphasized or deemphasized, and will vary from contest to contest, even for a particular athlete. You are not exactly the same every time you compete, and neither are the circumstances.

1. Internal conditions:

1. Motivation: How motivated are you to do well on the upcoming task? Does this usually affect your performance?
2. Emotion: How do you feel? Good, bad, or some other specific feelings?
3. Physical condition: Do you see yourself as physically ready and able to do well?
4. Attitude of importance: Does the upcoming event seem important to you? Does this usually help or hinder your performance?
5. Knowledge: Do you have all the knowledge and information necessary to do well? Do you feel comfortable with the necessary information, or is it unclear, too complex, or too extensive? Are the informational aspects of the event obscuring appropriate emotional readying?
6. Anticipated outcome: Do you anticipate success or failure? Which usually leads to better performance?
7. World significance: Do you see your performance as having importance beyond your own circumstances; that is, will it significantly affect other people? Does this tend to help or hinder performance for you?
8. Confidence in self: Do you feel confident that you will perform well? How does this usually affect performance? Remember the difference between anticipated outcome and confidence: One is your feeling about overall success or failure, while the other refers only to how well you feel you'll perform.
9. Confidence in others: Do you feel confidence in any other people with whom you may be cooperating during the performance?
10. Locus of control: Do you see the performance outcome as being under your own control, under someone else's, or under no one's (luck, divine intervention, and so on)? Under which circumstances do you usually perform best?
11. Attention focus: To what extent is all your attention focused on the upcoming event? Are distractions to concentration a factor? With what degree of concentration do you usually perform best?

2. External, general conditions:

1. Environment: Where and when will the performance occur? What is the weather, time of day, and so on? How do these factors usually affect you?
2. Equipment: Do you have the necessary equipment? Are you familiar with it?
3. Person contact: Do you have contact with others immediately prior to and during performance? Will this help or hurt?
4. Warmup: How much (if at all) does your warmup affect performance?
5. Non-task intrusions: To what extent do issues not related to performance intrude on your attention? Does this help or hurt?
6. Considerations of cycle: Where does the upcoming event fall in the cycle of performances? How recent was your last event? Is this one of a long line of performances? How does each of your internal conditions fit into a cycle; for example, if you feel motivated to do well and usually perform well with that feeling, how recently and frequently have you been so motivated in the past?
7. Performance-bound occurrences: How do things that occur as part of the performance (falling behind in a competition, seeing another person do well or poorly, starting out well or poorly yourself) affect you?
8. Task difficulty: How difficult is the upcoming event going to be? How does this usually affect your performance?
9. Familiarity: How familiar are all aspects of the internal and external conditions listed here? How do these particular familiarities affect performance? What part does ritual behavior play in helping you to feel ready to do well?
10. Reinforcers: What factors contribute to your wanting to perform at this particular time and place? Have these usually led to good performance? Will you be positively or negatively reinforced for good and bad performance? What specific reinforcers, either from others or from you, are operating in this event.

These are the main factors to be considered. Rather than having you try to apply them blindly, let me remind you of the overall perspective implicit in the readying approach by emphasizing three points:

First, in studying the preceding lists of performance factors, note the overlap between positive and negative factors. Everything can be either a potential help or a potential hindrance. In an effort to simplify preparations, coaches characteristically teach that certain feelings, thoughts, or conditions are always helpful (e.g., anxiety, fear of the event, and eagerness). The Readying Approach suggests otherwise, saying that any given factor can be either a positive or a negative influence, depending on the individuals and events involved. (The seeds of this perspective are beginning to become evident in today's athletic world, as people are willing to assume that certain factors, particularly the significance of the event, can help or hinder, depending on individual circumstances.) Thus, creating an individual profile of performance patterns, based on these various factors, is the most efficient approach.

Second, the fact that Factor Areas 3 and 4 are interactions of person and task needs to be emphasized. Certain decisions about how best to prepare yourself cannot be made only on the basis of who the person is or what the task is; they must be combined. If this sounds obvious, consider how widespread is what I call the *Prime Coaching Fallacy*: Because the sport I coach is what it is, everyone needs to do (or think or feel) certain things; otherwise, they can't be ready to perform well. This represents a direct jump from Factor Area 1 to areas 3 and 4: from the task to the practice and preparation. Some coaches who have recognized the problems with this jump are beginning to pay attention to individual characteristics, usually in terms of the few "psych cases" on their team. The hard job is to combine task and person considerations without giving precedence or overwhelming importance to either one.

Let's look at an example. Coach Jones is a college football coach. Two athletes on his team, Tom and Dick, are both important to the team's success and are having big matchups this week. Tom is at practice as usual all week, working hard, so Coach Jones "knows" he'll be ready. But Dick had a bad week. He missed one practice session because of an exam, and then was sick the next day and stayed home. And the third day wasn't too good because he was weak and couldn't work out hard. When game time comes, Coach Jones thinks Tom will be ready but Dick won't be.

By these traditional standards, Coach Jones has explanations for any pattern of performance that Dick, the "slacker," may show:

If he does well, Dick is exceptional—he succeeded in spite of the week's problems, overcoming his handicap.

If he does poorly, Coach Jones "knew" it all along, so it's no surprise.

In spite of the fact that Dick may have done well without good, steady practice (and every coach knows this to happen, at least from time to time), Coach Jones still maintains his belief that hard, steady effort is the way to insure doing well. The alternative is rarely considered: Dick may have done well not *in spite* of his layoff, but *because* of it. Perhaps his individual readying should include a layoff, and less hard work than Tom. That's what I mean by looking for the individual determinants of good performance.

This is one example of how people can maintain beliefs in spite of evidence to the contrary, but it is not meant to show that hard, steady practice is wrong; in fact, it's probably necessary for most people to do well. The point is that "most" people is not the same as "all" people, so designing practice or preparation procedures that are uniform for all athletes will ensure some poor performances. This is even truer of other factors, like emotions and thoughts, that are much less easy to apply to most people.

The third and final point is this: The list of factors outlined above is, by definition, incomplete. Anything, listed or not, can be an important factor in determining individual performance. This outline is based on study and observation of a great many athletes in different sports; it should cover most of the common points to be considered: But *most* and *common* are not good enough. Each individual must find which of these factors and which other factors affect his or her performance. That's why the Readying Approach has two phases: observation and application. If the coach or athlete expects to skip the self-observation phase and go directly to applying the things I have said about the four areas, he or she will greatly diminish the power and utility of the Readying Approach.

Checklist for Coaches and Athletes

PUTTING IT ALL TOGETHER

The mind is a complicated thing; it can take in so many pieces of information and behave in so many different ways that it makes the most complex computer look like a toy. This book has focused on using the mind to get the body ready for physical competition, and even that comparatively small chore has included many facets of the mind's functioning, as well as many other things that athletes and coaches can do to get ready. How can you possibly coordinate all these facets at once? How can you integrate all you have learned about your own readying into one comprehensive, useful plan? How can you juggle elements that are so hard to see or touch?

I wish there were a simple answer to these questions, but there isn't. Putting it all together takes practice and time: You try this, you try that, you keep what works for you and discard what doesn't. It is a process of learning and growing, of knowing more and more about yourself.

Some suggestions can help you go about this process. First, set out on this task in a step-by-step manner. Don't expect to revolutionize your own readying all at once; if it were that simple, every athlete would already be reaching his or her potential, and every coach would field perfectly prepared teams. Give yourself an ample trial period for each new technique you try, and try not to be in a hurry to see dramatic changes. Even for athletes who do see relatively quick improvements, it usually takes a few months before the new readying step becomes a comfortable part of their readying. The emphasis here is not on quick remedies, but on steady improvement.

Equally important is the need to avoid assuming that I have "said it all" here, or that the Readying Approach can do it *for* you. You have to do it, and these techniques are merely your tools. Tools don't build a house; people using tools do. My words and suggestions, and the techniques themselves, have as their goal making you think about yourself and your own readying. They are guides on where to look and how to proceed, but the exact content of your readying changes is up to you. If the many strategies laid out here do not prod you into seeing yourself in different ways, then they can have only limited effect. No one fully understands exactly what makes each individual different, or how chemistry makes the difference between great and not-so-great teams, or how everything has to fit together to achieve high-level competitive success. This book is a step in that direction, but only a step in a search that you, as a coach or athlete committed to improving your performance, must continue.

We can identify seven main points that serve as the foundation for each of the specific techniques; they can be used as a quick review, even after you have incorporated the Readying Approach into your own preparatory procedures. Especially when you feel that you have done the mechanics of your readying correctly but the results have not met your expectations, refer back to these concepts and apply them in your own way to your situation.

Fundamental Units—In readying, there are three human units to consider: *thoughts*, *feelings*, and *behaviors*. Dealing only with behaviors will not get the job done. When an athlete is performing beneath his or her capabilities in competition, look for reasons and solutions in each of the three areas, which comprise all that we are. Everything the athlete does or says can be classified in one of these three categories. Use them as your first step in assessing any readying issue.

The Basic Tools of Learning and Change—There are three: *reinforcement*, *shaping*, and *modeling*. While thoughts, feelings, and behaviors are the raw materials, reinforcement, shaping, and modeling are the methods of working with these raw materials. These three tools are based on the human mind's natural approach to dealing with the world. Whatever the goal, a moment or two of thought concerning how to use one or more of these tools can only help. The behavior of your athletes is the product of what learning they have already done; it

Putting It All Together

reflects what has been reinforced, shaped, and modeled. These three tools go far beyond the limited value of verbal descriptions in getting into the athlete's performance pattern. They give the coach, and the athlete who builds them into his or her workouts, some real leverage. As Chapter 4 pointed out, if you master nothing but reinforcement, you can still be one heck of a coach or athlete.

Observation and Action.—There are two steps in solving any readying problem: first, observing closely to see exactly what is going on, and what helps or hinders; and second, taking action. Both phases need to be tailored to the individual athlete, but there's no way that this can be done in the action phase if it isn't done first in the observation phase. Keep the two separate, and be sure to take the time to observe your own actions carefully before jumping at a solution. For coaches, this often means asking the athlete what he or she thinks is going on, instead of just telling him or her to try something new. Use the APIS with some serious thought, and then take whatever action seems appropriate.

Additionally, there are things that coaches can watch out for in their athletes: physical signs that can indicate what is going on inside the athlete, usually in terms of tension. Before competition, check out these behaviors:

Hands. Are the hands open and relaxed or in a tight fist? Both hands in tight fists is usually indicative of excessive tension, while completely open hands usually indicate less than optimal arousal. I've seen athletes have one hand clenched (usually the hand they favor) and the other open, which indicates a mid-range of tension. Which is best varies with the individuals, but the extremes can warn the observant coach.

Head and Neck. Flexibility is again the key here. Some athletes don't rotate their head on the neck naturally when they are extremely tense. If you approach them from the side they may move only their eyes, or they may turn their whole body mechanically, instead of first turning their head in your direction. These extremes suggest some relaxing intervention, maybe just some words aimed at loosening him or her up.

Trunk and Gait. Does the trunk of the athlete's body rotate naturally when he or she walks? The ideal is a mid-range flexibility somewhere between the tight walk of a robot and the loose walk of a clown.

The best time to observe these signs is when the athlete is walking out to warm up. The extremes tend to be most pronounced at that time, and it still leaves the coach a little time to intervene. Of course, that is also a very busy time for coach and athletes alike, but it's worth the trouble to make these observations, especially if the athlete has indicated in some other way questionable readiness. After all, what is more important at this time than readying?

The better you observe, the better you will ready. You don't go into competition without information about the game, so don't try to do your readying without first gathering some information.

Energy and Control—The athlete needs to play with as much energy as he or she can control. If too much emphasis is put on energy, high-spirited but mistake-filled play occurs; if too much emphasis is placed on control, the natural flow of the athlete at play is disrupted, leading to limited aggressiveness, range, and so on. This is a classic coach's dilemma, and which factor to emphasize with each athlete is one of the first decisions you must make when building any individual readying program. Almost every athlete is stronger in one or the other, and needs training in the weaker area.

The goal is to balance the two. A natural flow of activity, springing from the athlete's childlike desire to play, must be organized into a particular way of doing things. Often two or more coaches can work together to build this balance, with one emphasizing arousal while the other models self-possession and control. The happy marriage of these two attributes makes for the best athletic play, and any readying countdown must address itself to these issues.

Routine and Flexibility—The need for structure, routine, familiarity, and order must be counterbalanced by flexibility. Because I've already described in detail what I mean by routine, and because most coaches and athletes naturally establish some pattern, I'll focus on flexibility here.

Flexibility is the opposite of rigidity. Flexibility means that, no matter what you normally expect all athletes to do, you can tolerate some deviation. This shows itself in three ways. First, and most central, is the realization that *Peak Performance* is about *individual* readying, and that individual differences in readying are not only to be tolerated but also to be encouraged. Essentially, the Readying Approach is a personal one. Athletic competition has two main elements: the particular sport, and the person who will do the playing. Heretofore, most theories of how to prepare for competition have been based almost solely on what the sport is, what it demands, and so on. Football players are to be prepared in one way, hockey goalies in another, and swimmers in another. The Readying Approach turns this around and says, "Whatever the sport is, it's the person playing it who should determine what kind of readying needs to be done." This is a fundamental shift, and requires flexibility from coaches and athletes. Of course, the ideal preparation involves both of these perspectives; *Peak Performance* emphasizes the latter because it is underemphasized today.

Flexibility also involves the recognition and acceptance of fluctuations in athletic performance. No one is perfect every day, and growth is not always perfectly steady. While patterns of effort and accomplishment should be steady, real people don't work that way. Coaches and athletes should both know this, not because it provides an excuse for laziness and failure but because the fluctuations of your life can be used to your advantage. Inadequate coaches and athletes won't tolerate fluctuation, good ones will tolerate it, and experts will use it. Maintaining flexibility in your approach to your sport is in no way detrimental to order and ritual. In fact, if your readying countdowns are well-planned and ordered, so that you can feel satisfied with your efforts in this area, you will be much more likely to be able to tolerate whatever smaller fluctuations do occur.

And third, flexibility shows itself as creativity and curiosity. Both coach and athlete should constantly be seeking new approaches to readying. The Readying Approach is not meant to be just one more lock-step list of instructions for you to follow—it is much more important that you look for and try new things, maintaining an attitude of openness to innovation and change. Be creative in your readying, and you will naturally find what readies you best.

Performance and Outcome—The appropriate goal of positive readying is *performance* at or near the top of the individual's range—not winning. Obviously, good performance and winning go hand in hand, but on those occasions when they don't it is critical to focus on performance. If the readying process is cluttered with concerns about winning, which is something you essentially can't control, it detracts from the focus on performance. This wastes energy and diffuses attention, which are central to good play. The only worthwhile goal for any athlete is to be the best he or she can be.

Responsibility and Opportunity—Each athlete is ultimately responsible for his or her own performance. You continually have the opportunity to better yourself and your play, and the committed athlete accepts this responsibility. *Peak Performance* is an attempt to expand the number of arenas in which you can control your performance. No longer must you do your physical workouts and blindly try to "make" yourself, in some highly emotional but undefined way, ready to play. Here you are given the nuts and bolts of readying: what it means to be ready and how to bring about such a state. Each individual must help him- or herself, and not look to others to make him or her ready.

Moreover, I always encourage athletes to see this as an opportunity. Undoubtedly, there are things in this book that you haven't tried, and now you can. Competitive sports require application and work but should also be play. Approach them with this in mind, and it will seem like a real opportunity to know the joy of reaching out to your limits. The brief episodes of effort and achievement in competition will grow, and they will stay with you in other areas of life.

These are the seven major points, but there are other things, too: the Readying Spot, coach-athlete communication, imagery, attitudes, attention, the countdown, the *feeling*, and so on. What all of these have in common is the concept of readying itself. There are many different ways to look at the world of sport: as play, as work, as a sign of what is wrong with our society or what is right with it. The perspective here is that of getting yourself ready to perform, whatever the context of the performance. The Readying Approach can be used in almost any performance situation: a musical recital, a final exam, or in learning any new skill. When performance is part of the activity, getting yourself psychologically ready is an integral part of the task.

In fact everything you do can be seen as readying. All that you do readies you for the next performance. The challenge is to learn how to get yourself ready, to take a step back from the performance itself. Readying relates to performance the way that cooking relates to eating: You don't want to be a "raw" athlete whose main attribute is physical potential, and you certainly don't want to go into competition half-baked. That's why we all need a recipe for good, comprehensive readying.

In whatever preparatory work you do, make getting your mind right a priority. Don't let the word *psychological* throw you; all it really means is the thoughts and feelings that you have inside. These things are familiar to you, and calling this method of readying *psychological* means simply that you will be paying more attention to these already familiar parts. You know what it feels like to be ready for competition;

getting that sense of mental and emotional readiness should be high on your list, right alongside the physical readying. Taking this psychological approach to getting yourself ready won't undermine your physical training techniques or your sense of game strategy or any other part of your competitive self. It will simply add to these other facets of sport. This will give you a total program of self-improvement, in which you use everything at your command to be consistently at the top of your game. After all, every real athlete knows that playing at the top of your game is what it's all about. So give it your best shot—get ready.

APPENDIX:
Evaluating athletes for
emotional energy and control

Physical ability is the single most important attribute of the successful athlete; but once an individual possesses the necessary physical skills to compete at a high level, psychological characteristics determine how successful that athlete will be at performing consistently well in actual competition. Peak performance requires both physical and mental superiority.

Consequently, a complete plan for evaluating athletes must include psychological assessment. This approach identifies athletes who are psychologically equipped to compete well—who can play with both emotional energy (intensity) and control (poise). It also assesses whether coach and athlete are a good fit and could reasonably expect to progress toward their ultimate goal, top performance.

Competent psychological evaluation requires more than merely having the athlete fill out a questionnaire that gives one, all-encompassing, competitiveness score. There simply is no "winner" test. For this reason, this evaluation plan collects information about the athlete in three ways: by having him or her fill out a personal athletic survey, by talking with the athlete, and by watching his or her "mental game" in actual competition. The process yields an overall athletic profile: a brief description of the athlete's mental/emotional strengths and weaknesses, so that the coach can make knowledgeable selections from among athletes of similar physical abilities.

The evaluation requires five main steps and is carried out by a trained sport psychologist, the coach, and the athlete.

ATHLETE ASSESSMENT PLAN

Phase	Activity	Participants
I.	Physical Assessment	Coaches, trainers, etc.
II.	Psychological Assessment A. Athletic Performance Improvement Survey B. Structured Interview C. Observation in Competition D. Emotional Energy and Control Profile	Athlete Athlete and Sport Psychologist Sport Psychologist Sport Psychologist
III.	Athlete/Coach Personal Interview	Athlete/Coach
IV.	Coach/Evaluator Meeting	Coach and Sport Psychologist
V.	Final Selection of Athletes	Coach

ATHLETE-ASSESSMENT OUTLINE

I. Selection of Athletes Based on Physical Abilities. First, the coaches, trainers, scouts, and other staff familiar with the physical demands of the sport select from the entire group of available athletes those who meet at least the minimum physical standards necessary to compete well. The emphasis is not only on selecting the top physical specimens but also on identifying athletes who meet minimum physical standards. Then, psychological assessment is carried out only on this physically-able group of athletes. This preliminary physical selection process: (a) quickly eliminates the athletes who physically could not compete well, while (b) keeping in the pool of potential athletes those who have only moderate physical skills but who may prove to be exceptional competitors on the psychological testing to follow. Final athlete selection then rests on the combination of physical and psychological strengths and weaknesses.

II. Psychological Assessment by Sport Psychologist. Once the athlete has passed the initial physical checkpoint, he or she meets with the sport psychologist for evaluation of mental and emotional qualities. Evaluation consists of four main parts:

1. First, the athlete is given the Athletic Performance Improvement Survey, or APIS (Appendix B). This self-administered, 73-item survey asks the athlete for information about how he or she prepares for competition and under what conditions he or she performs best. It is used by the sport psychologist in rating, on the APIS Rating Sheet, the athlete's experience and knowledge of positive performance conditions. Such knowledge and experience are good indicators of the athlete's ability to perform well when it's time to do so.

2. The sport psychologist meets with the athlete to conduct the Structured Interview. Using the Sample Question sheet as a guideline, the evaluator helps the athlete to discuss attitudes, emotional strengths and weaknesses, social environment, competitiveness, and overall attitude toward the sport in question. The evaluator then rates the athlete's responses on the Structured Interview Rating sheet.

3. The third stage of the general psychological assessment is to observe the athlete in actual competition. The sport psychologist takes note of the athlete's sureness of action, powers of attention and concentration, knowledge of the sport, aggressiveness, reactions under pressure, effort, and self-control in competition. The evaluator specifically does not assess the athlete's physical abilities; rather, psychological training permits closer observation of the mental and emotional aspects of competing. After observing the athlete, the evaluator fills out the Observation in Competition Rating sheet.

4. In order to put this information into a concise, manageable form that will be useful to the coach, the sport psychologist fills out the athlete's Emotional Energy and Control Profile sheet, which combines the ratings from each assessment technique: self-report (APIS), interview, and observation. It is this final Profile Sheet which will be shared with the coach.

The most important mental attribute the athlete needs in order to perform well is *emotional energy*—energy to play hard, to be intense, and to practice long hours. But when emotional energy is very high in competition, athletes sometimes get out of control—they make mistakes, lose their precision and fluidity. That's why the second important mental attribute of the superior athlete is *control*. Psychologically, top athletes bring high emotional energy to their sport and can remain poised and planful even in the extreme ranges of energy and effort. It is the balance of these two mental attributes that is critical, as reflected in the Profile Sheet. Additionally, it includes other important points about the individual athlete. Finally, a short summary and overall rating of the athlete's psychological profile are provided.

III. Personal Interview with Coach. After being evaluated by the sport psychologist, the athlete meets with the coach (or coaches) with whom he or she would be working later. In contrast to the objective, clinical information gathered in Phase II, this coach/athlete meeting is meant to be a "get to know each other" session. The coach's task is to get a feel for how well he or she could work with this athlete. This personal assessment is often a critical step in choosing the select few athletes who are found to be both physically and psychologically suited to compete well and who fit well with the coach's style of training.

IV. Coach/Evaluator Meeting. Coach and sport psychologist share their impressions of each athlete. The coach brings knowledge of the physical skills of the athlete and feelings about how well the athlete will work under him or her; the sport psychologist brings attitudinal, emotional, and behavioral data that describes the athlete's strengths and weaknesses in terms of the psychological ability to compete well.

V. Final Selection of Athletes. A combination of these perspectives yields the final, selected athletes—the ones who (1) are physically skilled, (2) are psychologically suited to do well, and (3) fit into the coach's plans for overall competitive success.

ATHLETIC PERFORMANCE IMPROVEMENT SURVEY (APIS) RATING

Based on the insightfulness and completeness of the athlete's responses on the APIS, rate the athlete's overall level of experience and knowledge about him- or herself in preparing to perform well in this sport. Circle the appropriate rating.

> Exceptional— Extensive and complete readying knowledge of self in competition given in exceptional clarity and detail.
>
> Above Average— Has good knowledge of self in competition and a specific plan of readying.

> Average— Answers all questions, but no clear picture of a definite readying style emerges.

> Below Average— Only vague self-awareness, usually of strictly physical things like rest, food, and so on.

> Poor— No awareness of readying factors in preparing self for competition.

SAMPLE QUESTIONS FOR STRUCTURED INTERVIEW BETWEEN ATHLETE AND EVALUATOR

1. How (and when) did you get interested in this sport?
2. Describe yourself as an athlete, compared to others, in terms of how you play the game (especially your strengths and weaknesses as a competitive athlete).
3. What are the 2–3 biggest contests you've ever faced? Describe.
4. Do you feel you know how to prepare yourself? How do you?
5. Do you like to compete?
6. How do you usually feel before competing? In a "big" contest?
7. Do you feel you can control your emotions in big contests, or do they sometimes "take over"?
8. How do family and friends feel about you playing this sport?
9. How do you feel about making (or possibly making) this team?
10. How badly do you want to do this?

STRUCTURED INTERVIEW RATING

Circle the appropriate rating for each performance factor.

1. General Attitude and Motivation—What is this athlete's general attitude toward this sport (event, position, etc.)?

> Exceptional—His or her top priority, without question.
> Above Average—Evidence of long and strong commitment.
> Average—Definitely wants to play.
> Below Average—Unsure but interested in trying.
> Poor—Is being pushed to compete.

2. Competitiveness—How competitive is this athlete?

Exceptional—Talks at length and with feeling about competition; seems to thrive on it.

Above Average—Cites an example or two of thriving on competition.

Average—States that he or she likes competition, but no other evidence is present.

Below Average—Prefers non-competitive sport but is willing to try competing.

Poor—Fears competition.

3. Experience—How much competitive experience has this athlete had in this particular sport (or event or position)?

Exceptional—Many years.

Above Average—More than most his or her age.

Average—An appropriate number of contests for his or her age and ability.

Below Average—Five or fewer contests.

Poor—None or one contest.

4. Confidence—How confident is this athlete in his or her ability to work hard and perform well?

Exceptional—Supremely confident.

Above Average—Very sure of self and ability at all but the highest levels.

Average—Confident, but aware of the ups and downs, the high abilities of opponents, etc.

Below Average—Feels he or she might do well with hard work and luck.

Poor—Very unsure.

5. Emotional Control—How good is this athlete at controlling strong emotions before competition?

Exceptional—Very comfortable with strong emotions before competition.

Above Average—Almost always in firm control before competition.

Average—Usually in control, with occasional lapses.

Below Average—Sometimes shaky before competition.

Poor—Often out of control before competition.

6. Social Support—What is the athlete's level of support from family and friends for competing in this sport?

Exceptional—Everyone's behind it as a top priority.
Above Average—Steady, strong interest from family and friends.
Average—Interest is generally positive, but other things are more important in their eyes.
Below Average—General disinterest from family and friends.
Poor—Definite opposition from family and friends.

7. Early Developmental Set—For how long has this athlete wanted to play this sport? How committed has he or she been to it?

Exceptional—Encouraged with first steps as a child.
Above Average—Longer than most people his or her age.
Average—An appropriate length of time for his or her age and ability.
Below Average—A season or two.
Poor—It's a new idea.

OBSERVATION-IN-COMPETITION RATING

Circle the appropriate rating for each performance factor.

1. Aggressiveness—How good is the athlete at attacking the task, to take control over the competition?

Exceptional—Always attacks with strength and purpose; forces opponents to respond.
Above Average—Usually attacks with strength and purpose.
Average—Is mid-range, attacking and responding at times.
Below Average—Occasionally acts aggressively, usually not.
Poor—Acts defensively only in response to opponent.

2. Concentration—How good is the athlete at looking where he or she should on each separate play?

Exceptional—Full attention all the time.
Above Average—Rarely distracted at any time.
Average—Usually attends correctly.
Below Average—Occasionally attends well but often is looking in the wrong place.
Poor—Rarely attending correctly, easily distracted.

3. Sureness of Actions—How sure and definite are the athlete's movements?

> Exceptional—Always sure, firm, and with good balance.
> Above Average—Usually sure and definite.
> Average—Mid-range; does some things with balance and sureness, others not.
> Below Average—Sometimes sure but usually tentative.
> Poor—Very tentative, unsure, often off-balance.

4. Game Sense—How familiar is the athlete with the strategies, movements, and overall flow of the sport (event, position, etc.)?

> Exceptional—Anticipates everything; never out of position.
> Above Average—Anticipates well.
> Average—Anticipates some things but is occasionally out of place.
> Below Average—Responds but never anticipates.
> Poor—Looks lost and out of place.

5. Attention Span—Overall, how long can the athlete keep his or her mind on competition?

> Exceptional—Full attention throughout competition.
> Above Average—Only one or two distractions in entire competition.
> Average—Attends well in periods of twenty to thirty minutes, then rests for five to ten.
> Below Average—Attends well for a few minutes at a time.
> Poor—Scattered, erratic attention.

6. Control under Pressure (Stress)—How good is the athlete at staying in control in high-pressure situations?

> Exceptional—Always has sense of purpose; even calms others who need it.
> Above Average—Usually remains calm and purposeful.
> Average—Is calm until things really get tough, then errs.
> Below Average—Occasionally keeps cool, but usually not.
> Poor—Errs when pressed, by over-trying or becoming upset.

7. Observed Energy and Effort—How much energy does the athlete show in competition?

Exceptional—Always energetic with obviously full effort throughout.

Above Average—High energy, with only a few down periods.

Average—Periods of intensity mixed with shorter flat spots.

Below Average—Some good energy, but overall shows definite signs of flatness.

Poor—Lazy and uncaring throughout.

8. Observed Self-Control in Competition—How much control does the athlete show throughout a whole competition?

Exceptional—Always composed, attentive, sure, and ready to act.

Above Average—Usually attentive, sure, and in control.

Average—Periods of good control mixed with sloppiness.

Below Average—Some control, but often erratic and sloppy.

Poor—Almost always stressed, unsure, and over-reaching.

EMOTIONAL ENERGY AND CONTROL PROFILE

Athlete's Name ___M. G. (Sample)___

1. Does this athlete have the necessary emotional energy to play with full effort and intensity, to work hard, and to be committed to the sport?

Indicators of Emotional Energy	Rating
General Attitude and Motivation	Exceptional
Competitiveness	Exceptional
Aggressiveness	Above Average
Observed Energy and Effort in Competition	Above Average
Social Support	Above Average
Early Developmental Set	Above Average

2. Can this athlete show control (poise) along with intensity; i.e., can

this athlete use energy effectively and with purpose, even in the heat of competition?

Indicators of Emotional Control	Rating
Experience	Exceptional
Confidence	Above Average
Concentration	Exceptional
Sureness of Actions	Exceptional
Game Sense	Exceptional
Emotional Control	Above Average
Attention Span	Exceptional
Control Under Pressure	Exceptional
Observed Self-Control in Competition	Exceptional
Knowledge of Individual Reading	Average

3. When does this athlete perform best?

When he feels challenged by the opposition and feels that he has a responsibility to teammates. (Good captain material.)

4. Summary description of athlete:

Strengths: Excellent all around. Plays with both great energy and full control, even under pressure. Even leads teammates by example.

Weaknesses: If anything, doesn't know how good he is. Could improve pre-game routine.

5. Rating: Energy   Control   Overall

Exceptional   Exceptional   Exceptional

A top psychological athlete.

**EMOTIONAL ENERGY AND CONTROL
PROFILE**

Athlete's Name ___J. L.   (Sample)___

1. Does this athlete have the necessary emotional energy to play with full effort and intensity, to work hard, and to be committed to the sport?

Indicators of Emotional Energy	Rating
General Attitude and Motivation	Average
Competitiveness	Average
Aggressiveness	Below Average
Observed Energy and Effort in Competition	Below Average
Social Support	Below Average
Early Developmental Set	Below Average

2. Can this athlete show control (poise) along with intensity; i.e., can this athlete use energy effectively and with purpose, even in the heat of competition?

Indicators of Emotional Control	Rating
Experience	Above Average
Confidence	Above Average
Concentration	Below Average
Sureness of Actions	Average
Game Sense	Average
Emotional Control	Poor
Attention Span	Average
Control Under Pressure	Below Average
Observed Self-Control in Competition	Below Average
Knowledge of Individual Reading	Poor

3. When does this athlete perform best?

No obvious pattern. Gets by on physical superiority; doesn't know how to prepare himself to be consistent or aggressive.

4. Summary description of athlete:

Strengths: Has played a long time and beleives in himself, because of prior successes.

Weaknesses: Plays with low energy and sometimes uncaring attitude. Is very suspect emotionally — could fall apart under pressure or taunting. Probably used to play better and harder than he does now.

5. Rating:

Energy	Control	Overall
Below Avg.	Below Avg.	Below Avg.

Talented, but a questionable risk as a performer.

EMOTIONAL ENERGY AND CONTROL PROFILE

Athlete's Name _____R.B. (Sample)_____

1. Does this athlete have the necessary emotional energy to play with full effort and intensity, to work hard, and to be committed to the sport?

Indicators of Emotional Energy	Rating
General Attitude and Motivation	Above Average
Competitiveness	Average
Aggressiveness	Average
Observed Energy and Effort in Competition	Average
Social Support	Average
Early Developmental Set	Above Average

2. Can this athlete show control (poise) along with intensity; i.e., can this athlete use energy effectively and with purpose, even in the heat of competition?

Indicators of Emotional Control	Rating
Experience	Exceptional
Confidence	Average
Concentration	Above Average
Sureness of Actions	Above Average
Game Sense	Above Average
Emotional Control	Above Average
Attention Span	Exceptional
Control Under Pressure	Above Average
Observed Self-Control in Competition	Exceptional
Knowledge of Individual Reading	Exceptional

3. When does this athlete perform best? In big games, when much is expected of her. When she pushes herself.

4. Summary description of athlete:
   Strengths: Very experienced. Knows how to prepare herself and play with control.
   Weaknesses: Only average competitiveness, aggressiveness, and overall energy.

5. Rating:

Energy	Control	Overall
Average	Exceptional	Above Avg.

Knows the game; is good when it counts. Needs to be pushed to be more aggressive; if so, may do very well.

EMOTIONAL ENERGY AND CONTROL PROFILE

Athlete's Name _D. J. (Sample)_

1. Does this athlete have the necessary emotional energy to play with full effort and intensity, to work hard, and to be committed to the sport?

Indicators of Emotional Energy	Rating
General Attitude and Motivation	Above Average
Competitiveness	Exceptional
Aggressiveness	Exceptional
Observed Energy and Effort in Competition	Exceptional
Social Support	Average
Early Developmental Set	Above Average

2. Can this athlete show control (poise) along with intensity; i.e., can this athlete use energy effectively and with purpose, even in the heat of competition?

Indicators of Emotional Control	Rating
Experience	Average
Confidence	Average
Concentration	Above Average
Sureness of Actions	Average
Game Sense	Average
Emotional Control	Average
Attention Span	Above Average
Control Under Pressure	Average
Observed Self-Control in Competition	Below Average
Knowledge of Individual Reading	Average

3. When does this athlete perform best? _When she feels confident and under control._

4. Summary description of athlete:

Strengths: _Overall energy, hustle, and competitiveness are exceptional. A very hard and eager worker._

Weaknesses: _Sometimes plays wildly and out of control._

5. Rating:

Energy	Control	Overall
Exceptional	Average	Above Avg.

Overall, is Above Average primarily because she is willing to work so hard.

275

APPENDIX:
Athletic Performance
Improvement Survey

Name _____ Sport _____

The purpose of this survey is to help you improve your performance either in a specific area or in general. Answering these questions will help you to do so in three ways:

1. By reminding you of the important factors that you feel can influence your performance;
2. By suggesting other factors that you may not have considered but that can affect your performance; and
3. By pointing out which of these factors are under your control and which are not.

This will help you to map out the conditions under which you perform best, and how to arrange those conditions so that you can perform better.

General
1. Describe the conditions under which you best perform your sport. Include as many different things (physical, emotional, mental, social, and so on) as you can. If you need additional space, please use the reverse side.

2. Is there anything that you like to do before or after a performance that helps you to do better?

Yes_____ No_____

If you answered *Yes*, please describe what you do.

On the following questions, you will be given three choices: Circle T if the statement is true, F if the statement is false, and ? if you are not sure or need to think about it, or if it seems irrelevant to you.

Remember that there are no right or wrong answers. Simply state your *opinion* on each item. When do *you*, as an individual, perform best? Also *please circle* any item you feel to be particularly important to your performance.

Familiarity

3. T   ?   F   I perform best when I have specific knowledge about what activities I'll be performing, when, and with whom.

4. T   ?   F   I perform best when my task is familiar to me.

5. T   ?   F   I perform best when my physical surroundings are familiar to me.

6. T   ?   F   I perform best when my mental and emotional states are familiar to me.

Positives

7. T   ?   F   I perform best when I am in good physical condition.

8. T   ?   F   I perform best when all my attention is on my task.

Significance

9. T   ?   F   I perform best when my performance is important not only to me, but also to many others.

10. T   ?   F   I perform best when how I do is important to me.

11. T   ?   F   I perform best when how I do is important to my future.

Failure and Success

12. T   ?   F   I perform best when failure seems very possible.

13. T ? F   I perform best when I feel confident that I will perform well.

14. T ? F   I perform best when I feel confident that others around me will perform well.

15. T ? F   I perform best when I feel that success or failure is under my control, and not under someone else's.

16. T ? F   I perform best when I anticipate success.

Warmup

17. T ? F   I perform best when I warm up fully and at length.

18. T ? F   I perform best when I have contact with others just prior to performing.

Feelings

19. T ? F   I perform best when I feel unemotional.

20. T ? F   I perform best when I feel highly motivated.

21. T ? F   I perform best when I feel anxious.

22. T ? F   I perform best when I feel eager to perform.

23. T ? F   I perform best when I feel angry.

24. T ? F   I perform best when I feel loving.

25. T ? F   I perform best when I feel some other way. (Please describe: _____)

Practice

26. T ? F   I perform best when I have practiced my task regularly.

27. T ? F   I perform best when I have practiced my task hard.

28. T ? F   I perform best when my task is one that I have practiced to do well at a specific time.

29. T ? F   I perform best when I have practiced my task a lot.

30. T ? F   I perform best when I have practiced my task alone.

31. T ? F   I perform best when I have practiced my task very recently.

32.	T	?	F	I perform best when I have practiced my task in parts, instead of always practicing the whole performance.
33.	T	?	F	I perform best when I have practiced my task with continuous effort, instead of having vacations mixed in.

Outside factors

34.	T	?	F	I perform best when my task is difficult.
35.	T	?	F	I perform best when I like my task.
36.	T	?	F	I perform best when my task gets support from my friends and family.

Prior performance

37.	T	?	F	I perform best when my task is one that I have performed (not practiced) recently.
38.	T	?	F	I perform best when my task is one that I have done well before.
39.	T	?	F	I perform best when my task is one that I have performed (not practiced) many times before.

More feelings

40.	T	?	F	I perform best when my task involves being emotional.
41.	T	?	F	I perform best when my task involves feeling a specific emotion. (Describe: _____)

Mind

42.	T	?	F	I perform best when my task involves a lot of discipline and self-control.
43.	T	?	F	I perform best when my task involves intense concentration.
44.	T	?	F	I perform best when my task involves using my memory.
45.	T	?	F	I perform best when my task requires high intelligence.
46.	T	?	F	I perform best when my task involves talking.

47. T ? F   I perform best when my task involves solving problems.

Relations with people

48. T ? F   I perform best when my task is fun.
49. T ? F   I perform best when my task involves competition.
50. T ? F   I perform best when my task involves cooperating with others.
51. T ? F   I perform best when my task is completely individual, involving no competition or cooperation.

Duration

52. T ? F   I perform best when my task is very short (less than one minute).
53. T ? F   I perform best when my task is relatively short (one to thirty minutes).
54. T ? F   I perform best when my task is slightly longer (thirty minutes to two hours).
55. T ? F   I perform best when my task is long (over two hours).

Feedback vs. self-paced

56. T ? F   I perform best when my task allows me to get feedback as I am performing.
57. T ? F   I perform best when my task involves reacting to someone or something, instead of going at my own pace.

Physical abilities

58. T ? F   I perform best when my task involves a lot of physical movement.
59. T ? F   I perform best when my task involves precise, small muscle movement.
60. T ? F   I perform best when my task involves full-body, large muscle movement.
61. T ? F   I perform best when my task involves speed in movement.

62.	T	?	F	I perform best when my task involves quick reactions.
63.	T	?	F	I perform best when my task involves endurance and stamina.
64.	T	?	F	I perform best when my task involves physical strength.

Mental complexity

65.	T	?	F	I perform best when my task involves a lot of thought.
66.	T	?	F	I perform best when my task involves speed in thought.
67.	T	?	F	I perform best when my task involves seeing and responding to many things.
68.	T	?	F	I perform best when my task involves doing many different things.

General externals

69.	T	?	F	I perform best when the weather is a certain way. (Describe: _____)
70.	T	?	F	I perform best at certain times of the day or night. (Describe: _____)
71.	T	?	F	I perform best in a certain place. (Describe: _____)
72.	T	?	F	I perform best when I eat before performing.
73.	T	?	F	I perform best when I have had plenty of sleep.

Wrap-Up

Are there any other factors not mentioned here? If so, complete one or more of the following:

I perform best when _____

I perform best when _____

I perform best when _____

GLOSSARY

Achievement goal: A common source of motivation, based on the desire for accomplishment and success.

Acquisition curve: The pattern in which most material is learned. Usually, skills taught first or last are best retained, while material taught in the middle is harder to retain. (See **Learning.**)

Action phase: The second part of the overall readying process, which involves taking control over readying and making appropriate changes; follows the **Observation phase.**

Activation: Pure excitement and arousal, without accompanying emotional feelings like anxiety or tension.

Affiliation goal: A common source of motivation, based on the desire for acceptance and recognition by other people as "one of the group."

Anticipated outcome: Thoughts and beliefs about winning or losing an upcoming event, as distinguished from confidence about one's upcoming performance.

Anxiety: A feeling characterized by uncertainty, discomfort, and an overall negative sense of being; nevertheless, a common source of the arousal necessary for good performance.

APIS (Athletic Performance Improvement Survey): A checklist of positive performance conditions for the individual athlete; part of the observation phase of readying, it is usually the first concrete step in the new readying routine.

Arousal: The cumulative product of all emotions and physical activators; mid-range arousal is associated with top performance. Arousal is the one name for the combined effects of everything the athlete is feeling at any one time; as such, it is the intermediate step between any single emotion and athletic performance.

"As if" behavior: A technique in which the athlete learns to try new positive skills by being instructed to behave "as if" he or she were some particular star athlete.

Attention: The process of putting one's mind (through the senses of sight, sound, and so on) on a given object, person, or task.

Attention-clearing and focusing technique: An individual readying technique that involves sweeping through all possible distractions in the mind before an event, resulting in complete attention on competition when the event begins.

Attention span: The length of time a person is able to keep his or her mind on a given object, person, or task; attention spans vary, depending on the abilities of the person, the material attended to, and the manner in which the material is presented.

Attention reinforcement: The reinforcing of a behavior simply by attending to it. Any words or actions of the coach in the direction of an athlete, regardless of the approving or disapproving nature of such attention, make it more likely that the behavior will occur again. All attention is essentially reinforcing.

Attitude: A network of thoughts centered around a particular object, person, or task.

Bad-call workouts: A method of preparing athletes for bad breaks and hostile environments by purposely injecting such events into regular practices.

Behavior: Strictly, any action that is physically observable; more loosely, both external and internal activities. For the coach, the athlete's behavior consists of what is observable; for the athlete, both external actions and internal states are manipulatable behaviors. Both kinds of behavior follow all principles of learning, such as reinforcement, ignoring, and so on.

Behavior chain: A series of small behaviors that together form one overall skill or activity; an important concept in the shaping process.

Bolster period: Following a period of instruction, a short period of time in which the athlete rests and mentally reviews material; a method of avoiding the negative effects of mental fatigue and attention slippage; a time of mental review and rehearsal. (See Mental rehearsal.)

Buzz of emotions: A state in which the athlete is feeling a mixture of different things, as opposed to one emotional state; an undesirable mental state, indicative of lack of control over necessary internal readying.

Challenge technique: A practice technique to train for performance under actual competitive pressure by singling out an individual athlete for a measured performance in front of his or her peers; the individual's performance determines the team's next activity.

"Child's play" imagery: A form of positive imagery involving the remembrance and reproduction of the sheer joy of playing as a young child, without external performance pressures.

Chunking: A memory-aiding technique that involves grouping bits of information to be remembered into chunks of three to four bits; bits related around one theme are the best chunked.

Cognition: Thought; the process of thinking, as opposed to feeling, perceiving, sensing, and behaving.

Cognitive anxiety: One of the two forms of anxiety, chracterized by unwanted negative thoughts, worries, inability to concentrate, and overall lack of control over the mind to prevent it from racing or from considering negative possibilities. (See **Somatic anxiety.**)

Cognitive cycle: The precompetition readying cycle having to do with thoughts, studying, and attitudes.

Cognitive mediation: The process by which thoughts and words are used as learning aids in the teaching of physical skills through modeling and shaping.

Competency drive: A source of motivation based on the human desire to manipulate the world, to handle whatever is being attempted. (See **Mastery.**)

Complexity of behaviors: The extent to which the athlete is required to do many different physical things during performance.

Complexity of cues: The extent to which the athlete is required to respond to many diffent things during performance.

Concentration: The state of attentiveness to the task at hand, made up of such factors as **Attention span, Selective attention,** and **Orienting response.**

Confidence: A feeling of self-assurance and faith in one's ability to perform well.

Consistency of reinforcement: A major determinant of the effectiveness of reinforcement over the long run.

Countdown: The readying routines, rituals, and exercises used in the final precompetition period, lasting from one to forty-eight hours.

Countdown markers: During the countdown period, the activities and events used as timing signposts to get the athlete ready by synchronizing all cycles, and cueing the athlete as to precisely when competition will begin.

Creative worrying: See Negative imagery.

Crucial conditions: The two factors, one internal and one external, that are important for the readying of any individual athlete; products of the APIS.

Cycle: A period of time in which patterns repeat, rising and falling at predictable intervals; specifically, the timing of three main readying channels during the countdown period. (See Cognitive, Emotional, and Physical cycles.)

Danger zone: Pertaining to cycles within the countdown period, the period immediately prior to competition when further physical or mental practice can have a negative effect on subsequent performance.

Desire for success: A source of motivation involving the simple attraction of doing well for positive reasons, as opposed to striving to avoid failure. (See Fear of failure.)

Discipline: Control; training that molds physical skills and mental faculties, giving a sense of self-control and direction; not necessarily punishment.

Dressing ritual: A timing marker used in the countdown period, consisting of a slow, patterned process of undressing and putting on one's uniform. It is used as a time for mental and emotional readying, the internal equivalent of putting on the external armor to go into battle (competition).

Drives: Internal sources of motivation to perform well, arising from some of our basic human needs and wants. (See Competency, Mastery, Social drives, and Rewards.)

Early Developmental Set: An overall attitude favorable to athletic performance, based on the individual's childhood history of believing in, valuing, and striving for athletic success.

Emotions: Feelings, as distinguished from thoughts, behaviors, and physical sensations; the affective part of mental functioning.

Emotional cycle: The precompetition readying cycle having to do with feelings and the arousal resulting from feelings.

Emotional flexibility: The ability to feel different things at different times with varying intensities.

Emotional stability: The ability to feel strong feelings without losing control over one's thoughts and actions; emotional balance.

Energy: The capacity for being active and performing; the driving force underlying all activity; includes physical, emotional, and mental energy. (See **Arousal.**)

Equilibrium: A state of balance; the normal, resting state of the body and the mind; "ground zero."

External factors: Performance and readying conditions outside of the athlete's head, including the people, things, and activities going on around the athlete. (See **Internal factors.**)

External locus of control: A belief that whatever happens is determined primarily by things, people, and events outside of the athlete's control, including luck and fate. (See **Locus of control.**)

Extinction: The process by which behaviors, thoughts, and feelings are done less and less until they disappear entirely; this can occur with wanted or unwanted behaviors, and is the result of ignoring, punishing, and the *lack* of positive reinforcement.

Familiarity: A positive practice, readying, and performance condition characterized by common, expected events, people, and places. (See **Routine.**)

Fear of failure: A source of motivation involving striving to avoid the negative consequences of failure, as opposed to trying to do well for simply positive reasons. (See **Desire for success.**)

Fear of success: An emotional characteristic preventing full effort and commitment to athletic achievement, stemming from a fear of giving one's all and thereby finding out for sure that it's not enough to win.

Feedback pattern: The pattern in which the sport gives information to the athlete about how well he or she is doing during competition.

The Feeling: A technique for producing the unique set of feelings and thoughts that lead to top performance for each individual athlete; it is a particularly individual set of feelings, tied to specific people and events, and it does not usually fall into the common emotional categories, like simple anxiety, psyching, and so on.

Glossary

Fight or flight reaction: A physical reaction, usually accompanied by strong emotions, that corresponds to a rush of arousal and prepares the body to respond quickly and with force.

Flexibility: The ability to do, think, feel, and tolerate different things in different situations; the ability to try new things and to continue to function well when things don't go exactly as you planned.

Floating anxiety: A general, unspecific sense of uncomfortable uncertainty; worry that cannot be tied to a specific source, but follows you around when you are trying to do other things.

Fluctuation: A natural part of all practice and performance; a fundamental characteristic of human beings that leads to unavoidable ups and downs.

Free play: A state of playing with ultimate freedom and energy without the need for control or rules; childlike play.

Game sense: Knowledge of your sport, including understanding play and anticipating actions.

Hazard: The event that marks the beginning of a downward trend in motivation or performance; the specific event marks the switch from positive attitudes to negative ones and is thus a prime target for coach-athlete discussion.

Homeostasis: A relatively stable balance among all the various parts and cycles of the body.

Homeostatic mechanism: A process by which the body continually seeks to gain a state of balance among all its parts and cycles.

Identification: The process by which people (especially young children) learn to talk and act like highly respected models (like parents, heroes, and so on); the underlying mechanism of the modeling process.

Ignoring: A major teaching technique, involving the removal of all attentional reinforcement in order to decrease the likelihood of the athlete repeating an unwanted behavior; the appropriate counter-technique to positive reinforcement.

Imagery: The process of seeing pictures or images in the mind; used in several different readying techniques, it is the application of one's imagination to the readying process.

Immediacy of reinforcement: A major determinant of the effectiveness of reinforcement.

Individual differences: A fundamental factor in human preparation and performance, making one strategy or approach to any task impossible; the recognition of individual differences in needs, practice regimens, and top performance conditions is the hallmark of top-flight readying.

Information intake: The mental process of getting information into the brain; only the first step in learning.

Information retention: The mental process of keeping information in the brain once it gets in; the second step in learning.

Information use: The physical use of learned information; the top priority step in the learning process.

Interference: The mixing of two or more activities in a way that hinders the action of one or both; in readying, there is **Interference of cycles** of emotions, thoughts, and behaviors during the countdown period, and there is **Interference of memory** or other mental processes; both are to be avoided.

Internal clock: The automatic timing mechanism inside the mind, it is always aware of how long until competition; it is aided and impressed upon the body by the use of countdown rituals and timing markers. (See **Countdown marker.**)

Internal factors: Performance and readying conditions inside the athlete's head, including thoughts, feelings, and images, as opposed to external people and events. (See **External factors.**)

Internal locus of control: A belief that whatever happens is determined primarily by the actions of the athlete him- or herself, both in readying and in competition. (See **Locus of control.**)

Key phrase: The one phrase from the relaxation technique that is most powerful in bringing a feeling of relaxation to each individual athlete. The phrase that can best be used by itself, quickly and effectively, in tight spots or just before competition.

Kinesiology: The study of body mechanics and how they relate to physical movement, especially in sports.

Learning: The acquiring of knowledge and skill, both mentally and physically, but not necessarily the **Performance** of the skill; an athlete may have learned how to perform a skill, giving him or her the *capacity* to do it, but actual performance is the next step.

Learning aids: External devices, such as written or recorded material, that can help in the learning process.

Learning history: The prior events in the athlete's life that affect his or her current behaviors, emotions, attitudes, and learning readiness.

Learning principles: Rules and strategies, including the areas of attention, presentation, and reinforcement, that govern how well something will be learned.

Locus of control: The belief of the athlete as to who or what determines his or her readiness, performance and outcome in competition. (See External and Internal locus of control.)

Long-term memory: A memory function of the brain, largely separate from short-term memory, which can be aided by cognitive mediation and practice. (See Short-term memory.)

Maintenance: The process of keeping up desired behaviors by periodically reinforcing them even after they are initially learned.

Marking reinforcement: The use of reinforcement not as a reward but as a marker to indicate precisely the desired behavior from among a series of behaviors.

Mastery drive: A source of motivation based on the human desire to control and master the world, originally as a means of survival (See Competency drive.)

Mental: Referring to all that goes on in the mind: thoughts, attitudes, images, and emotions.

Mental blueprint: An image or picture in the mind of an action to be taken by the body; a mental plan of action.

Mental energy: The driving force underlying all activity of the mind, as distinguished from physical energy; almost all activities require both types of energy, and both will be depleted by any practice or competition event; physical rest will replenish only physical energy, and mental rest is required to replenish mental energy.

Mental errors: Mistakes caused by improper mental readiness, falling into two categories: being mentally too loose or too tight; they are structurally the same as physical errors and respond to the same kinds of coaching reaction as do physical errors. (See Type A and Type B mental errors.)

Mental fatigue: The state of depleted mental energy, which can be present even when physical energy is high, and which leads to mental errors.

Mental rehearsal: The planning in the mind of actions to be taken later by the body, usually using imagery and mental blueprints; an important readying and practicing technique. (See Bolster period.)

Mental set: An attitudinal framework or setup; the overall mood and attitude the athlete has at any given time.

Modeling: The teaching and learning of skills through example and demonstration; governed by the salience, status, and perceived similarity of the demonstrator to the observer; a major principle of learning. (See Identification.)

Model salience: The "watchability" and power of the person demonstrating a skill; it depends on the beliefs and preferences of the person watching (the athlete), and is a major determinant of the effectiveness of the modeling.

Model status: The level of social enviability of the model; it depends on the beliefs and preferences of the person watching (the athlete), and is a major determinant of the effectiveness of the modeling.

Momentum: A sense of the general flow of events during competition, including which side has it, how strong it is, and how long it is likely to last.

Motivation: A set of attitudes that causes a person to act, serving as an incentive for his or her actions; the major attitude that underlies the athlete's level of effort and participation in his or her sport.

"My hero" imagery: A form of positive imagery involving the athlete imagining him- or herself playing exactly like his or her most revered athletic hero.

Negative imagery: The use of mental images that arouse anxiety and other emotions of distress; it can be used either (1) so that the distressing thoughts can be worried about intensely and efficiently and then set aside, leaving the athlete with a lower anxiety level at game time; or (2) so that the distressing thoughts can be used as a source of greater overall anxiety and arousal at game time.

Negative reinforcement: The increasing likelihood of a desired behavior by removing the negative aspects of not doing it (e.g., gripping and throwing a baseball correctly is reinforced because it leads to the avoidance of blisters and arm trouble).

Nonphysical reinforcers: Along with social and physical reinforcers, one of the three main categories of reinforcers; examples are money and time off, things that are not social and do not satisfy a basic physical desire.

No-trial learning: The process of learning a behavior without formal practice, through the channels of careful observation, identification, and modeling.

Observation phase: The first part of the overall readying process, involving surveying the individual athlete's strengths, weaknesses, and top readying conditions; precedes the Action phase.

Orienting response: First part of all attention processes, in which the person first trains his or her senses on an object, person, task, or event; usually an automatic, involuntary reaction to anything new or changing.

Outcome: The result of competition, as determined by standards outside the athlete's head, such as the score, margin of victory, and so on; winning and losing, as opposed to Performance.

Overlearning: The strategy of drilling responses to important cues so many times that they become automatic in actual competition, taking little time and requiring no thought.

Paralysis through analysis: The interruption of energies and natural, free-flowing performance by too much thought; this can occur during readying (caused by too much or misplaced study) or during competition (caused by too little rehearsal and practice), and is destructive of good play. (See Interference and Overlearning.)

Peak performance: Performance at the top of the individual athlete's range of possible performances.

Perceived similarity of model: The extent to which the observer of a demonstration sees the demonstrator as being similar in some important ways; it is a major determinant of the effectiveness of the modeling.

Perception: The taking in of information on the sensory or physiological level, as distinguished from (and preceding) thoughts or feelings.

Performance: The actions of the athlete in competition, within his or her individual range of possible performances, as opposed to winning or losing. (See Outcome.)

Personality: An individual's long-standing attitudes, moods, and behaviors in dealing with his or her life, as opposed to States of mind.

Physical cycle: The precompetition readying cycle having to do with the body itself—muscles, physical energies, and so on.

Physical reinforcers: Along with social and nonphysical reinforcers, one of the three main categories of reinforcers; examples are water, food, and rest, things that satisfy a basic physical desire.

Physical sensations: The basic information taken in through our sense organs, as opposed to emotions, thoughts, and behaviors.

Physiological: Pertaining to the physical, chemical, and biological aspects of the body.

Positive imagery: The use of mental images that arouse good feelings and desirable physical performances. (See Mental rehearsal.)

Glossary

Positive reinforcement: The increasing in likelihood of a desired behavior by providing something valued by the athlete when he or she does the desired behaviors. (See Social, Physical, and Nonphysical reinforcers.)

Pressure: A state of urgency or stress, leading to increased tension and arousal; as such, it can be good or bad for performance, depending on the situation and the individual.

Primacy: The principle of learning that says that things taught at the beginning of a session (however long or short) will be learned best. (See Acquisition curve, Recency.)

Prime coaching fallacy: The belief that athletic skills should be taught or that readying should be done in a prescribed way that depends only on the sport itself, without considering individual differences among athletes.

Problem-solving thought: A specific kind of thinking that deals with figuring things out, analyzing them, and generally solving problems; analytic, scientific thinking.

Psyched-up: A general, imprecise readying term found in popular usage to refer to all kinds of mental readiness; usually it refers to feeling high levels of arousal and eagerness to play, with commitment and purpose. (See Activation.)

Psychological readying: Mental preparation for competition; preparation that attends to the athlete's thoughts, emotions, attitudes, and knowledge relevant to top performance of the sport.

Psychological tools: The specific mental exercises and techniques that serve the same purpose as physical tools—to be used in appropriate situations in order to more easily accomplish a desired goal, namely, psychological readiness. (See Readying techniques.)

Psychology: The science of mind and behavior, including thoughts, emotions, attitudes, performance, and the learning of skills.

Punishment: The decreasing in likelihood of an unwanted behavior by responding to that behavior with something disliked by the doer (athlete); the appropriate teaching response for stamping out intolerable behaviors.

Range of performance: The spread, from the worst to the best, of all levels of play that the individual athlete is physically capable of reaching in competition.

Reactive sports: Sports (or positions within sports) that require the athlete to respond to the opponent's actions, as opposed to **Self-paced sports** like figure skating and gymnastics.

Reactivity level: The intensity and range with which the athlete typically experiences feelings; how emotionally reactive he or she is.

Readying: The process of doing whatever is necessary to make it easier for the athlete to perform at a high level in competition; this ranges from taking a practice swing on the tee to a forty-eight-hour **Countdown.**

Readying spot: A technique in which the athlete goes to a specific place at a specific time, outside the events of normal daily routine, and puts his or her mind on his or her sport for a set amount of time; the setting in which individual readying techniques such as imagery and relaxation are used.

Readying techniques: Structured mental exercises used to put the athlete in the specific frame of mind in which he or she performs best. (See **Psychological tools.**)

Recency: The principle of learning that says that things taught at the end of a session (however long or short) will be learned best. (See **Acquisition curve, Primacy.**)

Reinforcement: Following a desired behavior by something that increases the likelihood that that behavior will occur again; the single most important principle of learning; reinforcement refers to behaviors, not athletes—it is the behavior that is reinforced, as opposed to the person having earned a **Reward** by doing the behavior.

Reinforcer: Anything that increases the likely repetition of the behavior it has followed. (See **Social, Physical,** and **Nonphysical reinforcers.**)

Relationship: The pattern of interaction between two or more people, including behaviors, attitudes, and emotions.

Relaxation: The state of experiencing lowered muscular or mental tension; the process of achieving this state.

Relaxation phrases: A series of self-suggestive statements used to reach a state of lowered tension.

Response: Any behavior done by a person in reaction to an event, person, word, or anything else; technically, all behaviors are responses. (See **Stimulus, Stimulus response theory.**)

Reward: A compensation earned through the production of an **Outcome,** as opposed to the doing of any specific, desired behavior; behaviors are reinforced, while people are rewarded for achieving outcomes.

Ritual: Patterned, repetitive behavior used to provide a sense of **Familiarity** and continuity; a pattern used during the **Countdown** period to allow the athlete to control his or her readying environment. (See **Routine.**)

Routine: Patterned, repetitive behavior; also, patterned conditions of practice, readying, and performance used to reduce the amount of mental energy needed to attend to new, unexpected, or unfamiliar things. (See **Familiarity.**)

Selective attention: The capacity to put one's mind on one thing when a number of things are present; screening out distractions.

Self-learning model: An approach to the teaching and learning situation that emphasizes aiding and allowing the student to explore and learn, with less regard for direct instruction from the teacher.

Self-paced sports: Sports (or positions within sports) that are begun and timed at the athlete's own pace, as opposed to **Reactive sports** like soccer; for example, in baseball, pitching is self-paced while hitting and fielding are reactive.

Self-suggestion: The technique of putting thoughts and actions into one's own mind, usually in a relaxed and quiet setting, to prepare the mind and body for future action.

Sensorizing: Imagining an activity in such a way as to focus on all the physical senses as much as possible, as opposed to merely thinking about the activity; the sensory information includes what would be seen, heard, smelled, and felt while doing the imagined behavior.

Sensory channels: The five physical senses, which are our first line of information intake from the world: sight, hearing, taste, smell, and touch.

Shaping: The training of a behavior through the reinforcement of small steps that gradually approximate the overall desired behavior; a major principle of learning.

Short-term memory: A memory function of the brain, largely separate from long-term memory; evidence of short-term recall of information does not necessarily indicate that long-term recall will occur. (See **Long-term memory.**)

Significance of event: The extent to which the world outside of the participants will take note of an athletic event; the attitude of the athlete about the importance of an event.

Social drive: A source of motivation based on the human desire for positive contact with and positive regard from other people. (See **Social reinforcers.**)

Social environment: All the people within the athlete's physical surroundings and mental awareness, as well as the behaviors of those people as they relate to the athlete; coaches, teammates, friends, relatives, and all that they do.

Social reinforcers: Along with the physical and nonphysical reinforcers, one of the three main categories of reinforcers; examples are praise, affection, acceptance, and pats on the back—things (especially words) that are indicative of positive contact with and positive regard from other people.

Somatic anxiety: One of the two forms of anxiety, characterized by physical tension and symptoms such as tight muscles, upset stomach, and headaches; the physical side of distressing emotions. (See Cognitive anxiety.)

State of mind: A temporary, manipulatable thought, feeling, or attitude, as opposed to a more long-standing personality Trait; states are what you think or feel at any specific time, while traits are your overall, long-term mental and behavioral habits; states are the appropriate targets of mental readying techniques.

Stimulus: Anything that arouses an activity or response from a person; an event, person, or object to which the athlete attends and responds. (See Response.)

Stimulus response theory: The part of psychology that deals with how people react to things and how things (events, tasks, and other people) cause people to act; deals with the interaction between the athlete and his or her world.

Stop-start technique: An attention-training technique that teaches the athlete how to control the stopping and starting of attention on a given subject; focusing and unfocusing attention in a purposeful way, to gain control over one's powers of attention. (See Attention span, Selective attention.)

Study:rest ratio: The mixture of study time and rest time that is best for each individual person and each subject, to ensure good attention to and learning of material. (See Work:rest ratio.)

Symbolic thought: Complex thinking, unique to humans and higher primates, that involves symbols; examples are the use of letters and words, numbers, and concepts; moving from any Learning aid to physical action requires some symbolic thought, and this is often a weak spot in athletic training.

Tag: A nickname the athlete gives to him- or herself as part of an overall image of him- or herself performing in a desired way. (See **Positive imagery**.)

Target behavior: The specific skill that is being taught or learned; a specific piece of an overall skill—the smaller, the better. (See **Behavior chain**.)

Tension: The general term for the state of stress, tightness, or anxiety; the opposite of **Relaxation**, and a main contributor to **Arousal**.

Thoughts: Statement (words) inside the head, as distinguished from emotions, behaviors, and physical sensations.

Time out: A punitive response to undesired behavior, consisting of completely removing the athlete from all contact with both other people and the task at hand; stopping all **Attentional reinforcement**; commonly, running laps or banishment from the game.

Trait: A long-standing personality characteristic; long-term mental and behavioral habit, which may or may not affect psychological readying to perform.

Type A mental errors: Mistakes of looseness, inattention, and lackadaisical play; respond well to coaching emphasis.

Type B mental errors: Mistakes of tightness, pressure, and too much emotionality; respond poorly to coaching emphasis.

Warmup: The physical equivalent to psychological readying, especially in the countdown period.

Work:rest ratio: The mixture of working time and rest that is best for each individual person and each task, to ensure good attention and high energy when working.

INDEX

Control *(cont.)*
    78–79, 138, 140, 150, 240, 258, 263–73
Countdown:
  markers, 150–53
  period, 139–54
Creative worrying *(see* Techniques)
Crucial conditions, 159–60, 169
Cycles, 141–46, 224–27, 249, 259
  attention, 121–23, 136
  cognitive, 47, 142–44, 211–12
  danger zone, 143
  emotional, 32, 136, 142, 144–45, 211–12
  interference between cycles, 145
  momentum, 216–20
  physical, 29, 128, 136, 142–43

Danger zone *(see* Cycles)
Discipline, 76, 132–34, 221, 248
Dressing ritual, 147–48, 152
Drives, 51–53, 56
  achievement goal, 52
  affiliation goal, 52
  competency, 52
  mastery, 52–53
  physical, 51, 84
  rewards, 51–52
  social, 51–52

Early Developmental Set, 49–50, 55, 57, 68, 248
Emotions, 109, 194–99
  control, 11–12, 45, 188–94, 247
  cycles *(see* Cycles)
  flexibility, 11–12, 247
  reactivity levels, 11–12, 247
Energy:
  control/energy balance *(see* Control)
  emotional, 14–16, 44–45, 128–29, 225, 263, 265
  mental, 14, 128–29, 144, 225
  physical, 14, 128, 225
Equilibrium, 171
Excitement *(see* Activation)
External factors, 5–6, 151, 159, 199–200, 250–52
External locus of control *(see* Locus of control)
Extinction *(see* Learning principles)

Familiarity *(see* Routine)
Fear, 32–36
  of failure *(see* Motivation)
  of success, 35–36
Feedback patterns, 246
The Feeling (see Techniques)
Fight/flight reaction, 33–34
Fine-motor coordination, 15, 34
Flexibility:
  emotional flexibility *(see* Emotions)
  in coaching, 108, 138, 259
  in readying, 258–59
Floating anxiety *(see* Anxiety)
Fluctuation *(see* Cycles)
Focusing *(see* Attention)
Free play, 133, 182
Fun, 6–7, 53, 132–34, 136, 221, 240
Fundamental units, 256

Game sense, 136

Hate *(see* Anger)
Hazard, 56–57
Homeostasis, 188
Hypnosis, 168

Identification, 58, 111
Ignoring *(see* Techniques)
Imagery, 172–73
  "Child's Play," 181–82
  "My Hero," 183
  negative *(see* Techniques)
  positive *(see* Techniques)
  relaxation *(see* Techniques)
Individual differences:
  in abilities, 13, 120–21, 137
  in practice, 108, 124, 136–37
  in readying, 2–8, 11–12, 31–32, 70–71, 114, 145–47, 150, 154, 178, 212, 253–54
Information intake & retention *(see* Presentation of materials)
Interactional style, 147–48
Interference:
  of cycles *(see* Cycles)
  of memory, 131–32
Internal clock, 147, 150, 226
Internal factors, 5–6, 140–41, 151, 159, 228, 250–51
Internal locus of control *(see* Locus of control)

Reinforcement *(cont.)*
    physical, 84–86
    positive, 88–91, 98–99, 108, 236–37
    social, 77, 84, 86–87
    verbal, 86–87
Relationship between coach/athlete, 58,
    76–78
Relaxation:
    phrases *(see Techniques)*
Repetition, 128–29, 210
Responsibility, 73–76, 224, 259–60
Reversal, 215–16, 218
Rewards vs. reinforcers, 88, 92, 100
Rituals, 141, 146–49, 151
Routine, 71, 118, 128–29, 131, 146–49,
    227–29, 258–59

Selective attention (*see* Attention)
Self-learning model, 6–7, 109, 137, 212,
    260–61
Self-paced sports *(see Task characteristics)*
"Sensorizing," 209–210
Senses, 123–24, 172–73, 209–210
Shaping *(see Techniques)*
Short-term memory *(see Learning princi-*
    ples)
Significance of event, 69–72, 247
Slow starts, 214, 224–27
Social drives *(see Drives)*
Social environment, 249–50
Social reinforcers *(see Reinforcement)*
Somatic anxiety *(see Anxiety)*
States of mind vs. personality, 3–4, 47, 165
Stimulus/Response, 82, 100, 223
Stop/start technique *(see Techniques)*
Strategy, 237, 239
Structure, 128, 149, 154, 228, 249, 258
Studying *(see Techniques)*
Study/Rest ratio *(see Techniques)*
Success, 8, 24, 26, 28, 42, 53, 215
Superstition, 146
Symbolic thought, 124

Tag, 184
Talking (how to), 161–65
Target behaviors *(see Behaviors)*
Task characteristics, 244–47
Team spirit, 40–44, 113, 135
Techniques, 155–213
    attention clearing & focusing, 18, 72,
        169, 201–206, 240
    bad-call workouts, 230
    challenges, 135
    creative worrying *(see Negative im-*
        agery)
    The Feeling, 44, 140, 169, 194–201
    ignoring, 42, 93–95, 97–100, 223, 234,
        239–40
    modeling *(see Modeling)*
    negative imagery, 169, 187–94, 206
    positive imagery, 132, 169, 178–187
    Readying Spot, 23, 153, 166–69, 173,
        186, 189, 202, 213
    relaxation, 18, 169–78
    shaping, 102–110
    stop/start:
        for anxiety, 188–91
        for attention, 121–22
    studying, 169, 206–212
    study/rest ratio, 207–208
    time-out, 96–97
Tension, 37, 171, 177–78, 203
Time-out *(see Techniques)*
Tough loss, 232–33
Travel *(see Away games)*
Type A mental errors *(see Mental)*
Type B mental errors *(see Mental)*

Ultimatums, 54–55, 218–19

Warm-up, 128, 143, 152, 176
Winning, 4–5, 66–67
Worrying *(see Anxiety)*